PROFESSIONAL RESPONSIBILITY

By

LESLIE W. ABRAMSON

University of Louisville
School of Law

Exam Pro

WEST®

A Thomson Reuters business

Mat #41030660

© 2010 Thomson Reuters
   610 Opperman Drive
   St. Paul, MN 55123
   1–800–313–9378

Printed in the United States of America

ISBN 978–0–314–26475–6

PROFESSIONAL RESPONSIBILITY

Preface

To the student:

This book consists of three objective examinations in professional responsibility, containing a total of 180 objective questions. Each exam consists of sixty objective problems followed by four multiple-choice answers. Each exam is intended to take two hours and five minutes, thereby approximating the Multistate Professional Responsibility Examination [MPRE].

The purpose of this book is twofold: to assist 1) law students, and 2) law graduates. For law students, every professional responsibility course is taught differently in different sequences, using different books. At the end of the course, there will be a final examination, possibly with multiple choice examination questions. Regardless of whether there are multiple choice questions on your law school examination, it is highly likely that prior to sitting for the bar examination or being licensed as an attorney you will have to successfully pass the MPRE. That is the second purpose for this book. Many students do not take the MPRE until several weeks after taking the bar examination. This book is intended to help you refresh your recollection about your professional responsibility course during those weeks when you have serious reservations about whether your brain can absorb more material. Following this *Preface* is a *Table of Topics* to assist you in locating ethics topics which may appear on your law school examination and/or the MPRE. Each exam has an answer key with explanations for the best answer to the problem. The answer keys also explain why the other proposed answers are incorrect, or are not the best possible choice.

The exam problems cover the following general topics: regulation of the legal profession, the lawyer-client relationship, client confidentiality, conflicts of interest, competence and legal malpractice, litigation and other forms of advocacy, communications with non-clients, different roles of the lawyer, safekeeping property, advertising and solicitation, duties to the public and the legal system, and judicial ethics. For a book reviewing the professional responsibility course, consult *Acing Professional Responsibility*, (Thomson Reuters 2009), ISBN number: 13: 9780314199652. That book contains text, outlines, bullet points, sample essay questions and answers, and mini-checklists to teach the basics and fine points of professional responsibility.

The chief purpose of this book is to provide you with a comprehensive set of objective exam questions, to assist with exam and MPRE preparation. Working through these problems should enhance your understanding of professional responsibility and the appropriate analysis of rules, cases, policy and practices.

PROFESSOR LESLIE W. ABRAMSON

University of Louisville
 School of Law
September 2010

PROFESSIONAL RESPONSIBILITY

Table of Exam Topics

ADVERTISING AND SOLICITATION

Advertising	EXAM 1	PROBLEM 12
	EXAM 1	PROBLEM 15
	EXAM 1	PROBLEM 33
	EXAM 2	PROBLEM 53
	EXAM 3	PROBLEM 32
	EXAM 3	PROBLEM 59
Solicitation	EXAM 1	PROBLEM 15
	EXAM 1	PROBLEM 34
	EXAM 2	PROBLEM 11
Group legal services	EXAM 1	PROBLEM 34
Referrals	EXAM 3	PROBLEM 33
Communicating about fields of practice	EXAM 1	PROBLEM 33

CLIENT CONFIDENTIALITY

Lawyer-client privilege	EXAM 1	PROBLEM 43
	EXAM 2	PROBLEM 43
	EXAM 3	PROBLEM 9
	EXAM 3	PROBLEM 40
Work product doctrine	EXAM 3	PROBLEM 40
Ethical duty of confidentiality	EXAM 1	PROBLEM 1
	EXAM 1	PROBLEM 16
	EXAM 2	PROBLEM 33
	EXAM 3	PROBLEM 22
	EXAM 3	PROBLEM 50
Disclosures authorized by client	EXAM 1	PROBLEM 17
	EXAM 1	PROBLEM 36
	EXAM 1	PROBLEM 40
	EXAM 1	PROBLEM 41
	EXAM 1	PROBLEM 55
	EXAM 2	PROBLEM 1
	EXAM 3	PROBLEM 21

COMMUNICATIONS WITH NON–CLIENTS

Truthfulness in statements to others	EXAM 1	PROBLEM 36

	EXAM 2	PROBLEM 47
	EXAM 3	PROBLEM 24
Communications with represented persons	EXAM 1	PROBLEM 46
	EXAM 2	PROBLEM 17
	EXAM 3	PROBLEM 20
	EXAM 3	PROBLEM 49
Communications with unrepresented persons	EXAM 2	PROBLEM 56
	EXAM 3	PROBLEM 20
Respect for rights of third persons	EXAM 1	PROBLEM 31
	EXAM 1	PROBLEM 46

COMPETENCE AND LEGAL MALPRACTICE

Competence	EXAM 1	PROBLEM 13
	EXAM 1	PROBLEM 44
	EXAM 2	PROBLEM 49
Diligence and care	EXAM 2	PROBLEM 50
	EXAM 2	PROBLEM 51
	EXAM 3	PROBLEM 48
Limiting liability to clients	EXAM 2	PROBLEM 24
	EXAM 3	PROBLEM 28
	EXAM 3	PROBLEM 57

CONFLICTS OF INTEREST

Multiple client conflicts	EXAM 1	PROBLEM 19
	EXAM 1	PROBLEM 42
	EXAM 1	PROBLEM 56
	EXAM 1	PROBLEM 58
	EXAM 1	PROBLEM 59
	EXAM 2	PROBLEM 10
	EXAM 2	PROBLEM 16
	EXAM 2	PROBLEM 42
	EXAM 2	PROBLEM 48
	EXAM 2	PROBLEM 58
	EXAM 3	PROBLEM 1
	EXAM 3	PROBLEM 2
	EXAM 3	PROBLEM 46
	EXAM 3	PROBLEM 51
	EXAM 3	PROBLEM 53
	EXAM 3	PROBLEM 56
Lawyer's personal interests	EXAM 1	PROBLEM 37
	EXAM 1	PROBLEM 47
	EXAM 3	PROBLEM 45
	EXAM 3	PROBLEM 46
Former client conflicts	EXAM 1	PROBLEM 2
	EXAM 1	PROBLEM 23

	EXAM 1	PROBLEM 29
	EXAM 2	PROBLEM 2
	EXAM 2	PROBLEM 3
	EXAM 2	PROBLEM 15
	EXAM 3	PROBLEM 7
	EXAM 3	PROBLEM 29
	EXAM 3	PROBLEM 54
	EXAM 3	PROBLEM 56
Prospective client conflicts	EXAM 1	PROBLEM 60
	EXAM 3	PROBLEM 37
Imputed conflicts	EXAM 1	PROBLEM 38
	EXAM 1	PROBLEM 47
	EXAM 2	PROBLEM 2
	EXAM 2	PROBLEM 16
	EXAM 2	PROBLEM 57
	EXAM 3	PROBLEM 15
	EXAM 3	PROBLEM 30
	EXAM 3	PROBLEM 38
	EXAM 3	PROBLEM 51
	EXAM 3	PROBLEM 56
Acquiring an interest in litigation	EXAM 1	PROBLEM 11
	EXAM 1	PROBLEM 20
	EXAM 1	PROBLEM 38
	EXAM 1	PROBLEM 39
Business transactions with clients	EXAM 1	PROBLEM 11
	EXAM 1	PROBLEM 35
	EXAM 2	PROBLEM 14
	EXAM 3	PROBLEM 53
	EXAM 3	PROBLEM 57
Third party compensation and influence	EXAM 1	PROBLEM 10
	EXAM 3	PROBLEM 3
Lawyers in government service	EXAM 2	PROBLEM 60
	EXAM 3	PROBLEM 4
	EXAM 3	PROBLEM 5
	EXAM 3	PROBLEM 16
	EXAM 3	PROBLEM 44
	EXAM 3	PROBLEM 54
Former judge or other third party neutral	EXAM 1	PROBLEM 51
	EXAM 3	PROBLEM 17
	EXAM 3	PROBLEM 55

DIFFERENT ROLES OF THE LAWYER

Lawyer as advisor	EXAM 2	PROBLEM 45
	EXAM 2	PROBLEM 46
Lawyer as evaluator	EXAM 2	PROBLEM 45

	EXAM 2	PROBLEM 46
Lawyer as third party neutral	EXAM 1	PROBLEM 51
	EXAM 2	PROBLEM 45
Special prosecutorial responsibilities	EXAM 1	PROBLEM 49
	EXAM 2	PROBLEM 37
	EXAM 2	PROBLEM 38
	EXAM 2	PROBLEM 39
	EXAM 2	PROBLEM 54
	EXAM 3	PROBLEM 19
Nonadjudicative proceedings	EXAM 2	PROBLEM 28
	EXAM 2	PROBLEM 29
Representing an entity	EXAM 1	PROBLEM 18
	EXAM 2	PROBLEM 25
	EXAM 2	PROBLEM 40
	EXAM 2	PROBLEM 41
	EXAM 2	PROBLEM 59
	EXAM 3	PROBLEM 43

DUTIES TO THE PUBLIC AND THE LEGAL SYSTEM

Pro bono service	EXAM 1	PROBLEM 14
Accepting court appointments	EXAM 1	PROBLEM 7
	EXAM 1	PROBLEM 14
Serving legal service organizations	EXAM 2	PROBLEM 29
Law reform activities	EXAM 2	PROBLEM 28
Criticism of judges	EXAM 3	PROBLEM 6
Political contributions	EXAM 1	PROBLEM 54

JUDICIAL ETHICS

Ex parte communications	EXAM 3	PROBLEM 36
Disqualification	EXAM 1	PROBLEM 8
	EXAM 1	PROBLEM 45
	EXAM 1	PROBLEM 53
	EXAM 2	PROBLEM 12
	EXAM 3	PROBLEM 11
Extrajudicial activities	EXAM 2	PROBLEM 13
	EXAM 2	PROBLEM 55
	EXAM 3	PROBLEM 23
	EXAM 3	PROBLEM 41

LAWYER-CLIENT RELATIONSHIP

Limits of scope of representation	EXAM 1	PROBLEM 36
	EXAM 1	PROBLEM 50
	EXAM 1	PROBLEM 52
Client with diminished capacity	EXAM 1	PROBLEM 32

	EXAM 2	PROBLEM 20
	EXAM 2	PROBLEM 31
	EXAM 3	PROBLEM 31
Decision-making authority	EXAM 1	PROBLEM 30
	EXAM 2	PROBLEM 30
	EXAM 2	PROBLEM 59
	EXAM 3	PROBLEM 31
	EXAM 3	PROBLEM 58
	EXAM 3	PROBLEM 39
Termination of lawyer-client relationship	EXAM 1	PROBLEM 21
	EXAM 1	PROBLEM 32
	EXAM 1	PROBLEM 36
	EXAM 2	PROBLEM 21
	EXAM 2	PROBLEM 22
	EXAM 2	PROBLEM 52
	EXAM 2	PROBLEM 59
	EXAM 3	PROBLEM 12
	EXAM 3	PROBLEM 52
Communications with the client	EXAM 1	PROBLEM 28
	EXAM 1	PROBLEM 30
	EXAM 3	PROBLEM 58
Fees	EXAM 1	PROBLEM 11
	EXAM 1	PROBLEM 47
	EXAM 2	PROBLEM 9
	EXAM 2	PROBLEM 44
	EXAM 3	PROBLEM 7

LITIGATION AND OTHER FORMS OF ADVOCACY

Meritorious claims	EXAM 1	PROBLEM 6
	EXAM 1	PROBLEM 57
	EXAM 3	PROBLEM 37
Candor toward the tribunal	EXAM 1	PROBLEM 3
	EXAM 1	PROBLEM 4
	EXAM 1	PROBLEM 22
	EXAM 1	PROBLEM 26
	EXAM 1	PROBLEM 52
	EXAM 1	PROBLEM 57
	EXAM 2	PROBLEM 4
	EXAM 2	PROBLEM 19
	EXAM 2	PROBLEM 21
	EXAM 2	PROBLEM 22
	EXAM 2	PROBLEM 23
	EXAM 3	PROBLEM 18
	EXAM 3	PROBLEM 25
	EXAM 3	PROBLEM 26

	EXAM 3	PROBLEM 27
Fairness to opponent	EXAM 1	PROBLEM 48
	EXAM 2	PROBLEM 4
	EXAM 2	PROBLEM 59
Improper contacts with judge and jurors	EXAM 2	PROBLEM 36
	EXAM 3	PROBLEM 42
	EXAM 3	PROBLEM 60
Trial publicity	EXAM 2	PROBLEM 32
Lawyer as witness	EXAM 1	PROBLEM 5
	EXAM 2	PROBLEM 56

REGULATION OF THE LEGAL PROFESSION

Judicial power to regulate lawyers	EXAM 2	PROBLEM 7
	EXAM 3	PROBLEM 14
Regulation after admission	EXAM 1	PROBLEM 16
	EXAM 1	PROBLEM 25
	EXAM 2	PROBLEM 6
	EXAM 3	PROBLEM 60
Reporting professional misconduct	EXAM 1	PROBLEM 16
	EXAM 2	PROBLEM 8
	EXAM 3	PROBLEM 34
Unauthorized practice of law	EXAM 1	PROBLEM 9
Multi-jurisdictional practice	EXAM 1	PROBLEM 9
	EXAM 1	PROBLEM 24
Fee division with a nonlawyer	EXAM 3	PROBLEM 35
Law firm and other forms of practice	EXAM 1	PROBLEM 35
	EXAM 2	PROBLEM 26
	EXAM 2	PROBLEM 27
Responsibilities of law partners	EXAM 1	PROBLEM 44
	EXAM 1	PROBLEM 52
	EXAM 3	PROBLEM 47
Supervisory and subordinate lawyers	EXAM 1	PROBLEM 35
	EXAM 1	PROBLEM 44
	EXAM 1	PROBLEM 46
	EXAM 2	PROBLEM 34
	EXAM 2	PROBLEM 35
	EXAM 2	PROBLEM 56
	EXAM 3	PROBLEM 10
Restriction on right to practice	EXAM 1	PROBLEM 27
	EXAM 3	PROBLEM 39

SAFEKEEPING PROPERTY

Safekeeping property	EXAM 1	PROBLEM 32
	EXAM 2	PROBLEM 5

	EXAM 2	PROBLEM 18
	EXAM 3	PROBLEM 8
Disputes about trust fund property	EXAM 2	PROBLEM 18

TABLE OF RULES

Model Rule of Professional Conduct	Exam–Problem
1.1	1–13, 1–44, 2–49
1.2	1–50
1.2(a)	2–30, 3–31, 3–58
1.2(c)	1–50, 2–59
1.2(d)	1–36, 1–50, 3–39, 3–52
1.3	2–51, 3–47, 3–48
1.4	1–55
1.4(a)	1–28, 1–30, 3–58
1.4(b)	2–59
1.5	2–10, 3–7
1.5(a)	1–47
1.5(c)	2–44
1.5(d)	1–11, 2–9
1.5(e)	2–10, 3–7
1.6	1–23, 1–31, 1–36, 1–41, 1–55, 3–31, 3–56, 3–60
1.6(a)	1–1
1.6(b)	1–17, 1–36, 1–40, 1–41, 1–55, 2–1, 3–21
1.7	1–19, 1–42, 1–56, 1–58, 1–59, 2–58, 3–1, 3–2, 3–46, 3–56
1.7(a)	1–58, 2–10, 2–16, 2–48, 2–58, 3–51, 3–53
1.7(b)	1–42, 1–58, 2–10, 2–42, 2–48, 3–51, 3–53
1.7(c)	3–51
1.8	1–37, 1–47, 2–24, 3–45, 3–46
1.8(a)	1–11, 1–35, 2–14, 3–53, 3–57
1.8(c)	1–47, 3–45
1.8(d)	1–38
1.8(e)	1–39
1.8(f)	3–3, 3–58
1.8(g)	1–10
1.8(h)	2–24, 3–28, 3–57
1.8(i)	1–11, 1–20

Model Rule of Professional Conduct	Exam–Problem
1.8(j)	1–37, 3–46
1.8(k)	1–38, 1–47, 3–45
1.9	2–33
1.9(a)	1–2, 3–7, 3–54
1.9(b)	1–29, 2–2, 2–3, 3–7, 3–29, 3–54
1.9(c)	1–23, 2–15
1.10	2–10, 2–57, 3–56
1.10(a)	2–2, 2–16, 3–38, 3–51
1.10(b)	3–15, 3–30
1.10(c)	2–16
1.11(a)	2–60, 3–4, 3–16, 3–44
1.11(b)	2–60, 3–5
1.11(c)	2–60, 3–4, 3–51
1.11(d)	3–54
1.11(e)	3–44
1.12(a)	1–51, 3–17, 3–55
1.12(b)	1–51, 3–17
1.12(c)	1–51, 3–17, 3–55
1.13	2–40, 2–41
1.13(a)	1–18, 2–25, 2–58
1.13(b)	1–18, 2–25, 2–41, 2–58, 2–59, 3–43
1.13(c)	1–18, 2–25, 2–40
1.14	2–20
1.14(a)	1–32
1.14(b)	2–20, 2–31, 3–31
1.15(a)	2–5, 2–18, 3–8
1.15(b)	2–5
1.15(c)	2–5, 2–18
1.15(d)	1–32
1.15(e)	2–18
1.16	1–50, 2–52, 2–59, 3–52
1.16(a)	1–21, 1–36, 2–21, 2–52, 3–12
1.16(b)	1–21, 2–22, 2–52, 3–12
1.16(c)	2–21
1.16(d)	1–21, 1–32, 3–12, 3–52
1.17	2–26
1.17(c)	2–26
1.17(d)	2–26

Model Rule of Professional Conduct	Exam–Problem
1.18	2–33, 3–22
1.18(a)	2–33, 3–37
1.18(b)	3–37, 3–50
1.18(c)	1–60, 3–37
1.18(d)	1–60, 3–37
2.1	2–45, 2–46, 3–53
2.3	2–45
2.3(a)	2–46
2.3(b)	2–46
2.3©	2–46
2.4(b)	1–51, 2–45
3.1	1–6, 1–53
3.3	1–26, 1–52, 1–57, 2–19, 2–21, 2–22, 3–25, 3–26
3.3(a)	1–3, 1–4, 1–22, 1–52, 1–57, 2–4, 2–19, 2–21, 3–18, 3–27
3.3(b)	2–22, 2–23
3.3(c)	1–22, 3–18
3.3(d)	1–57, 3–25
3.4(a)	1–48, 2–59
3.4(c)	1–48, 2–4
3.4(d)	2–4
3.4(e)	1–48
3.4(f)	1–48
3.5(b)	3–42, 3–60
3.5(c)	2–36
3.6(a)	2–32
3.6(b)	2–32
3.6(c)	2–32
3.7	2–56
3.7(a)	1–5
3.7(b)	1–5
3.8(b)	1–49
3.8(c)	1–49, 2–37
3.8(d)	2–54, 3–19
3.8(e)	1–49, 2–38
3.8(f)	2–39
3.8(g)	1–49
3.9	2–28
4.1	1–36, 2–47

Model Rule of Professional Conduct	**Exam–Problem**
4.1(a)	2–47, 3–24
4.1(b)	1–36
4.2	1–46, 2–17, 3–20, 3–49
4.3	2–56, 3–20
4.4	1–46
4.4(a)	1–46
4.4(b)	1–31
5.1	3–47
5.1(a)	1–44, 1–52
5.1(b)	1–52
5.2(a)	2–34
5.3	1–35, 1–46, 2–35, 3–10
5.3(a)	2–35, 2–56
5.4(a)	3–35
5.5	1–9
5.5(b)	1–24
5.5(c)	1–24
5.6(a)	1–27, 3–39
5.6(b)	3–39
5.7(a)	1–35
5.7(b)	1–35
6.1	1–14
6.2	1–7
6.2(b)	1–14
6.2(c)	1–7
6.3(a)	2–29
6.3(b)	2–29
6.4	2–28
6.5	2–27
7.1	1–15, 1–33
7.2(b)	3–33
7.2(c)	1–15, 3–59
7.3(a)	1–15, 1–28, 1–34, 2–11
7.3(b)	1–15
7.3(d)	1–34
7.4(d)	1–33
7.5(a)	3–32
7.5(b)	3–32

Model Rule of Professional Conduct	**Exam–Problem**
7.5(c)	3–32
7.6	1–54
8.2(a)	3–6
8.3(a)	1–16, 2–8, 3–34
8.4(a)	3–60
8.4(b)	1–16, 2–6
8.4(c)	2–7, 3–14
8.4(d)	3–51
8.5(a)	1–25

Model Code of Judicial Conduct	**Exam–Problem**
2.4	2–13
2.9	3–36
2.11	1–8, 1–53, 2–12, 3–11
3.1	2–13
3.8	3–23
3.10	3–23
3.12	2–55
3.13	2–55, 3–41
3.14	2–55
3.15	2–55
4.1	2–13

Table of Contents

Exam 1 1

Answer Key Exam 1 117

Exam 2 39

Answer Key Exam 2 155

Exam 3 79

Answer Key Exam 3 193

Answer Sheets 231

PROFESSIONAL RESPONSIBILITY

Exam #1—60 Problems and Questions

Continental Towing Company is the nation's largest operator of towboats. A large Spanish corporation has been trying to acquire Continental. Very few people at Continental know about the acquisition possibility and the corporate CEO has instructed those few (including Lawyer Maris, the General Counsel) not to tell anyone about it. The takeover almost certainly would result in the Spanish company selling off most of Continental's operations business with nothing remaining of the current Continental business but the small manufacturing entity. Lawyer Jordan is the Associate General Counsel for Continental and seeks your advice. Two years ago, she learned from a recently-fired executive (who was her mentor) that Lawyer Maris had secretly tried to take over Continental without the corporate CEO's knowledge. Last week, Continental's outside counsel told her that Lawyer Maris and he were plotting the takeover by the Spanish corporation so that they could begin their own towing operation.

QUESTION:

1. Which of the following is true?

    A. Lawyer Maris violated his ethical duty of confidentiality to the organization.

    B. Lawyer Maris did not violate his ethical duty of confidentiality to the organization.

    C. Lawyer Maris had no duty of confidentiality to the organization.

    D. Lawyer Maris must not disclose confidences of the client, but may disclose the client's secrets.

* * *

1

Lawyer Larry has practiced law for four years. LaVerne Smith comes to his office to tell him about concerns she has about her job situation. Last summer, she became the assistant women's basketball coach at New State College, a highly successful program. Since her arrival, LaVerne has overheard several of the older players refer to tardy financial payments that they were expecting from boosters of the basketball program. Because such payments violate the rules of the National Collegiate Athletic Association (NCAA), LaVerne believes that she should talk to the NCAA compliance officer at the college. She asks whether it would be better if Lawyer Larry contacted the compliance officer, Shirley Crane, so that LaVerne is not perceived as a whistle-blower which she fears could result in the loss of her job. As Lawyer Larry interviews LaVerne, he realizes that two years ago he represented Shirley Crane when she divorced her first husband. That representation has concluded.

QUESTION:

2. Can Lawyer Larry represent LaVerne?

   A. Lawyer Larry can represent LaVerne, only because her case is factually different from Shirley's earlier divorce case.

   B. Lawyer Larry can represent LaVerne, only if Lawyer Larry does not use information relating to his former representation of Shirley to her disadvantage.

   C. Lawyer Larry can represent LaVerne, if Lawyer Larry does not use information relating to his former representation of Shirley to her disadvantage because her case is unrelated and factually different from Shirley's earlier divorce case.

   D. Lawyer Larry cannot represent LaVerne, because he has represented Shirley within the last two years.

* * *

Lawyer Schurman represents plaintiffs in civil litigation. At a pretrial conference conducted prior to the settlement of a client's case, Lawyer Schurman was opposing a summary judgment motion filed by the opposing party. In preparing to oppose the summary judgment motion, Lawyer Schurman became aware of several cases with dicta directly against his client's legal position but did not disclose the cases to the court or opposing counsel.

QUESTIONS:

3. What is Lawyer Schurman's ethical obligation, if any, as to the cases he found?

A. Lawyer Schurman has no ethical obligation to disclose cases that he believes contain only dicta.

B. Lawyer Schurman's ethical obligation is that he must disclose the cases in his response to the summary judgment motion and a later disclosure is never allowed.

C. Lawyer Schurman's ethical obligation is to disclose the cases to the court and to elaborate on their adverse implications for his client.

D. Lawyer Schurman's ethical obligation is to disclose the cases to the court no later than his oral argument at the pretrial conference.

4. In preparing to oppose the same summary judgment motion, Lawyer Schurman realizes that his client testified in his deposition about a fact important to the case that Lawyer Schurman knows is false. Lawyer Schurman's ethical obligation, if any, as to his client's deposition testimony is to:

A. Refuse to represent his client in future cases.

B. Refuse to disclose the false testimony because a deposition is not part of a judicial proceeding.

C. Disclose the nature and extent of his client's misleading testimony to the court, if his client is unwilling to tell the truth.

D. Disclose the existence of the false testimony to the opposing counsel.

* * *

A lawsuit was filed recently by First Bank against Sims, in which the law firm of Smith and Jones represents the plaintiff. The suit alleges that prior to leaving the bank's employ in 2007, Sims made fraudulent loans to himself through several fictitious accounts. Lawyer Travis, who is now an associate attorney at Smith and Jones and is assigned to *First Bank v. Sims*, worked at First Bank as a loan officer while in law school. During that time, he was assigned to Sims's loan area and worked on "one or two" of Sims's personal accounts.

QUESTION:

5. Can the firm of Smith and Jones be disqualified from representing First National Bank by virtue of Lawyer Travis's imminent testimony as a witness in *First Bank v. Sims*?

A. Yes, because there is a current conflict of interest between the firm's representation of the bank and its employment of Lawyer Travis who will testify as a witness.

B. Yes, if Sims has been a referral source of business for the law firm.

C. No, because Lawyer Travis never learned confidential information from Sims while working at the bank.

D. No, as long as neither Smith nor Jones is lead counsel in the case of *First Bank v. Sims.*

* * *

Prosperous Perot, who is one of Lawyer Smith's regular clients, asks Lawyer Smith to file a suit against the United States Government seeking to have the federal budget declared unconstitutional. Lawyer Smith advised Prosperous Perot that the suit is baseless, but Lawyer Smith finally agreed to file the suit on receipt of a $100,000 retainer.

QUESTION:

6. Is Lawyer Smith subject to discipline?

A. Yes, because it is unethical to present a claim not warranted under existing law unless it can be supported by a good faith argument for reversal, or modification, or extension of existing law.

B. Yes, because no portion of the fee was earned when Lawyer Smith accepted the retainer.

C. No, because Lawyer Smith fully advised Prosperous Perot that the suit was baseless and Prosperous Perot paid the retainer after giving informed consent confirmed in writing.

D. No, if a fee in these circumstances is not excessive.

* * *

One of the prestigious lawyers in the community is Lawyer Ballantine, who has been appointed by the court to represent an accused rapist who is indigent.

QUESTION:

7. Lawyer Ballantine:

A. Should refuse to take the case if he has read about the case in newspapers and believes the defendant is probably guilty.

B. May refuse to take the case if doing so would hurt his reputation, because a lawyer's reputation is his stock in trade.

C. Should take the case unless it requires him to align himself against influential members of the community.

D. Should not take the case if the intensity of his personal feeling may impair the effective representation of the prospective client.

* * *

At the start of the pretrial conference in the case of *Twitter v. Pfeezer, Inc.*, the trial judge announced that he owns 10,000 shares of the stock of Pfeezer, Inc. worth $1,900,000. He further offered to recuse himself from the case if the attorneys prefer. Counsel for Twitter and counsel for Pfeezer, Inc. briefly discussed the matter privately, and then each said on the record: "We have no problem, Your Honor." The trial judge then declared the disqualification waived. The trial judge believed that his financial interest is substantial.

QUESTION:

8. Did the trial judge act properly?

A. No, because the parties cannot waive such a disqualification.

B. No, because the judge did not secure a proper waiver of the parties and lawyers.

C. Yes, because any disqualification was waived.

D. No, because the trial judge should not have threatened to recuse himself when his financial interest was so minor.

* * *

The majority shareholder of Corleone Collection Agency, Inc. is Lawyer Corleone. When the agency's collection efforts have not been successful, Lawyer Corleone has told the agency's manager, Sarducci, to write a letter on Lawyer Corleone's legal letterhead.

The letter states that the matter has been referred to Lawyer Corleone and that a lawsuit will be filed in five days if payment is not received. Corleone does not personally review each letter before Sarducci signs and sends it.

QUESTION:

9. Can Lawyer Corleone be disciplined for his conduct?

   A. Yes, because Lawyer Corleone may not appear to threaten suit to gain advantage in a civil case.

   B. Yes, because Corleone Collection Agency, through Sarducci, is engaging in the unauthorized practice of law.

   C. Yes, because the letter is a blatant threat.

   D. No, because Sarducci is authorized to act as Lawyer Corleone's agent.

* * *

Having negotiated a settlement on behalf of twenty-two airplane accident victims, Lawyer Joe Bushkin reasonably believes that the settlement is beneficial to all of the plaintiffs who each will receive between $350,000 and $2,250,000 in damages. Defendants have stated clearly that all twenty-two plaintiffs must settle in order for the settlement to be effective with any of the plaintiffs. Bushkin is worried that, by revealing the details of the settlement to each of the twenty-two plaintiffs, the entire settlement will be upset.

QUESTION:

10. If Bushkin discloses the settlement details to each of the twenty-two participants in writing, can he be disciplined?

   A. No, but he would be violating his ethical aspirations for the twenty-two plaintiffs.

   B. Yes, because to do so might upset the entire settlement.

   C. No, because unless he advises each of the individuals of the participation of each person in the settlement, they cannot provide informed consent.

   D. Yes, because he would reveal confidential information.

* * *

Lawyer Lane represented Client Calvin in a divorce. Under the divorce decree, Client Calvin's former spouse is obligated to pay Client Calvin $50,000 a year in maintenance. Client Calvin's former spouse has paid nothing. Client Calvin contacts Lawyer Lane and asks Lawyer Lane to sue the former spouse. Lawyer Lane agrees and suggests that if he collects the arrearage, Lawyer Lane's fee will be a one-half interest in Client Calvin's mail-order business.

QUESTION:

11. Is the fee arrangement permissible?

   A. This fee arrangement is not permissible; contingent fees are never proper in domestic relations cases.

   B. This fee arrangement is not permissible, because a lawyer can never enter into a business transaction with a client.

   C. This fee arrangement is not permissible, because a lawyer cannot acquire a proprietary interest in the cause of action or the subject matter of the litigation.

   D. None of the above answers is correct.

* * *

QUESTION:

12. Under the advertising and solicitation cases decided by the United States Supreme Court,

   A. States must forbid in-person solicitation where a significant motive for the lawyer's solicitation is the lawyer's pecuniary gain.

   B. States cannot enact an absolute prohibition on mail advertisements sent to a general audience. However, states can enact an absolute prohibition on "targeted" mail advertisements sent to a select group of individuals, e.g., all persons who recently have bought a home.

   C. States cannot put any restrictions on the timing of mail advertisements sent to person known to be in need of legal services.

   D. None of the above answers is correct.

* * *

Chris Client contacted Lawyer Lyle and asked Lawyer Lyle to represent her in an antitrust case. Lawyer Lyle has no experience in antitrust cases. Lawyer Lyle knows Attorney Alice who is an exceptional antitrust lawyer in another law firm.

QUESTION:

13. What can Lawyer Lyle do in regard to the representation of Chris Client?

   A. Lawyer Lyle must decline to represent Chris Client because he is not competent in antitrust cases.

   B. Lawyer Lyle may refer the case to Attorney Alice and Attorney Alice may share the fee with Lawyer Lyle, even if Lawyer Lyle does no work and even if Chris Client is not consulted.

   C. If Lawyer Lyle refers the case to Attorney Alice, he can only share in the fee if Lawyer Lyle does some work. Lawyer Lyle's fee must be in proportion to the work done.

   D. None of the above answers is correct.

* * *

QUESTION:

14. On the issues of *pro bono* services and acceptance of court appointments,

   A. The United States Supreme Court has held that states cannot require lawyers to engage in *pro bono* work.

   B. The Model Rules of Professional Conduct require lawyers to engage in fifty hours of *pro bono* work every year.

   C. The Model Rules of Professional Conduct encourage, but do not require, lawyers to engage in *pro bono* work. Lawyers are advised to do a majority of their work by helping provide legal services to persons of limited means.

   D. A lawyer cannot decline a court appointment except where the lawyer is not competent to handle the case.

* * *

QUESTION:

15. Which of the following is true about advertising and solicitation under the Model Rules of Professional Conduct?

    A. In-person solicitation for pecuniary gain is prohibited.

    B. Targeted mailings to those known to be in need of legal services are always permitted.

    C. Lawyers cannot compare their services with those of other lawyers because such comparisons cannot be substantiated.

    D. Advertisements must contain the name of at least one person who is responsible for the ad.

* * *

QUESTION:

16. Which of the following statements is true about lawyer discipline?

    A. Under the Model Rules of Professional Conduct, a lawyer who is convicted of a felony must be disciplined.

    B. A lawyer who knows that another lawyer has violated any Rule of Professional Conduct must report it. Failure to do so may subject the non-reporting lawyer to discipline, unless the information is protected by the rules on confidentiality.

    C. The duty to report the violation of a Rule of Professional Conduct by another lawyer is limited to offenses that raise a substantial question about the lawyer's honesty, trustworthiness or fitness as a lawyer. Failure to report may subject the non-reporting lawyer to discipline, unless the information is protected by the rules on confidentiality.

    D. None of the above answers is correct.

* * *

Attorney defended Jones in a criminal assault case. Before trial, Jones told Attorney in confidence that he beat up the victim without provocation. Due to Attorney's hard work, coupled with a stroke of luck, the jury found Jones not guilty. Then Jones refused to pay

Attorney's fee. Attorney wrote to Jones as follows: "The jury found you not guilty, but your victim can still sue you for civil damages. If you do not pay my fee, and if I have to sue you to collect it, I will have to reveal the whole truth in open court, to explain why the amount of my fee is reasonable. Think this over carefully. I hope to receive your check by return mail."

QUESTION:

17. Which of the following is most nearly correct?

    A. Even though heavy-handed, Attorney's letter was proper because he was simply explaining to Jones the consequences of refusing to pay the fee.

    B. If Attorney sues Jones to collect the fee, Attorney will be subject to discipline because a lawyer is prohibited from using a civil suit to collect a fee.

    C. If Attorney sues Jones to collect the fee, Attorney may reveal Jones's confidential communications, but only to the extent necessary to establish his claim against Jones.

    D. Attorney's letter was proper because a lawyer is required to settle fee disputes amicably if possible.

* * *

Lawyer Miles does all of the outside legal work for his client Coffee Inc. He has just discovered that Coffee Inc. has been importing beans infested with a fungus known to cause illness in humans, and he believes that any future shipments of tainted beans would violate a federal statute regarding the knowing importation of adulterated foods. Lawyer Miles expresses his opinion to the vice-president of operations at Coffee Inc., who tells Lawyer Miles that no changes will be made regarding the planned importation of beans.

QUESTION:

18. Which of the following is the best answer?

    A. Miles would not be subject to discipline if he first revealed the problem to the shareholders, the ultimate owners of the corporation.

    B. Miles would not be subject to discipline if he first revealed the problem to the Board of Directors of Coffee Inc.

C. Miles would not be subject to discipline if he revealed the information to no one.

D. Miles would be subject to discipline if he first disclosed Coffee Inc.'s illegal conduct to the appropriate governmental agency.

* * *

Betty and Don Draper have been married for ten years. Both of them are lawyers but they work in different law firms. Betty currently represents Gravity Corp. in a lawsuit against Dropsy, Inc., a client of Don's partner, Roger.

QUESTION:

19. In deciding whether Roger can represent Dropsy, Inc., which of the following is the best answer?

A. Roger would be subject to discipline, because if Don could not represent Dropsy, Inc., neither can Roger.

B. Roger would be subject to discipline, because his representation of Dropsy, Inc. is materially limited by his acquaintance with Betty and Don.

C. Roger would not be subject to discipline.

D. Roger would not be subject to discipline as long as Don does not share in the fee.

* * *

After Michael was arrested for stealing a diamond ring that he was wearing at the time of his arrest, the local prosecutor approached the victim (who is not the prosecutor's client) of the theft and offered to buy the ring that day because she greatly admired it.

QUESTION:

20. Which of the following is the best answer?

A. The prosecutor is subject to discipline if she buys the ring before the case of *State v. Michael* is completed.

B. The prosecutor is subject to discipline if she buys the ring.

C. The prosecutor is not subject to discipline if Michael clarifies that he makes no claim to ownership of the ring.

D. The prosecutor is not subject to discipline if Michael consents to the purchase.

* * *

QUESTION:

21. In a non-litigation matter:

   A. A lawyer may withdraw if the representation will result in a violation of the Rules of Professional Conduct or other law.

   B. A lawyer must withdraw if the client has used the lawyer's services to perpetrate a crime or fraud.

   C. A lawyer may withdraw if the representation will result in an unreasonable financial burden on the lawyer, but only if the withdrawal can be accomplished without having a material adverse effect on the interest of the client.

   D. A lawyer may withdraw if the client persists in a course of action involving the lawyer's services that the lawyer reasonably believes is criminal.

* * *

Attorney Bob Cranfill represents Andrew Kuhn at his sentencing hearing following his criminal conviction. The pre-sentence investigation indicates that Andrew has no prior criminal record, and the trial judge asks Andrew whether that is true. After Andrew confirms the information in the pre-sentence investigation, the trial judge places Andrew on probation. Attorney Cranfill knows from an independent inquiry and from questioning Andrew that Andrew does have a criminal record and that the pre-sentence investigation is incorrect.

QUESTION:

22. When Judge Wrigley asks Attorney Cranfill whether he has anything to say, does Attorney Cranfill have an ethical obligation to correct the record?

   A. No, because Attorney Cranfill would violate his duty of confidentiality if he disclosed the information about Andrew's prior record.

   B. Yes, because Andrew has committed perjury which can be imputed to Attorney Cranfill.

C. No, because Andrew made the false statement, not Attorney Cranfill.

D. Yes, because Attorney Cranfill is prohibited from offering evidence that he knows to be false and from making a false statement of material fact to a tribunal.

* * *

When Lawyer Simon represented Hyman in connection with a murder investigation ten years ago, Hyman repeatedly assured Lawyer Simon that he was innocent. Because the investigation proved inconclusive, Hyman was never formally charged with any crime and Lawyer Simon's representation of Hyman ended. Currently, Lawyer Simon represents Client Burlingame in a child custody dispute between Burlingame and her ex-husband. Burlingame tells Lawyer Simon in confidence about a murder committed ten years ago by a person named Hyman, who was helped after the murder by her ex-husband. The details offered by Burlingame make it clear to Lawyer Simon that her former client Hyman did commit the murder.

QUESTION:

23. What is Lawyer Simon's ethical disclosure obligation?

A. If there is no statute of limitations on the crime of murder, Lawyer Simon may reveal Burlingame's information to the police without her consent.

B. Lawyer Simon must reveal the information to the police because Hyman's evasion of the law is a continuing crime.

C. Lawyer Simon may reveal the information to the prosecutor without the consent of either Hyman or Burlingame, provided that he asks the prosecutor not to disclose the source of the information.

D. Lawyer Simon must keep the information in confidence unless Burlingame consents to have it revealed.

* * *

Clarence has practiced law in New Jersey for sixteen years, and is a member of only the New Jersey Bar. After a powerful hurricane extensively damaged property and injured hundreds of people on the Gulf Coast, Clarence decided to offer assistance to the people in that region by relocating his New Jersey law practice to the Gulf Shore in Mississippi for the winter months. Clarence closed his Newark, New Jersey office for six months and notified all of his clients where they could reach him and that he would return to his Newark office on June 1. When he left New Jersey in late November, he had no clients from Mississippi and had no cases arising out of any conduct in Mississippi. Beginning December 1, Clarence opened a law office in a trailer on the Gulf of Mexico beach just off a main highway.

QUESTION:

24. Is Clarence subject to discipline?

    A. Yes, a lawyer who is not licensed in a jurisdiction can never maintain an office there or hold himself out as practicing in that state.

    B. Yes, because Clarence has never been admitted to practice anywhere outside of New Jersey.

    C. Yes, unless Clarence is practicing in Mississippi temporarily and associates himself with a lawyer admitted to practice in Mississippi who actively participates in Clarence's cases.

    D. Yes, unless Clarence has a national license to practice law.

* * *

In the previous question, assume that Clarence is practicing in Mississippi during those six winter months. However, he persists in refusing to return the phone calls of any clients who have paid him a retainer fee to represent them.

QUESTION:

25. Which of the following best describes Clarence's potential for discipline?

    A. Clarence is subject to discipline in New Jersey because that is where he is admitted to practice law.

    B. Clarence is not subject to discipline in Mississippi because that is where he has violated the Rules by failing to communicate with clients.

    C. Clarence is not subject to discipline in New Jersey because his misconduct occurred outside New Jersey.

    D.   Answers A and B are correct.

* * *

When Lawyer Lanier interviewed Client Cal, the subject of the representation related to probating the will of Client Cal's sister. Client Cal disclosed to Lawyer Lanier he knew about three wills that his sister had written. After reading all three wills, Lawyer Lanier told Client Cal that generally all three wills contained the same information, but that Client Cal would realize the greatest benefit from the second will. Thereafter, with Lawyer Lanier's assistance, Client Cal submitted his sister's second will for probate without disclosing to the Probate Judge any information about the other two wills.

QUESTION:

    26. Which of the following best describes Lawyer Lanier's situation?

        A.   Lawyer Lanier is subject to discipline for presenting a will for probate without disclosing the existence of a later will.

        B.   Lawyer Lanier is not subject to discipline because no one can have more than one will.

        C.   Lawyer Lanier is not subject to discipline because all three wills were more or less identical.

        D.   Answers B and C are both true.

* * *

Lawyer Lackey has been practicing with the firm of Osborne and Glick for ten years. During that time, his practice has grown in the area of maritime law. In the beginning, his maritime clients were clients of the law firm. As his reputation grew, a large number of new clients came to the firm because of Lawyer Lackey. He now has decided to leave his firm to practice with several lawyers he has met.

QUESTIONS:

    27. Which of the following best describes how the legal needs of Lawyer Lackey's current clients will be met?

        A.   The clients who belonged to Osborne and Glick when Lawyer Lackey arrived must stay with that firm, and the rest of the clients can decide whether to go with Lawyer Lackey or stay with Osborne and Glick.

B.   The clients who came to Osborne and Glick after Lawyer Lackey arrived must go with Lawyer Lackey to his new firm, but the other clients can decide for themselves whether to go with Lawyer Lackey or stay with Osborne and Glick.

C.   All of Lawyer Lackey's clients can decide for themselves which lawyer or law firm to use for legal services.

D.   None of Lawyer Lackey's clients at Osborne and Glick can be his clients after he leaves that firm.

* * *

28. Which of the following describes Lawyer Lackey's notice to his clients about his departure from Osborne and Glick?

A.   It is permissible for Lawyer Lackey to send a letter announcing his new affiliation to Osborne and Glick clients whose matters he is handling.

B.   It is permissible for Lawyer Lackey to personally contact all Osborne and Glick clients about his new affiliation.

C.   It is mandatory for Lawyer Lackey to send a notice announcing his new affiliation to Osborne and Glick clients whose matters he is handling.

D.   It is mandatory for Lawyer Lackey to send targeted mail to all Osborne and Glick clients about his new affiliation.

* * *

Lawyer Little has practiced commercial litigation for thirteen years with Pernick and Hinerfeld, a law firm of more than 200 lawyers. Lawyer Little became so successful that she accepted an offer from one of her firm's chief competitors, Barber and Richmond. After she arrived at Barber and Richmond, Lawyer Little and her new law partner Lawyer Rodes began to represent the Jaye Corporation, a client of Pernick and Hinerfeld when Lawyer Little practiced there. Her old firm was so aggravated by Lawyer Little representing Jaye Corporation that it moved to disqualify both Lawyer Little and

Lawyer Rodes from representing Jaye Corporation in *Jaye Corporation v. Coan Industries, Inc.* In that case, Pernick and Hinerfeld represented an old client of that firm, Coan Industries, Inc.

QUESTION:

29. Under the Model Rules, which of the following describes how the trial judge should decide the motion to disqualify Lawyer Little and Lawyer Rodes?

   A. The court should grant the motion if Coan Industries, Inc. was a client of Pernick and Hinerfeld while Lawyer Little practiced there.

   B. The court should grant the motion if Lawyer Little socialized with Coan Industries, Inc.'s Chief Executive Officer while she was a lawyer at Pernick and Hinerfeld.

   C. The court should deny the motion if Lawyer Little knew no confidential information about Coan Industries, Inc. after having practiced at Pernick and Hinerfeld.

   D. The court should deny the motion to disqualify Lawyer Little if she is screened from participating in *Jaye Corporation v. Coan Industries, Inc.*

* * *

Lawyer Harriet is a solo practitioner who represents Client Charlie in a breach of contract case. Yesterday, the opposing side sent twenty interrogatories calling for detailed responses; the interrogatories must be answered within thirty days under the Rules of Civil Procedure for that state. Lawyer Harriet receives those interrogatories just before leaving town for a four-week vacation in Mexico.

QUESTION:

30. Which, if any, of the following describes Lawyer Harriet's obligation?

   A. Lawyer Harriet is subject to discipline if she never sends the interrogatories to Client Charlie for him to assist in answering.

   B. Lawyer Harriet is subject to discipline if she waits to return from her vacation to forward the interrogatories to Client Charlie.

C. Lawyer Harriet is subject to discipline if she does not send the interrogatories to Client Charlie and instead answers them, although she knows that her information in Client Charlie's files cannot satisfactorily comply with the requests for information.

D. Answers A, B and C are correct.

* * *

Lawyer Ben has been litigating personal injury cases for ten years, but he is not yet comfortable with many of the new customs and practices regarding technology. In fact, sometimes he becomes confused when faxing information to his client and to the opposing counsel in some of his cases. For example, last week when he intended to fax important correspondence between himself and Client Daniels, instead he accidentally included those documents in a bundle of papers which he faxed to opposing counsel, Lawyer Brandon, as answers to interrogatories. It is clear to Brandon that these documents were not intended to be sent to him from Lawyer Ben.

QUESTION:

31. What, if any, obligation does Lawyer Brandon have upon receiving the privileged documents from Lawyer Ben?

A. Lawyer Brandon is subject to discipline if he fails to inform Lawyer Ben immediately.

B. Lawyer Brandon is subject to discipline if he returns the documents unread to Lawyer Ben.

C. Lawyer Brandon is subject to discipline if he forwards the documents to Client Daniels.

D. A and C are both correct answers.

* * *

Client Turpin, a widow, received an unsolicited mailing for estate planning services from Lawyer Lewis. A month later, Lawyer Lewis visited with Client Turpin at her home. Following the viewing of a videotape prepared by Lawyer Lewis and a presentation by her explaining estate planning instruments, Client Turpin signed an engagement letter and gave Lawyer Lewis a check for $1,995 for her legal fees. Brenda, a daughter of Client Turpin, was present with her mother during the videotape and presentation. Three months later, Client Turpin's health deteriorated, and she was hospitalized. Family members of Client Turpin called Lawyer Lewis and informed them of Client Turpin's hospitalization and declining health. Lawyer Lewis came to the hospital with a revocable living trust agreement, last will and testament, and business and health care powers of attorney forms. Because Client Turpin was incapacitated, Lawyer Lewis advised Client Turpin's daughter to execute and sign the legal documents on behalf of her mother. The daughter signed the trust, will, and powers of attorney as instructed. Lawyer Lewis took no further action to protect Client Turpin's legal interests as to her estate. After the local probate court rejected the will alleged to be Client Turpin's, her daughter and her family retained another lawyer to probate Client Turpin's estate. In addition, on behalf of Client Turpin's heirs, the new lawyer made a demand on Lawyer Lewis for the return of $1,995 for legal fees and payment to cover the costs associated with the intestate probate of the estate. Lawyer Lewis failed to respond to the demand, failed to return the $1,995 to Client Turpin's estate, failed to assist in the probate of the estate, and failed to take steps to the extent reasonably practicable to protect Client Turpin's estate.

QUESTION:

32. Which of the following is (are) true about Lawyer Lewis's ethical lapses?

    A. Lawyer Lewis is subject to discipline for failing to maintain a normal lawyer-client relationship with Client Turpin.

    B. Lawyer Lewis is subject to discipline for failing to return the $1,995 to Client Turpin's estate.

    C. Lawyer Lewis is subject to discipline for failing to take steps to protect Client Turpin's interests.

    D. Answers A, B and C are true.

* * *

For the past fifteen years, Lawyer Kramer has had a general practice along with two other lawyers with whom she shares office space. Because her law practice has evolved toward a fairly narrow specialization in family adoption law, she thinks that she would like to begin advertising that practice specialty.

QUESTION:

33. Which of the following statements about advertising specializations is false?

A.   She will be subject to discipline if she advertises in the local newspaper that she is a specialist in family adoption law and in child custody disputes.

B.   She will be subject to discipline if she advertises on the Internet that she is a specialist in family adoption law and in patent law.

C.   She will be subject to discipline if she advertises on cable television that she is a family adoption specialist, but only if the state where she is admitted to practice recognizes specialization through certification.

D.   She will be subject to discipline if she advertises on billboards that she is a family adoption specialist as a member of a group accredited by the American Bar Association and the name of the certifying organization is clearly identified in her ad.

* * *

The law firm of Able, Baker and Cohen realizes that its client base is getting older and that the firm must find new ways to attract clients. While the firm has explored advertising as a means of bringing in new business, the rate of new clients is slower than the projections the firm made when it initiated it advertising campaign. Thus, the law firm has decided to take an even riskier path toward client development by experimenting with solicitation of clients.

QUESTION:

34. Which of the following solicitation approaches will result in the law firm partners being subject to discipline under the Rules?

A.   The law firm partners can solicit other lawyers for new business.

B.   The law firm partners can contact their family members and close friends for new business.

C.   The law firm partners can join an existing prepaid legal services plan and solicit people not known by them to need legal services in a particular matter.

D.   Answers A, B and C are correct.

* * *

Lawyer Dee represents wealthy clients in divorce litigation. In addition to employing several investigators to assist her in the development of factual information necessary to litigate issues such as custody and asset ownership, Lawyer Dee also employs financial planners who guide her clients in decisions about investing property in which the clients have sole ownership. Client Corrine needs financial planning advice, which Lawyer Dee indirectly offers through ownership of a financial investment service located elsewhere in Lawyer Dee's office building.

QUESTION:

35. Which of the following is not true?

A. Lawyer Dee is subject to discipline if she fails to follow the ethical standards related to business transactions with a client.

B. Lawyer Dee is subject to discipline, because the financial planning services must be offered from her law office rather than having them dispensed from a separate office, even if it is adjacent to her law office.

C. Lawyer Dee is subject to discipline if she fails to supervise the non-lawyers in the delivery of the financial planning advice.

D. Lawyer Dee is not subject to discipline for offering law-related services to her clients.

* * *

Plaintiff Lawyer Lotz represents Client Clore in a car accident case in which the defendant's liability is clear. The only issue is the extent of Client Clore's damages, including a back injury. Two days ago, Lawyer Lotz wrote a demand letter to the insurance company indicating that Client Clore had never been in an accident before and never had any other injuries to his back. Today, Lawyer Lotz saw a friend of Client Clore's who knows she is representing Client Clore and asks whether she is handling Client Clore's first or second accident. Lawyer Lotz calls Client Clore immediately. Client Clore admits to her that a year before the car accident, he had hurt his back in a fall at his friend's house. Client Clore tells her that he never made a claim for the earlier injury and had not said anything about it because he was afraid it would ruin this case. Client Clore tells Lawyer Lotz that he will pursue the case no matter what and that he does not want to disclose the prior accident or injury.

QUESTION:

36. What is Lawyer Lotz's best course of action under the Rules?

A. Lawyer Lotz must disclose Client Clore's fraud if her failure to do so will assist Client Clore in perpetrating a fraud on the insurance company that will result in substantial financial injury.

B. Lawyer Lotz may disclose Client Clore's fraud if her failure to do so will assist Client Clore in perpetrating a fraud on the insurance company that will result in substantial financial injury.

C. Lawyer Lotz must not disclose Client Clore's confidential information.

D. None of the above answers is correct.

* * *

Lawyer Tony practices corporate law with a concentration in securities regulation. Client Chloe retained the services of Lawyer Tony about a securities issue related to her ownership of stock in a publicly-traded company, but their relationship quickly grew beyond the normal lawyer-client relationship. Lawyer Tony and Client Chloe began a dating relationship that soon became a sexual relationship. At about the time that they decided to live together, Client Chloe's case became more complex as she faced charges of insider trading.

QUESTION:

37. Which of the following best describes Lawyer Tony's ethical situation?

A. Lawyer Tony may continue to represent Client Chloe, if she consents to the continued representation.

B. Lawyer Tony may continue to represent Client Chloe is she consents after consulting another lawyer.

C. Lawyer Tony must withdraw from representing Client Chloe, but his law partner may represent her.

D. Lawyer Tony may continue to represent Client Chloe, because her case does not raise the potential for prejudice to her as a result of their relationship.

* * *

Lawyer Phillips represents Client Justin, a former high school football coach accused of causing the death of one of his players by denying him water during the hot weather of summer practices. Fearing he would not be able to afford the entire fee charged by Lawyer Phillips, Client Justin has signed over to Lawyer Phillips the literary rights to his story to about the ordeal of being a coach accused of homicide in the death of one of his beloved players. Although he was acquitted of the criminal charges, Client Justin still faces a civil wrongful death case for damages brought by the dead player's family. Lawyer Phillips is using the break between those two cases to seek a book contract for Client Justin.

QUESTION:

38. Which of the following describes Lawyer Phillips's situation?

   A. Lawyer Phillips is not subject to discipline, because Client Justin needs the money to pay her fee.

   B. Lawyer Phillips is not subject to discipline, because the focus of the book will be on Client Justin's criminal trial.

   C. Lawyer Phillips is subject to discipline, because she cannot acquire her client's literary or media rights for his case.

   D. Lawyer Phillips is subject to discipline, but someone else in her firm acquire the publication rights from Client Justin while the wrongful death case is pending.

* * *

Lawyer Lonnie has been appointed to represent Client Taylor who is accused of killing her husband after a long period of spousal abuse by him. Because Client Taylor is a lifelong local resident, the court released her on her own recognizance rather than setting a large monetary amount for her to post in order to obtain her pretrial release. However, Client Taylor, who is a stay-at-home mother, is quickly running out of money. Lawyer Lonnie has some discretionary funds available to him and he wants to give Taylor some cash to use for living expenses.

QUESTION:

39. What is the ethical course for Lawyer Lonnie to pursue?

A. Give her a reasonable amount of money to live on but only while her criminal case is pending.

B. Give her a free place to live until her criminal case is over.

C. Not advance her any money for living expenses.

D. Not represent her because he feels sorry for Client Taylor.

* * *

Admitted to practice for less than six months and practicing law by herself, Lawyer Luther's recent interview with a potential client left her clueless about how ethically to represent his interests. Lawyer Luther recalls studying and discussing the conflict of interest rules in law school but the reality of the client's immediate needs have her anxious about doing a good job for her client. As Lawyer Luther sees the situation, she would have to disclose her client's confidential information in order to obtain ethical advice about how to proceed.

QUESTION:

40. What is Lawyer Luther's ethical disclosure obligation?

A. Lawyer Luther may disclose her client's confidential information to obtain ethical advice under the Rules, but only if she first obtains her client's informed consent in writing.

B. Lawyer Luther must not disclose her client's confidential information to obtain ethical advice.

C. Lawyer Luther may disclose her client's confidential information to obtain ethical advice, but only if the disclosures are to a person who works with a bar association's ethics hotline.

D. Lawyer Luther may disclose her client's confidential information to obtain ethical advice, but only if she obtains assurance that the disclosed information will remain confidential with the person from whom she is seeking advice.

* * *

Lawyer Fitzgerald has represented consumers in environmental litigation for more than twenty years. Historically, his specialty is litigating against private corporate polluters. Recently, though, Lawyer Fitzgerald has represented some of those same corporations because she decided that her influence on their behavior might be greater if they listened to her legal advice. Her most recent case involved air pollution by a local rubber manufacturer. Through discussions with her corporate client's officers, Lawyer Fitzgerald has learned about a longstanding policy of ignoring the pollutants emanating from the corporate smokestacks which has resulted in large increases in the rate of lethal, incurable cancers in the neighborhoods adjacent to the local manufacturing plant.

QUESTION:

41. With this information, what is Lawyer Fitzgerald's ethical disclosure obligation?

A. Must disclose what she knows to the appropriate government authority.

B. May disclose what she knows in order to save lives.

C. Must not disclose any confidential information learned from her corporate client.

D. May disclose what she knows to prevent the corporation from going bankrupt.

* * *

Lawyer Willa is a partner in a local law firm. One of her clients, Metro Stoneware Corporation, has a large manufacturing plant with over 250 employees. Currently, Lawyer Willa is litigating a "right to strike" provision in its standard collective bargaining agreement with its employees. Metro Stoneware wants to nullify the broad interpretation that their employees' union prefers. One of Willa's other clients is a separate labor union with a collective bargaining agreement at the local underwear company. Coincidentally, that union is advocating a broad interpretation of its "right to strike" provision.

QUESTION:

42. Is Willa subject to discipline for advocating both sides of the same issue?

A. Yes, because the Rules treat this type of "positional conflict" as *per se* unethical.

B. Yes, but only if the two representations involve litigation.

C. No, if the underwear union gives its informed consent to the conflicting representation.

D. No, if the conflict does not materially limit her representation of one of her clients.

* * *

In the course of seeking professional advice from Lawyer Sarah, client Sam discloses that he committed the crime with which he is charged. Later that same day he tells his bank teller, grocery clerk and furnace repairman of his criminal acts.

QUESTION:

43. If a trial judge later orders Lawyer Sarah to disclose what Client Sam had told her that day, which of the following describes whether there has been a waiver of the lawyer-client privilege or the ethical duty of confidentiality?

A. There has been a waiver of both the lawyer-client privilege and the ethical duty of confidentiality; Lawyer Sarah must disclose what Client Sam told her.

B. There has been a waiver of the lawyer-client privilege but not the ethical duty of confidentiality; Lawyer Sarah must disclose what Client Sam told her.

C. There has been no waiver of either the lawyer-client privilege or the ethical duty of confidentiality; Lawyer Sarah must not disclose what Client Sam told her.

D. There has been a waiver of the ethical duty of confidentiality but not the lawyer-client privilege.

* * *

The law partnership of Ames and Bean employed Lawyer Lana as an associate lawyer. Client Cross hired Lawyer Ames to sue one of his competitors for tortious interference with contract. Too busy to do the research himself, Lawyer Ames assigned Lawyer Lana to do the necessary research and draft a complaint. Lawyer Lana had never filed a tortious interference claim and confined his research to state law. Any reasonably competent general practitioner would have discovered a more favorable body of parallel federal law. Ames eventually brought the case to trial on state law theories only, and Client Cross lost the case. If the case had been tried under the federal law, Client Cross would have won a large judgment.

QUESTION:

44. Which of the following is true?

    A. Lawyer Lana is liable for malpractice.

    B. If Lawyer Lana is liable for malpractice, then Ames also is liable.

    C. If Lawyers Lana and Ames are liable for malpractice, then Bean also is liable.

    D. Answers A, B and C are true.

    * * *

QUESTION:

45. Which of the following statements accurately describes the view of the United States Supreme Court on judicial disqualification?

    A. Judicial disqualification questions never involve constitutional issues.

    B. Judicial disqualification questions may involve constitutional issues.

    C. A judge's ruling cannot be set aside on grounds that the judge had a conflict of interest in the case when the judge was unaware of it at the time of the ruling.

    D. Answers B and C are correct.

    * * *

Investigator Ike works for the law firm of Dewey and Howe. After a client recently brought a potentially lucrative breach of contract case to the law firm, Lawyer Dewey filed a lawsuit on behalf of the client against Adversary Abner who is represented by Lawyer Cheatham. After Adversary Abner answered the complaint, Lawyer Dewey instructed Investigator Ike to invite Adversary Abner to go to lunch and find out as much about Adversary Abner and the case as possible without appearing to be too nosey.

QUESTION:

46. Which of the following describes Lawyer Dewey's ethical situation if Investigator Ike sends a long memo about Adversary Abner to Lawyer Dewey after the lunch?

A. Lawyer Dewey is not subject to discipline for sending Investigator Ike to interview Adversary Abner.

B. Lawyer Dewey is subject to discipline for sending Investigator Ike to talk to Adversary Abner.

C. Lawyer Dewey is subject to discipline only if Investigator Ike obtains privileged information from Adversary Abner.

D. Lawyer Dewey is not subject to discipline for sending Investigator Ike to talk to Adversary Abner unless Investigator Ike obtains privileged information from Adversary Abner.

* * *

Lawyer Lark's client arrived in the United States last year, without knowing anyone in the small town where Lawyer Lark practices law. The client came to Lawyer Lark when the client's first business venture failed, but Lawyer Lark achieved an outstanding outcome for her client. Realizing that she cannot ask her client to give her a large gift in appreciation for the surprising outcome to her tortious interference with contract case, Lawyer Lark has several ideas for recognition of her hard work.

QUESTION:

47. Which of Lawyer Lark's ideas will *not* subject her to discipline?

A. Lawyer Lark may draft an agreement by which her client, who is not related to Lawyer Lark, may give a substantial gift to Lawyer Lark's daughter to pay for her college education.

B. Lawyer Lark may ask her client to designate Lawyer Lark the executrix of his Last Will and Testament, although the size of the fee for being the executrix that is designated in the will is far beyond what is reasonable for either the fee of an executrix or for Lawyer Lark's fee for being the lawyer for the client's estate.

C. Lawyer Lark's client may ask Lawyer Lark's law partner to draft an instrument providing for a substantial gift to Lawyer Lark.

D. Lawyer Lark's client may ask Lawyer Stewart, who practices law in another downtown building, to draft an agreement which provides a substantial gift to Lawyer Lark.

* * *

QUESTION:

48. In representing a client accused of a crime, for which of the following curse of action may a lawyer encounter an ethical problem?

 A. A defense lawyer may ask the court's permission to violate its order of document disclosure because the documents are privileged.

 B. A defense lawyer may advise the defendant not to volunteer any information to the prosecutor.

 C. A defense lawyer can assert her personal opinion about the facts, as by asserting that a witness is lying.

 D. A defense lawyer may request that an unrepresented witness refuse to volunteer information if he is her client's relative whose his interests will not be adversely affected if the lawyer's request is honored.

* * *

QUESTION:

49. As part of prosecutors' special ethical responsibilities, which of the following need not be done by the ethical prosecutor?

 A. Prosecutors must provide defendants with a reasonable opportunity to obtain counsel by informing them of their right to have their own counsel.

 B. Prosecutors must negotiate directly with a *pro se* defendant.

 C. In the post-conviction context, prosecutors must promptly disclose to the court and the convicted defendant any new, credible and material evidence that creates a reasonable likelihood that he did not commit a crime for which he was convicted.

 D. Prosecutors may subpoena defense counsel to testify before a grand jury, unless defense counsel asserts the intent to assert the lawyer-client privilege if asked about communications with her client.

* * *

Client Kevin has sought the advice of Lawyer Will on several occasions in the past, but he sometimes believes that Lawyer Will's style of practicing law is somewhat eccentric. For example, Lawyer Will has an aversion to conflict and disagreements with others. As a result, Lawyer Will tries to avoid litigation situations, even on behalf of his past clients who are in need of his services. Last month, Client Kevin asked Lawyer Will to represent him in a dispute with his cable television provider about billing practices. Lawyer Will agreed to represent Client Kevin, with one stipulation: he would counsel Client Kevin about the matter but if the dispute had to be litigated, Client Kevin knew that he would have to find another lawyer.

QUESTION:

50. Is Lawyer Will subject to discipline for agreeing to represent Client Kevin under that condition?

    A.   Yes, because the client alone determines the scope of the representation.

    B.   Yes, because as long as the client is not asking his lawyer to assist in criminal or fraudulent conduct, the client dictates the scope of the representation.

— C.   No, because a lawyer may limit the scope of the representation if the client gives informed consent.

    D.   No, because a lawyer may limit the scope of the representation regardless of whether the client consents.

* * *

Lawyer Levine was trained and became certified as an mediator three years ago by the American Mediation Association. As she has become a more experienced litigator in family law cases, she also has increased the number of cases in which she mediates family law disputes around the state where she is admitted to practice law. Through mediating, she meets increasing numbers of lawyers and other members of the community where she lives.

QUESTION:

51. What is Lawyer Levine ethically permitted to do as a mediator?

A. When she wears her American Mediator Association badge identifying herself as a mediator, she does not have to explain to unrepresented persons that she does not represent them.

B. She cannot discuss further employment with either a party or a lawyer representing a party in the matter in which she is mediating.

C. She can never represent a party to the mediation in a future proceeding related to the mediation, without the consent of all mediation participants.

D. If she is disqualified from representing a party to the mediation in a future proceeding related to the mediation, no one else in her law firm can represent anyone in the future either, unless she is properly screened and receives no part of the fee paid to the law firm.

* * *

Lawyer Lyons is a senior associate in a medium-sized law firm of twenty-six lawyers. She is in her sixth year as an associate lawyer, hoping to become a partner in two more years. Her current cases include a matter which is scheduled for trial next month. The other lawyer in the case, Lawyer Lincoln, has been practicing at the firm for less than two years. After making his vacation plans, Lawyer Lincoln realized that his plans for being on vacation abroad include the time of the trial that he is helping Lawyer Lyons to prepare. Without contacting Lawyer Lyons, Lawyer Lincoln calls the opposing counsel and offers a totally false reason for seeking an agreement to ask the trial judge for a six-month continuance of the trial date. The stipulated motion to continue the case is approved by the trial court at the ensuing motion hour. Lawyer Lyons happens to learn about the continuance while checking her emails from the trial judge's court clerk. She confronts Lawyer Lincoln but does not contact the opposing counsel or the trial judge. While having dinner with Partner Peters a week later, Lawyer Lyons tells the partner about what Lawyer Lincoln has done. Partner Peters, who works in a different department of the firm from either Lyons or Lincoln laughs about the situation but otherwise does nothing.

QUESTION:

52. Which of the following describes the ethical situation for Lawyer Lyons and Partner Peters?

A. Both Lawyer Lyons and Partner Peters are subject to discipline for failing to take action after learning about

Lawyer Lincoln's false claim to opposing counsel and to the trial judge.

B. As Lawyer Lincoln's direct supervisor in the case, only Lawyer Lyons is subject to discipline for failing to take action after learning about Lawyer Lincoln's false claim to opposing counsel and to the trial judge.

C. As a partner in the law firm, only Partner Peters is subject to discipline for failing to take action after learning about Lawyer Lincoln's false claim to opposing counsel and to the trial judge.

D. Neither Lawyer Lyons nor Partner Peters is subject to discipline for failing to take action after learning about Lawyer Lincoln's false claim to opposing counsel and to the trial judge.

* * *

Judge Jackson and Prosecutor Paul were married for twelve years. Before their marriage, when they were dating an administrative order was entered that prohibited Judge Jackson from presiding over any criminal case in the county where Judge Jackson presides. After their divorce, a second administrative order was issued allowing Judge Jackson to begin accepting criminal cases, with no further limitations. That order allowed Prosecutor Paul to practice in front of Judge Jackson. Lawyer Liston, who represents a defendant accused of several felonies, filed a motion to disqualify Judge Jackson from presiding in the case.

QUESTION:

53. Under the Code of Judicial Conduct, how should Judge Jackson rule on Lawyer Liston's motion to disqualify?

A. Judge Jackson should grant the motion, because the Code clearly states that a judge's ex-spouse cannot appear before the judge

B. Judge Jackson should grant the motion, if her impartiality might reasonably be questioned because her ex-spouse is acting as counsel of record in the case.

C. Judge Jackson should deny the motion, because the Code of Judicial Conduct does not address the issue of an ex-spouse acting as counsel of record.

D. Judge Jackson should deny the motion, because she has a duty to sit in any case assigned to her court.

* * *

Lawyer King is deeply involved in local political matters, including judicial politics. When the judicial election campaigns begin for the judges who are elected every four years, Lawyer King is one of the first lawyers to contribute to both candidates for two reasons: so that she can claim to have backed the election winner, and so that she can realize some monetary benefit in the form of a judicial appointment. The size of her contribution is usually the equivalent of the average political contribution. When Lawyer King's law practice began to decrease, she decided to be more aggressive in realizing a benefit from her cumulative campaign donations. Last year, after Judge Pfeiffer was reelected, Lawyer King successfully requested to have her name placed at the top of the judge's list for court appointments such as exclusive positions like guardian *ad litem*. Since that time, Lawyer King has received dozens of such appointments.

QUESTION:

54. Is Lawyer King subject to discipline?

   A. Yes, because the Rules prohibit "play-to-pay" contributions like those made by Lawyer King.

   B. No, as long as Lawyer King's contribution did not exceed the legal limit for individual contributors.

   C. No, because Lawyer King's contribution was not excessive, compared to the contributions of other lawyers.

   D. No, because Lawyer King's motives for contributing to Judge Pfeiffer were not exclusively to obtain judicial appointments.

* * *

According to state statute, anyone who knows about child abuse within the state must report that person to the police regardless of how the person with knowledge acquired the child abuse information. While representing Client Cliff in his divorce case, Lawyer Lochridge learns from him that he has physically abused one of his four children since the child was three years old. The abused child apparently has never disclosed the abuse to his mother, his siblings, or anyone else. Client Cliff's chances of being awarded custody of any of his children are severely jeopardized if the trial judge learns about his abusive past.

QUESTION:

55. Which of the following describes Lawyer Lochridge's ethical choices?

A. She must disclose her client's abuse of his child, because the statute requires disclosure.

B. She may disclose her client's abuse of his child, after discussing the issue of disclosure with Client Cliff.

C. She must not disclose her client's abuse of his child, because the information is protected by the lawyer-client privilege.

D. She must not disclose her client's abuse of his child, because the information relates to her representation of Client Cliff.

* * *

As part of her standard employment contract, Lawyer Luther decided to include several provisions which she learned about in her law school course in professional responsibility. In addition to sections about aggregate settlements and third parties paying her fee, there is a section pertaining to each client's consent to Lawyer Luther's future conflicts of interest.

QUESTION:

56. Under which of the following circumstances would such a consent provision be valid under the Rules?

A. Such a consent provision may be given orally or in writing in this circumstance.

B. Such a consent provision does not have to be in writing,

C. Such a consent provision must be in writing, and must include a full disclosure of the material risks and reasonably available alternatives of going forward with or without Lawyer Luther as the client's counsel.

D. Such a consent provision is never valid.

* * *

Most of Lawyer Lotz's law practice relates to representing divorce clients, especially wives who need a temporary restraining order to have their abusive husbands removed from the home in order to protect themselves and their children. Lawyer Lotz's current divorce client is Client Catherine who apparently is prone to be just as abusive to her husband as he is toward her.

QUESTION:

57. At the *ex parte* hearing before Judge Judd on whether to issue a temporary restraining order, for which of the following courses of conduct is Lawyer Lotz *not* subject to discipline?

   A. Alleging a meritorious claim for Client Catherine to evict her husband from their home, but saying nothing about her abuse toward her spouse at the hearing.

   B. Failing to disclose spouse abuse in that state which is directly adverse to Client Catherine's position that women never abuse their spouses.

   C. Presenting evidence that Lawyer Lotz knows is false: that Client Catherine never abused her husband.

   D. Refusing to offer all factual information, both helpful and adverse, for Judge Judd to consider.

* * *

Lawyer Leslie represents many union members with any family law problems. Occasionally, her fellow lawyers retain her when they are contacted by the bar association in conjunction with possible disciplinary proceedings. Last month, she was surprised when one of her biggest family law competitors, Lawyer Samuels, retained her about an allegation that he had commingled some of his client escrow accounts with his private funds. At the time, Lawyer Leslie and Lawyer Samuels have six cases where they are counsel of record on opposite sides of the case.

QUESTION:

58. In which of the following situations is Lawyer Leslie *not* subject to discipline?

   A. She attacks Lawyer Samuels's credibility in the divorce cases where he is counsel of record and she is counsel for the adversary.

   B. She tempers her advocacy on behalf of her divorce client in the cases with Lawyer Samuels so as not to alienate Lawyer Samuels.

   C. She is charging Lawyer Samuels a fee that is twenty times the amount of the total fees she is charging the six divorce clients whose spouses are represented by Lawyer Samuels.

D. She obtains informed consent from her six divorce clients and from Lawyer Samuels, who must make full disclosures to his six divorce clients.

* * *

For six years, Lawyer Landers has represented AB. Corporation, which is the largest employer in the town where its only manufacturing facility is located. Three years ago, AB.'s president, Clint Johnson, asked Lawyer Landers to serve a four-year term on AB.'s board of directors. Serving on the board at its monthly meetings and on several committees has allowed Lawyer Landers to apply some of the knowledge that she acquired when she earned an M.B.A. degree long ago at Summit University, the same place where she earned her law degree. A recent board discussion about a pending patent application has made it clear to Lawyer Landers that Clint Johnson and the other board members did not understand whether she was giving legal advice as counsel to the corporation or business advice as a board member.

QUESTION:

59. If Lawyer Landers seeks ethical advice from the senior partner in her law firm, what is the correct advice to offer her?

A. Her only financial choice is to resign as a board member, but remain as lawyer for AB. Corporation.

B. If her independent professional judgment is compromised in the dual capacity, she may resign either as lawyer for AB. Corporaton or as a board member.

C. She must resign as a board member and as the lawyer for AB. Corporation.

D. She may remain as a board member and as lawyer for AB. Corporation, as long as she clarifies that the lawyer-client privilege applies anytime that she is present at a board meeting.

* * *

Company Abner is interested in suing Company Bates for breach of contract. Company Abner asks several law firms to present its qualifications, and Company Abner revealed significantly harmful confidential information about its proposed lawsuit with all of the law firms. Specifically, Company Abner's disclosures of confidential information with Law Firm Carey & Dyson were with Law Partner Fisher. Company Abner decides not to retain Law Firm Carey & Dyson, which is retained by Company Bates three months later to defend Company Abner's lawsuit of *Company Abner v. Company Bates*.

QUESTION:

60. Which of the following describes Law Partner Fisher's and Law Firm Carey & Dyson's ethical situation in regard to representing Company Bates in the lawsuit, assuming that Company Abner receives notice about the situation?

    A. Any lawyer in Law Firm Carey & Dyson can represent Company Bates.

    B. Law Partner Fisher is disqualified from representing Company Bates, but Law Firm Carey & Dyson may represent Company Bates.

    C. Law Partner Fisher is disqualified from representing Company Bates, but Law Firm Carey & Dyson may represent Company Bates only if Law Partner is effectively screened.

    D. Neither Law Partner Fisher nor Law Firm Carey & Dyson can represent Company Bates.

PROFESSIONAL RESPONSIBILITY

Exam #2—60 Problems and Questions

Lawyer Arthur practices law in Hartford, primarily representing plaintiffs in civil litigation. Recent events have made him concerned about the ethics of his behavior. After successfully obtaining a hefty settlement for Sam Jones in a personal injury case, Lawyer Arthur was troubled by the fact that, in preparing for trial, Jones had told him that he is a cocaine trafficker and plans to continue engaging in selling tainted cocaine which teenagers often consume. Lawyer Arthur contacted the local police about Sam's admissions to him.

QUESTION:

1. Did Lawyer Arthur violate the rules on confidentiality by reporting his client's admission?

   A. Yes, because he must not reveal confidences to others, but may disclose the client's secrets.

   B. Yes, because he must never reveal "information relating to representation of a client" without the client's consent.

   C. No, because he always may disclose information relating to his client's intent to engage in any future criminal conduct.

   D. No, if Lawyer Arthur reasonably believes that giving the information to the police would prevent Jones from committing a criminal act that Lawyer Arthur believes is likely to result in prevent reasonably certain death or substantial bodily harm to the area's teenagers.

* * *

A lawsuit was filed recently by First Bank against Paul Sims, in which the law firm of Smith and Jones represents the plaintiff. The suit alleges that prior to leaving the bank's employ in 2008, Sims made fraudulent loans to himself through several fictitious accounts. Prior to attending law school, an associate attorney at Smith and Jones, Lawyer Travis, worked at First National Bank as a loan officer assigned to Sims's loan area but does not recall working on any of Sims's personal accounts. Lawyer Travis also recently came to work for Smith and Jones after working for three years at the law firm of Wilson and Craig, which just completed the representation of Sims in connection with a lawsuit over a 2009 business dispute between Sims and a business partner. However, Lawyer Travis is unaware of any information about that case. Previously, Smith and Jones represented Sims when Sims was executor of the Dale estate during the early–2000s. The representation was routine, except for a fee dispute which was mediated. The law firm of Smith and Jones has asked you to review the relationships between Paul Sims and the firm.

QUESTIONS:

2. In the facts above, can the law firm of Smith and Jones be disqualified from representing First National Bank by virtue of the firm's prior work as counsel for an estate in which Sims was the executor?

  A. Yes, because Smith and Jones had learned confidential information about Sims.

  B. Yes, because the current representation against Sims and the prior representation of Sims are not the same "matter" under Rule 1.9.

  C. No, because no lawyer in the Smith and Jones law firm is disqualifiable under the rule of imputed disqualification.

  D. No, because the mediated fee was based upon a misunderstanding .

3. In the facts above, can the firm of Smith and Jones be disqualified from representing First National Bank by virtue of Lawyer Travis's prior employment at Wilson and Craig while that firm represented Sims in a lawsuit?

  A. Yes, because the Sims matter and the First National Bank matter are substantially related.

  B. Yes, because Lawyer Travis recalls that his Wilson and Craig colleagues had represented Sims.

C. No, only because the Sims matter and the First National Bank matter are substantially related.

D. No, because Lawyer Travis acquired no confidential information about Sims's breach of contract case while at Wilson and Craig.

* * *

Lawyer Kussy filed a negligence action against the Minutia Delivery Corp. for injuries sustained in a collision between Lawyer Kussy's client's auto and Minutia's delivery truck. Ten years prior to this case, Lawyer Kussy had represented Minutia Delivery Corp. for one month when he briefly and unsuccessfully attempted to collect their delinquent accounts. During pretrial discovery in the current case, Minutia's counsel properly seeks information about the plaintiff's medical experts who would testify about the plaintiff's physical injuries sustained in the collision. Lawyer Kussy responds to the defendant's interrogatories that he has retained Dr. Cecil Doan, who will testify about the nature and extent of the plaintiff's physical injuries. He includes Dr. Doan's opinions and the reasons for those expert conclusions. Upon receiving those answers from Lawyer Kussy, Minutia's counsel has the court clerk issue a subpoena for Dr. Doan's deposition. Although Dr. Doan is properly served with the subpoena, he fails to appear for the scheduled deposition. Minutia immediately moves to have Dr. Doan held in contempt for his failure to appear. (The jurisdiction has a local rule which requires a litigant to answer interrogatories fairly and not falsely or in a manner calculated to mislead.) Dr. Doan appears at a hearing to show cause why he should not be held in contempt, and testifies as follows: he met Lawyer Kussy at a party in Lawyer Kussy's neighborhood, with Lawyer Kussy telling Doan about the instant case that is set for trial next year. Dr. Doan denied (and brought along a credible corroborating witness) that he ever was retained as an expert witness by Lawyer Kussy because he never received any money from Lawyer Kussy. Further, he never agreed to testify for Lawyer Kussy and he never expressed any opinion about Lawyer Kussy's client's injuries. After hearing this testimony, the trial judge dismissed Minutia's motion, and referred Lawyer Kussy to the State Bar Association for possible charges of unethical conduct.

QUESTION:

4. Of the following, for which conduct is Lawyer Kussy not subject to discipline?

A. Representing an adversary of Minutia Delivery Corp. which he had represented ten years earlier.

B. Making a false statement about Dr. Doan's availability to testify.

C. Knowingly disobeying the local rule regarding discovery.

D. Failing to make a diligent effort to determine if Dr. Doan had agreed to be his expert

* * *

Lawyer Connie Jones recently represented a client in a lawsuit to recover a valuable necklace that had been wrongfully converted. The jury awarded Lawyer Jones's client the necklace as well as $250,000 punitive damages. When Lawyer Jones and the client signed a fee contract, they agreed that Lawyer Jones would receive 40% of all punitive damages. The client told Lawyer Jones that on a big recovery 40% is unfair. The client offered to pay Lawyer Jones 25%. The defendant in the case satisfied the judgment by giving Lawyer Jones the necklace and a check for $250,000 payable to Lawyer Jones. She immediately deposited the check in her client trust account and put the necklace around her neck until the fee dispute was resolved.

QUESTION:

5. Was it proper for Lawyer Jones to put the $250,000 check into her trust account or for her to wear the necklace?

A. Yes, it was proper to put all the money in her account but only for a brief period.

B. Yes, it was proper to put the money in her account for as long as necessary to resolve all disputes relating to the money.

C. Yes, it was proper for Lawyer Jones to wear the necklace until she saw her client at her office.

D. No, it was improper for Lawyer Jones to wear the necklace, but she may delay transferring the necklace to her client until the financial issues are resolved.

* * *

While driving home from a golf outing, a Highway Patrol officer gave Lawyer Homer Simson a traffic ticket for having a defective tail light. A traffic ticket is a criminal misdemeanor in Lawyer Simson's state.

QUESTION:

6. Can Lawyer Simson be disciplined for having received the traffic ticket?

  A. No, because the offense does not reflect adversely on the lawyer's fitness.

  B. No, because Lawyer Simson was not acting in a professional capacity.

  C. Yes, because the ticket shows a lack of respect for law.

  D. None of the above.

* * *

Lawyer Cowell has not practiced for years, but he still pays bar dues annually. When his good friend O'Leary lost his house due to a fire, Lawyer Cowell who is employed as an insurance adjuster inflated his estimate of O'Leary's actual losses hoping to receive a kickback from O'Leary. However, O'Leary refused to give Lawyer Cowell any money.

QUESTION:

7. Can Lawyer Cowell be disciplined for his conduct?

  A. No, because Lawyer Cowell did not engage in such conduct in his capacity as a lawyer.

  B. No, because he received no kickback.

  C. Yes, because he acted in a prohibited conflict of interest situation when he adjusted his friend's claim.

  D. Yes, because he submitted a fraudulent insurance claim.

* * *

While seeking legal advice from his lawyer, Lawyer Dardeen, Madhatter told Lawyer Dardeen that she has had financial problems because her former lawyer (Lark) has stolen money from her. Madhatter begged Lawyer Dardeen not to reveal this information because Lark is her sister-in-law. Lawyer Dardeen told her that unless she was willing to let him reveal the information, there is little that he could do. He assured her, though, that he would keep her secret.

QUESTION:

8. Can Lawyer Dardeen be disciplined for not revealing this information to the disciplinary authorities?

    A. Yes, because he must report such unfavorable information to the appropriate tribunal empowered to investigate it.

    B. No, because the information is confidential.

    C. No, unless the amount stolen is large.

    D. Yes, if Madhatter's concerns for Lark's wife are groundless.

* * *

Lawyer Nussbaum counsels and advises clients about tax matters and other transactions that are largely tax-motivated. If the client-taxpayer's treatment of the transaction is not challenged by the Internal Revenue Service, the transaction may result in a substantial reduction in taxes to the client. If, on the other hand, the transaction is not sustained, the taxpayer will at least be required to pay the tax he had hoped to avoid plus interest and possibly a negligence penalty.

QUESTION:

9. In advising a client on such a transaction with doubtful consequences, in which of the following fee arrangements would Lawyer Nussbaum be subject to discipline for the fee arrangements, assuming that the fee is not "unreasonable"?

    A. Lawyer Nussbaum and Client Clinton agree that the client will be charged a fixed fee which includes not only the planning of the transaction but which would also cover representation of the client in the event the client's return is selected for audit, both before the Internal Revenue Service and in possible litigation before the Tax Court. If either the audit or the Tax Court litigation did not ensue, the lawyer would still keep the fee.

    B. Lawyer Nussbaum and Client Clinton agree on a contingent fee where Lawyer Nussbaum is only to be paid if he accomplishes a tax saving for the client.

C. Lawyer Nussbaum and Client Clinton agree on a fixed fee coupled with a contingency on the outcome of the case providing it is also understood that the fixed fee applies irrespective of the outcome and that the contingency applies only to the tax saving effected.

D. Answers A, B, and C are all ethical fee arrangements.

* * *

Lawyer Choate represents Client Gore in the purchase of a home. For a fee of $3,000, the representation will last from August until December. In October, Client Kemp comes to Lawyer Choate about filing a $200,000 personal injury case against Client Gore on a contingent fee basis. The statute of limitations of the claim will run in November.

QUESTION:

10. How should Lawyer Choate ethically handle the situation?

A. Lawyer Choate should have another lawyer in his office handle the personal injury claim.

B. Lawyer Choate should transfer Kemp to another law firm but may claim a referral fee of one-third of the net fee.

C. Lawyer Choate may accept Kemp's case, if he makes a full disclosure to Kemp and Kemp consents.

D. Lawyer Choate cannot represent Kemp.

* * *

Attorney Bert practices largely in the areas of tax, wills and estates, and trusts. Attorney Bert learned of a new Internal Revenue Service regulation that may affect provisions in a will she prepared for former Client Ernie two years ago. Attorney Bert has not heard from former Client Ernie since she drew the will.

QUESTION:

11. Is Attorney Bert subject to discipline if she advises former Client Ernie of the new IRS ruling?

A. No, because Attorney Bert believes that the new rules may affect former Client Ernie's will.

B. No, unless Attorney Bert's motive is to secure employment by former Client Ernie.

C. Yes, because former Client Ernie is no longer a client.

D. Yes, because Attorney Bert would be soliciting legal business.

* * *

Judge Fox has been assigned to hear a suit brought by the local citizen consumer group against the local water company. There is no reason to doubt Judge Fox's complete impartiality in the case.

QUESTION:

12. Of the following, which circumstance would **not** require him to disqualify himself?

A. The spouse of the judge's sister is trial counsel for the utility.

B. The judge has personal knowledge that one of the key allegations in the complaint is absolutely false.

C. The judge's son, Joey (a minor living at home), owns two shares of a mutual fund, which owns .003% of the outstanding common stock of the utility.

D. The judge's nephew's spouse will testify as a material witness for the plaintiffs.

* * *

Judge Jones has lifetime tenure on the state Supreme Court. Her husband, Tom, is a candidate for election to the State Senate. Tom plans to hold a political gathering at their home to solicit funds for his campaign.

QUESTION:

13. Which of the following may Judge Jones do?

A. Make a brief, dignified speech on Tom's behalf, urging the guests at the gathering to contribute to Tom's campaign.

B. Send out invitations to the gathering on her trial judge stationery.

C. Act as hostess at the gathering.

D. Answers A, B and C are all incorrect.

* * *

Attorney Mary Ann represented Ginger in many contract negotiations over the years. Originally, all of the legal work involved employment for Ginger. Later, the work also involved various business dealings in which Ginger participated. Ginger came in last week and described a business venture in which she wished to invest. Mary Ann took this opportunity to ask Ginger if she would loan her the money to send her son to college. Ginger took out her purse and wrote the tuition check on the spot and told Mary Ann that she was thrilled to assist.

QUESTION:

14. Is Mary Ann subject to discipline?

A. Mary Ann is subject to discipline for accepting a loan from a client.

B. Mary Ann is not subject to discipline if the loan was the result of their friendship and not solely the result of the representation relationship.

C. Mary Ann is subject to discipline because Ginger did not consult another lawyer.

D. Mary Ann is subject to discipline because she did not present the loan proposal to Ginger in writing.

* * *

Attorney Fred was sued in 2008 by Slate. Slate claimed that Fred had committed malpractice in his representation of Slate in an employment contract dispute. Attorney Rubble represented Fred in the malpractice action. In 2010 Fred has filed a complaint against Dino. The complaint claims that Dino manufactured defective toasters.

QUESTION:

15. Which of the following is the best answer if Attorney Rubble represents Dino in Fred's case against Dino?

A. Attorney Rubble will be disciplined if he represents Dino because Rubble cannot be directly adverse to a former client.

B. Attorney Rubble is not subject to discipline because he has no prior relationship with Dino.

C. Attorney Rubble would be subject to discipline if he used information about Fred gleaned from his representation of Fred to Fred's disadvantage.

D. Attorney Rubble would not be subject to discipline because the two matters are not the same or substantially related.

* * *

Attorney Blinky handled commercial litigation matters for World Bank and had done so for years. Attorney Brian, Blinky's associate, now has the opportunity to represent Fruit Truck Inc. in an action against World Bank. Fruit Truck claims that a World Bank armored car negligently caused a traffic collision which resulted in personal injuries to a Fruit Truck employee and property damage to Fruit Truck property.

QUESTION:

16. Is Blinky subject to discipline for his conduct?

A. Attorney Blinky would be subject to discipline if he represented Fruit Truck in this action, but Attorney Brian can do it ethically even without World Bank's consent.

B. Attorney Brian would not be subject to discipline as long as Attorney Blinky is screened.

C. Attorney Blinky or Attorney Brian could represent Fruit Truck without threat of discipline.

D. Attorney Brian would be subject to discipline if he accepted the Fruit Truck representation.

* * *

Lawyer Woodrow's clients are three shareholders of the Citizens for Better Education, Inc. (CBE), suing on behalf of themselves and others similarly situated. The defendants are CBE, Inc., a corporation, and Wayne Crosby, CBE's President. CBE and Wayne are represented by separate lawyers who have answered the complaint. Lawyer Woodrow's lawsuit alleges that Wayne misappropriated huge sums of CBE funds and that the CBE Board of Directors knew about Wayne's conduct but failed to stop him. Shortly after the complaint was filed, and without the knowledge or consent of either defense lawyer, Woodrow interviewed an assistant bookkeeper who works for CBE who brought CBE accounting records with her to the interview where she and Woodrow went over them in detail.

QUESTION:

17. Which of the following best describes whether Woodrow is subject to discipline?

    A. Woodrow is subject to discipline, because he should have obtained the consent of CBE's defense lawyer.

    B. Woodrow's conduct was proper, because the bookkeeper was not a party to the lawsuit.

    C. Woodrow is subject to discipline, because he should have obtained the consent of both defense lawyers.

    D. Woodrow's conduct was proper, because the bookkeeper was neither an official nor a high-ranking CBE employee under the control group test.

* * *

Lawyer Lynn represents Client Calvin in a personal injury case, which settled for $75,000. Lawyer Lynn deposited the settlement check in her law firm's trust account. Lawyer Lynn informed Client Calvin about receipt of the check and stated that her fee in the case was $25,000. Client Calvin argues that Lawyer Lynn is entitled to only $15,000.

QUESTION:

18. Which of the following describes the best ethical resolution of the situation?

    A. All of the money from the settlement must remain in the law firm's trust account until the fee dispute is resolved.

    B. The parties to the lawsuit must submit their fee dispute to arbitration.

    C. Lawyer Lynn must disburse $50,000 to Client Calvin and must retain $25,000 in the law firm's trust account until the dispute is resolved.

D. Lawyer Lynn is entitled to withdraw the amount of her fee which is not in dispute ($15,000), and must disburse $50,000 to Client Calvin. The remaining amount ($10,000) must remain in the law firm's trust account until the fee dispute is resolved.

* * *

Lawyer Luke represents Client Callie in a breach of contract case. Since the beginning of the representation, Lawyer Luke has realized that Client Callie is not dependable about keeping her word about anything. For example, when he forwarded interrogatories to her during discovery, she failed to return them which resulted in the trial court imposing discovery sanctions on Lawyer Luke and Client Callie. On the day the trial is supposed to begin, Client Callie has not appeared and the trial judge is unhappy with yet another problem with Lawyer Luke's reliability, vicarious or otherwise. When the trial judge asks Lawyer Luke where his client is, Lawyer Luke states to the court that he does not know. In fact, Client Callie had called him at his office just before he left to go to the courthouse, and she told him that she had decided to avoid the stress of the trial by taking a vacation at a resort in the Carribean.

QUESTION:

19. Which of the following best describes whether Lawyer Luke is subject to discipline?

   A. Lawyer Luke is subject to discipline, because he lied to the trial judge by telling the judge that he did not know where Client Callie was located.

— B. Lawyer Luke is not subject to discipline, because Client Callie's location is not a material fact.

   C. Lawyer Luke is not subject to discipline, because he did not intend to deceive the trial judge.

   D. Lawyer Luke is subject to discipline, because he perjured himself when he told the judge that he did not know Client Callie's location.

* * *

Lawyer Len has represented Client Redd for several years as Client Redd has become eligible for Social Security and Medicare entitlements from the federal government. Client Redd has become concerned about needing someone to visit him at his home twice a week to check on his physical condition. When Client Redd contacts Lawyer Len to employ a health care provider, Lawyer Len is distressed about Client Redd's generosity in wanting to compensate the health care provider at 20% above the normal rate.

QUESTION:

20. Which of the following describes Lawyer Len's ethical situation?

   A. Lawyer Len is not subject to discipline if he takes action to protect Client Redd who is not acting in his best interest.

   B. Lawyer Len is not subject to discipline if he substitutes his own judgment for what is a reasonable price to pay the health car provider, because Client Redd is exhibiting a "diminished capacity" by his willingness to contract for an excessive price to pay for a health care provider.

   C. Lawyer Len is not subject to discipline if he advises Client Redd to consider a reduced price for the health care provider.

   D. Lawyer Len is not subject to discipline if he immediately petitions a court to have a guardian appointed for Client Redd.

* * *

Lawyer Powell represents Client Jones in a murder prosecution. Yesterday, Client Jones told Lawyer Powell that he wants to testify at his trial to present an alibi defense. Client Jones had never mentioned an alibi defense to Lawyer Powell. Now it appears that his sister has agreed to lie for him and say that Client Jones was at her house babysitting with her kids at the time of the murder. When Lawyer Powell states that he cannot be a party to perjured testimony, Client Jones reminds him that he has the right to testify at his own trial. After Client Jones assures Lawyer Powell that he will tell the truth if he testifies, Lawyer Powell allows him to testify.

QUESTION:

21. Which is Lawyer Powell's best ethical approach to the situation?

   A. Lawyer Powell must call Client Jones's sister as a witness to reinforce Client Jones's alibi testimony.

B. The trial judge must grant Lawyer Powell's motion to withdraw from the case.

C. No solution exists because the Sixth Amendment to the Constitution cannot be undermined by Lawyer Powell's refusal to put his client on the stand.

D. If Lawyer Powell cannot dissuade Client Jones from testifying falsely, and if Client Jones reneges on his promise to testify truthfully, Lawyer Powell must take reasonable remedial measures, including disclosing the false testimony to the court.

* * *

Lawyer Cahill represented Client Clyde in his divorce litigation. After numerous meetings in which they gathered information about marital assets, Lawyer Cahill learned that Client Clyde had squandered the married couple's largest marital asset, an individual retirement account (IRA) containing $72,500. Just after the divorce petition was filed, Client Clyde withdrew the proceeds in the IRA in cash without the knowledge of his wife or Lawyer Cahill. A few days later, Client Clyde told Lawyer Cahill that he had cashed in the IRA but had lost the proceeds at a local restaurant. The trial judge held a hearing at which the division of the marital assets was contested. Both parties presented evidence that the marital assets included the IRA, which both parties valued at $72,500. Neither Lawyer Cahill nor Client Clyde disclosed to the court or the wife that the IRA no longer existed. The trial court entered a divorce decree, awarding to Client Clyde's ex-wife 50% of the proceeds from the sale of the parties' home and $36, 250 of the IRA. Client Clyde failed to pay his ex-wife the $36,250 as ordered and tried to discharge that financial obligation by filing a bankruptcy petition.

QUESTION:

 22. Which of the following describes Lawyer Cahill's ethical situation?

A. Lawyer Cahill is subject to discipline, because the Rules require him to promptly call upon Client Clyde to rectify the situation

B. Lawyer Cahill is subject to discipline for failing to inform the divorce court about the IRA to avoid assisting in Client Clyde's fraud on the court.

C. Lawyer Cahill is subject to discipline because the information about the IRA is confidential.

   D. Lawyer Cahill is not subject to discipline because he
       decided to continue his representation of Client Clyde,
       instead of withdrawing as soon as learned about the
       IRA.

* * *

Lawyer Linda represented Client Hamilton in several matters
during the past few years. Most recently, she represented him in his
role as a preferred creditor for the estate of Simione. Now, Client
Hamilton has requested that Lawyer Linda form a new corporation
for him, telling Lawyer Linda about Abner, an attorney he knew who
had been "milking" the Simione estate for four years and who was
about to become a judge. Abner needed to sell the estate's business,
Pacific Bowling Lanes, quickly in order to close the estate before he
took the bench. Client Hamilton had agreed to buy the bowling alley.
When Client Hamilton told Lawyer Linda that there was no time for
an appraisal of the business, Lawyer Linda said that she did not
want to hear about it. Lawyer Linda formed the corporation and had
no further involvement with Client Hamilton about the purchase of
Pacific Bowling Lanes. Later, (now) Judge Abner ruled against
Lawyer Linda in all of her cases. To retaliate, Lawyer Linda
prepared a memorandum detailing Client Hamilton's confidences
about Judge Abner, and sent it to the state attorney general's office,
the state bar association, the Internal Revenue Service (IRS), and
the local newspaper.

QUESTION:

23. Which of the following best describes Lawyer Linda's ethi-
    cal situation?

   A. Lawyer Linda is not subject to discipline, because she
       had a duty to report Abner's wrongdoing.

   B. Lawyer Linda is not subject to discipline, because she
       had the discretion to report Abner's wrongdoing.

   C. Lawyer Linda is subject to discipline, because her
       disclosure of Client Hamilton's confidential informa-
       tion was broader than the Rules permit.

   D. Answers A and B are both correct.

* * *

Lawyer Levin has been served with a show cause order relating to a
provision that he includes when he establishes a lawyer-client

relationship with his clients. In his standard retainer fee agreement, he includes a provision that future malpractice disputes between her and her clients must be submitted to binding arbitration.

QUESTION:

24. Based on the general agreement of the courts and bar association ethics opinions, how will a bar association disciplinary committee resolve the show cause order against Lawyer Levin, in this case of first impression in this state?

    A. Lawyer Levin's retainer fee agreement violates the prohibition against limiting a lawyer's malpractice liability.

    B. Lawyer Levin's retainer fee agreement violates the prohibition against limiting a lawyer's malpractice liability, unless her clients can consult another lawyer.

    C. Lawyer Levin's retainer fee agreement does not violate the prohibition against limiting future malpractice liability, as long as her clients can consult another lawyer.

    D. Lawyer Levin's retainer fee agreement does not violate the prohibition on limiting future malpractice liability, because binding arbitration clauses merely shift malpractice claims to another forum.

* * *

Continental Towing Company is the nation's largest operator of towboats. It also has a small manufacturing plant. A large Spanish corporation has been trying to acquire Continental. Very few people at Continental know about the acquisition possibility and the corporate CEO has instructed those few (including Maris, the General Counsel) not to tell anyone about it. The takeover almost certainly would result in the Spanish company selling off most of Continental's operations business with nothing remaining of the current Continental business but the small manufacturing entity. Jordan is the Associate General Counsel for Continental and seeks your advice. Last week, Continental's outside counsel told her that Maris and he were promoting the takeover by the Spanish corporation so that they could begin their own towing operation.

QUESTION:

25. Does Jordan have an ethical obligation to disclose her knowledge about the General Counsel's conduct and intent?

A. No, because she is not the General Counsel.

B. Yes, because she believes that some injury to the corporation will occur.

C. Yes, but she can speak only to the General Counsel.

D. Yes, because she believes that the General Counsel has acted or intends to act in a manner which is likely to result in substantial injury to the corporation.

* * *

After practicing for more than fifty years, John Tipton has decided to retire and move to a different state with his wife. His reputation as a lawyer in his small community is excellent. Tipton's nephew just graduated from law school and wants to move back to his hometown where Tipton has practiced.

QUESTION:

26. Which of the following best describes Tipton's ability to sell his law practice to his nephew?

A. Tipton may sell his entire law practice to his nephew.

B. If Tipton sells his law practice, he is prohibited from practicing law on his own or for anyone else in his home state.

C. Before and after he sells his law practice, Tipton cannot disclose to his nephew any confidential information about his client's cases.

D. Tipton's nephew has the discretion to increase his fees to be charged to Tipton's former clients.

* * *

Lawyer Lori graduated from law school ten years ago, but she enjoys doing "pay back" activities for her law school to show her appreciation for the legal education she received. This year, one of her "pay back" methods is to assist law students when they conduct Wills Clinics at senior citizen centers for ARP (Association of Retired Persons). After the law student interviews each senior citizen and types the draft of each simple Will, Lawyer Lori asks the senior citizen several questions before approving the Will for signing and self-acknowledgment.

QUESTION:

27. Which of the following best describes issues for Lawyer Lori as she participates in the Wills Clinic?

    A. Lawyer Lori is not subject to any discipline for participating in a service-oriented project like a Wills Clinic, even if one of her current clients has an ongoing real property title dispute with one of the senior citizens who is writing a Will that day at the Wills Clinic.

    B. Lawyer Lori is not subject to discipline if she knows that one of her current clients has an ongoing real property title dispute with one of the senior citizens who is writing a Will that day at the Wills Clinic.

    C. Lawyer Lori is subject to discipline if she knows that one of her current clients has an ongoing real property title dispute with one of the senior citizens who is writing a Will that day at the Wills Clinic.

    D. Lawyer Lori is subject to discipline if her law partner has a current client who has an ongoing real property title dispute with one of Lawyer Lori's senior citizen clients who is writing a Will that day at the Wills clinic.

* * *

Lawyer Stephanie has represented antitrust clients for almost twenty years, and she continues to represent them in both trial and appellate litigation. The Chief Judge of her federal district has asked her to be a member of a law reform effort to expedite commercial litigation such as antitrust, price discrimination, and copyright cases in the local federal courts. The Chief Judge wants Lawyer Stephanie to be a member of the local rules committee and to testify before a Congressional subcommittee on the topic of streamlining litigation.

QUESTION:

28. Which of the following is true of Lawyer Stephanie's ethical obligations if she accepts the Chief Judge's requests?

    A. Lawyer Stephanie is subject to discipline if she is a member of the local rules committee while she has antitrust clients.

    B. Lawyer Stephanie is subject to discipline is she fails to tell the Congressional subcommittee that she represents antitrust clients.

C. Lawyer Stephanie is not subject to discipline if she serves as a member of the local rules committee without disclosing that her clients may benefit from the committee's decisions.

D. Lawyer Stephanie is subject to discipline if she serves on the local rules committee without having a lawyer-client relationship with the committee.

* * *

Lawyer Lynn is the chairperson of Board of Directors for the local Legal Aid Society, which serves the legal needs of indigent clients in the Metro area. While serving on the Legal Aid Board for more than five years, she also is a law partner and the chairperson of her law partnership's Executive Committee in Metro.

QUESTION:

29. Which of the following best describes whether Lawyer Lynn is subject to discipline?

A. Lawyer Lynn is subject to discipline, because she cannot serve as chair of the Legal Aid Board and be on her law firm's Executive Committee.

B. Lawyer Lynn is subject to discipline if in her private practice she represents any client who is adverse to any Legal Aid client.

C. Lawyer Lynn is subject to discipline if she leads the Legal Aid Board to vote in favor of ordering that Legal Aid clients must stop suing a group of local public utilities, some of which are represented by her and her law firm.

D. Even if she as a board member does not participate in the Legal Aid decision, Lawyer Lynn is subject to discipline if the Legal Aid Board votes to stop representing clients who sue local public utilities, some of which are represented by her and her law firm.

* * *

Lawyer Frank represents his client in a personal injury case. There has been extensive discovery and motions for summary judgment have been filed for both sides. In addition, each side has agreed to several motions to continue the trial until a later time. Lawyer

Frank's client has steadfastly refused to take any settlement offer of less than $100,000, and she has even told Lawyer Frank, "You don't have to call me if they offer anything less than $100,000." Yesterday, the opposing side called Lawyer Frank about two matters: 1) a settlement offer of $90,000, and 2) if the settlement offer is rejected, a motion to continue the trial for another six months.

QUESTION:

30. Which of the following describes Lawyer Frank's obligation to contact his client after the telephone call?

A. Lawyer Frank must contact his client about approval for both the settlement offer and the motion to continue the case.

B. Lawyer Frank must contact his client about approval for the settlement offer, but not for approval of the motion to continue the case.

C. Lawyer Frank must contact his client about the motion to continue the case, but not the settlement offer.

D. Lawyer Frank does not have to contact his client about either the settlement offer or the motion to continue the case.

* * *

Lawyer Harris represents Client Moran who is charged with setting fire to several buildings. From several interviews with her client and observing his demeanor, Lawyer Harris is becoming increasingly concerned about her client's competency to go to trial or to participate in his defense.

QUESTION:

31. Which of the following describes what Lawyer Harris ethically should do?

A. Lawyer Harris is subject to discipline if she informs the court about her concerns relating to her client's competence

B. Lawyer Harris is subject to discipline if she testifies about both what Client Moran told her as well Client Moran's physical appearance.

C. Lawyer Harris is not subject to discipline if she testifies about Client Moran's physical appearance.

D. Lawyer Harris is not subject to discipline if she does nothing.

* * *

Prosecutor Peters recently oversaw the grand jury investigation that resulted in a seventeen-count cocaine trafficking indictment against a local drug kingpin named Mortimer. Within a day of the indictment, Prosecutor Peters met with the press twice to inform them about Mortimer and the charges he faced in the current case. A portion of his statement follows:

> Today we obtained an indictment against Rudy Mortimer, who is one of the biggest threats to our children in this community. Our investigation is ongoing and we have completed much of our preparation for trial. However, we need the help of everyone in this community to make sure that Mortimer never has the opportunity to spend another day having his people befriend our children in order to sell them illegal drugs. If you have information or you know anyone who may have information that is relevant to these crimes, please contact me or contact the police. It is time to put an end to the crimes that this man has used to profit at the expense of our kids. We all know about his two prior trafficking felony convictions, and this time we're going to put him away for good.

QUESTION:

32. Is Prosecutor Peters subject to discipline for his statements to the press?

A. Yes, he is subject to discipline for referring to Mortimer's prior convictions and the need to convict him.

B. Yes, he is subject to discipline for referring to Mortimer's prior convictions but not for emphasizing the need to convict him.

C. Yes, he is subject to discipline for emphasizing the need to convict Mortimer but not for referring to his prior convictions.

D. No, Prosecutor Peters is permitted to make any true statements to the press.

* * *

Client Cal came to Lawyer Lennox's office to talk to her about a breach of contract claim he wants to bring regarding a piece of real estate he attempted to sell earlier this year. Client Cal believes that he has a very good claim against Jill for reneging on a contract they signed for the sale of Client Cal's home. Client Cal was very excited at the time to have made the contract with Jill because it had become so difficult to sell the house during bad economic times. Client Cal had been in Lawyer Lennox's office for about ten minutes describing the circumstances of his claim when Lawyer Lennox received an urgent call from her father that her mother had become acutely ill and was on the way to the hospital. Apologizing to Client Cal, Lawyer Lennox rushed out of the office before Client Cal had even discussed a fee arrangement with Lawyer Lennox. After two weeks without hearing from Lawyer Lennox, Client Cal became impatient and decided to see another lawyer about his breach of contract case.

QUESTION:

33. Which of the following describes the ethical situation between Lawyer Lennox and Client Cal?

   A. Lawyer Lennox is not subject to discipline because she never discussed a fee arrangement with Client Cal.

   B. Lawyer Lennox is not subject to discipline if she reveals Client Cal's information to anyone.

   C. Lawyer Lennox is subject to discipline if she reveals Client Cal's confidential information.

   D. Lawyer Lennox is not subject to discipline because Client Cal had no reasonable expectation of becoming her client.

* * *

Lawyer Kim has been as associate lawyer at a large law firm in Metro for the past three years. For most of that time, she has been assigned to the litigation section where she has done most of her work for two lawyers—Partner Palmer and Partner Player—on their medical malpractice cases. In a recent case, Lawyer Kim became concerned that the assumption of risk defense being asserted by the partners she worked for is completely without merit. In fact, at the last pretrial conference, Judge James commented on the lack of evidence that seemed to have been put forth by Lawyer Kim and the two law partners she works for on that defense. When she asked the two partners about the substance of the assumption of risk defense in that case, Partner Palmer told her that something factually would turn up, and Partner Player told her to just keep doing as she was told. Realizing that she cannot take a frivolous position that lacks a factual basis, Lawyer Kim does not want to have discipline charges brought against her by the state bar association. Yet, she doesn't want to be fired if she decides not to follow the course dictated by Partner Player.

QUESTION:

34. Of the following, which describe Lawyer Kim's ethical course of action?

    A. If confronted by Judge James or by bar association charges that she has no factual support for her client's defense of assumption of risk, Lawyer Kim can state that she is following the orders from Partners Palmer and Player.

    B. If she is fired for not following the orders from Partners Palmer and Player, Lawyer Kim can sue them for wrongful discharge.

    C. Lawyer Kim is ethically responsible for her actions, despite being ordered by Partners Palmer and Player to pursue the frivolous defense of assumption of risk.

    D. Answers B and C are correct.

* * *

Lawyer Kuric works for a law firm as an associate lawyer. In the real estate section of the firm, she works for Partner Williams and Partner Clark. Paralegal Sosa and Paralegal Delk work for all three of the lawyers in the real estate section. When Paralegal Delk sits in on client interviews about new shopping center projects or commercial real estate foreclosures, he has difficulty controlling his inclination toward being a gossip about what he hears. Within a day of client interviews, everyone in the law firm knows about the real estate client's business and legal issues. Although she works for two partners in a medium sized law firm, Lawyer Kuric is worried about whether Paralegal Delk's gossipy nature could get her into trouble if he tells his friends at other law firms about the firm's client's cases.

QUESTION:

35. Which of the following best describes Lawyer Kuric's ethical situation?

    A. Lawyer Kuric is not subject to discipline for not having already discussed ethical aspects of his employment with Paralegal Delk.

B. Lawyer Kuric is not subject to discipline, because she is an employee of the law firm just like the paralegal employees.

C. Lawyer Kuric is already subject to discipline for failing to discuss the ethical aspects of his employment with Paralegal Delk.

D. Lawyer Kuric is subject to discipline for any improper disclosure of confidential information by Paralegal Delk, even if she had already discussed the ethical aspects of his employment with him.

* * *

As a new prosecutor assigned to litigate domestic violence cases, Lawyer Laurie is anxious to be as effective as possible. After the jury returned a guilty verdict in her first trial and was released from their jury duties, she waited outside the courtroom to speak to each of the twelve jurors to find out how she can improve her trial techniques for her future trials.

QUESTION:

36. Does Lawyer Laurie face any ethical sanctions for speaking to the jurors after the verdict?

A. Lawyer Laurie is subject to discipline if the law prohibits such contact with the jurors.

B. Lawyer Laurie is not subject to discipline, even if the jurors requested no contact.

C. Lawyer Laurie is not subject to discipline if she did not harass or coerce the jurors.

D. Answers A and C are correct.

* * *

Prosecutor Petrie has issued a complaint charging Donald Dorchester with second-degree burglary, which is a felony carrying a maximum penalty of ten years imprisonment. At his initial appearance, Dorchester elected to represent himself in defending the burglary charge. Based on her prior experiences with *pro se* defendants, Prosecutor Petrie finds that communicating and negotiating with such defendants is very difficult because of the need to explain so many things to that defendant.

QUESTION:

37. What is Prosecutor Petrie's ethical stance in this case?

   A. Prosecutor Petrie must negotiate directly with Donald Dochester.

   B. Prosecutor Petrie may request that the trial judge communicate plea offers to Donald Dorchester.

   C. Prosecutor Petrie may persuade Donald Dorchester to waive his right to a preliminary hearing.

   D. Prosecutor Petrie may not question Donald Dorchester at her office without the presence of a standby counsel.

* * *

Prosecutor Painter is certain that Lawyer Jacobs knows relevant evidence about his client who is charged in an indictment with three counts of federal money laundering. Based on information from a reliable informant, Prosecutor Painter believes that Lawyer Jacobs has had communications with his client that are not protected by the lawyer-client relationship.

QUESTION:

38. Which of the following describes Prosecutor Painter's ethical duty in this situation?

   A. Prosecutor Painter is subject to discipline for issuing a subpoena for Lawyer Jacobs unless she reasonably believes that Lawyer Jacobs has information that is not protected from disclosure by any applicable privilege.

   B. Prosecutor Painter is subject to discipline for issuing a subpoena for Lawyer Jacobs unless she reasonably believes that the evidence she is seeking is essential to the successful completion of his client's prosecution.

   C. Prosecutor Painter is subject to discipline for issuing a subpoena for Lawyer Jacobs unless she reasonably believes that there is no other feasible alternative to obtain the information.

   D. All of the above answers are correct.

* * *

Last year, Prosecutor Alston hired a public relations person to be the spokesperson for her office when it was necessary to communicate with journalists and media representatives. Until recently, the public relations person did his job in an exemplary manner. Last week, however, Prosecutor Alston asked her spokesperson to address questions from the press and media outlets on an indictment that the grand jury returned in a case. What Prosecutor Alston did not know is that her public relations spokesperson's girlfriend was the victim in the assault. The spokesperson answered the questions posed by the press and media, but he then ranted about the certainty of the accused's guilt and the heinous nature of the charge.

QUESTION:

39. What is Prosecutor Alston's ethical position in this matter?

   A.   Prosecutor Alston is subject to discipline for any statements made by her spokesperson.

   B.   Prosecutor Alston is subject to discipline for an statements made by her spokesperson that had the effect of depriving the defendant of a fair trial.

   C.   Prosecutor Alston is not subject to discipline for statements made by anyone other than herself.

   D.   Prosecutor Alston is not subject to discipline for statements made by her spokesperson if she trained her spokesperson about which statements to the press were proper and which were improper.

* * *

Lawyer Edward is vice-president and general counsel of a small, publicly-traded corporation that services equipment at manufacturing facilities. Recently he learned from reliable managerial sources within the company about several significant misstatements of corporate holdings on its balance sheet; such misstatements may be the source of public and private litigation by the Securities and Exchange Commission and by shareholders. As general counsel, Lawyer Edward spoke to the persons he believes to be the persons responsible for the balance sheet misstatements. When they refused to follow his advice about correcting the corporate balance sheet, he spoke to the President of the company and to the Board of Directors. To his consternation, neither the President nor the Board of Directors wanted to take immediate action, preferring to transfer the suspected persons elsewhere in the company.

QUESTION:

40. What is Lawyer Edward's ethical obligation, if any?

A. Must resign as general counsel immediately.

B. Must not report the balance sheet irregularities, because it is confidential information.

C. Must report the balance sheet irregularities to the Securities and Exchange Commission.

D. May report the balance sheet irregularities to an outside entity.

* * *

QUESTION:

41. Of the following duties, which are the professional responsibilities imposed by the Securities and Exchange Commission on lawyers who represent corporations which issue publicly-traded securities?

A. The lawyer's reporting of wrongdoing must relate to the representation of the entity.

B. A lawyer's reporting duty pertains to wrongdoing that is likely to cause substantial injury to the entity.

C. The reporting requirements apply to a lawyer who has been retained by the entity to investigate wrongdoing that is reported by someone else.

D. Answers A, B and C are all incorrect.

* * *

Lawyer Lemon has a concurrent conflict of interest, based upon her representation of one client in a civil case whose interests are directly adverse to another client whom she represents in a separate civil case. She believes that both of her current clients will consent to the conflict, but she is unsure about what else she needs to resolve.

QUESTION:

42. Which of the following is *not* an accurate description of a factor which Lawyer Lemon must consider prior to proceeding with the conflicted representation?

A. She must believe that she can competently and diligently represent all of her clients affected by the conflict.

B. She must decide whether some other law precludes her from accepting the conflicting representations.

C. Her representation of the conflicting interests does not involve representing one client against another in the same litigation.

D. Both clients must consent to the conflicting representations.

* * *

QUESTION:

43. In the following statements, which involve(s) potential successful invocation of the evidentiary lawyer-client privilege?

A. In response to a request from her lawyer, the client sends the lawyer several strands of hair from her head.

B. A client makes statements to her lawyer in her lawyer's reception area where there are other clients waiting to see that lawyer.

C. A prospective client communicates to a lawyer, but the lawyer declines to represent that person.

D. Answers A and C are both correct.

* * *

Contingent fee arrangements provide that a lawyer will receive a fee if she is successful in obtaining a recovery for her client. While they are customarily used by plaintiff's counsel, there is no *per se* ethical prohibition against their use by defense counsel. During the past decades, however, contingent fees have become a favorite target of lawyer critics. In response, the Model Rules have imposed requirements that are specific to contingent fee arrangements.

QUESTION:

44. Which of the following are required in contingent fee situations?

A. Any contingent fee agreement must be in writing.

B. The agreement must be signed by the client.

C. The agreement must describe if the percentage to be charged, unless it depends on how far the case proceeds.

D. A and B are both correct.

* * *

Lawyer Lawson represents Client Cotton in many of his businesses' real estate and commercial transactions. Sometimes, Client Cotton asks her for legal advice and sometimes he seeks her opinion about the commercial advantages of the "deals" that he wants to make with other business entities. Last week, Client Cotton asked Lawyer Lawson to investigate a matter and write an opinion letter for the prospective buyer of one of his small companies.

QUESTION:

45. In which lawyer role would that assignment by Client Cotton ethically place Lawyer Lawson?

A. Advisor

B. Evaluator

C. Negotiator

D. Third-party Neutral

* * *

QUESTION:

46. Of the following situations, in which would a lawyer serving a client in the role of an evaluator not have an ethical obligations?

A. She has a duty to tell her litigation clients about forms of alternative dispute resolution.

B. She must reasonably believe that doing the evaluation is compatible with other aspects of the lawyer-client relationship with the client.

C. She must obtain her client's informed consent if she knows or reasonably should know that the evaluation is likely to affect the client's interests materially and adversely.

D.   Disclosure of the evaluation to a third party removes client confidentiality for information found in the evaluation, but other information relating to the evaluation that is not included in the evaluation remains confidential.

* * *

QUESTION:

 47. Of the following, when a lawyer is serving a client in the role of a negotiator, which of the following is false?

A. A negotiator has no duty to do any research for the other side of the litigation or transaction or to volunteer factual information that could weaken her client's position.

B. A negotiator cannot make false statements of material fact.

C. A negotiator's statements about her client's intentions about an acceptable settlement do not constitute material facts.

D. A negotiator may not exaggerate about facts and values.

* * *

Lawyer Longfellow represents Client Allen who is defending a breach of contract action regarding a contract with his former business partner, Clyde. Lawyer Longfellow also represents Client Bruce who is seeking a divorce from his wife, Della. Throughout pretrial discovery in *Clyde v. Allen*, Clyde's lawyer never identified his trial witnesses until two weeks ago when it became apparent that one of Clyde's important witnesses at trial will be Client Bruce.

QUESTION:

 48. Faced with this uncomfortable situation, in which of the following is Lawyer Longfellow not subject to discipline?

 A. Obtains written consent from Client Allen only, before cross-examining Client Bruce.

B. Obtains written consent from Client Bruce only, before cross-examining Client Bruce.

C. Obtains oral consent from both Client Allen and Client Bruce.

D. Withdraws from representing both Client Allen and Client Bruce.

* * *

Lawyer Learned has practiced law for less than one year. Most of the clients who have needed legal assistance in court were accused on driving offenses. In fact, she is becoming busier than her court schedule permits. Yesterday, a client consulted her about an antitrust case, which would be her first case that requires extensive research or court experience.

QUESTION:

49. Based on her legal experience, in which of the following is Lawyer Learned subject to discipline?

A. Asks an experienced litigator with an office on the same floor to be her co-counsel in the antitrust case.

B. Fails to ask an experienced litigator to be her co-counsel in the antitrust case.

C. Lacks competence to practice in the antitrust area when she accepts the case.

D. Accepts the antitrust case when she already knew that her workload was too heavy.

* * *

Lawyer Lofton has practiced law at the Public Defender's office for more than four years. Her court-appointed caseload has ebbed and flowed, but for the last year she believes that she has been representing more indigent clients than she should be.

QUESTION:

50. Which of the following is not among Lawyer Lofton's prescribed ethical choices?

A. She may ask the court to stop assigning any new cases to her until her caseload is reduced to an acceptable level.

B. She must inform her supervisor and seek relief, such as help with representing the current clients.

C. She must inform her supervisor and seek relief, but if the supervisor or his board of directors fail to help her she must seek to withdraw from some of her cases.

D. She must inform her supervisor and seek relief, but if the supervisor or his board of directors fail to help her she may seek to withdraw from some of her cases.

* * *

Lawyer Light's law practice focuses on domestic relations, including divorce, adoption and custody cases. At one time, she spent long days and nights on her cases, but recently her success in attracting clients has led her to spend more of her time on other pursuits than on her clients' cases. In addition, her tactics in court are questionable in the eyes of her peers and the judges in the Family Courts. Moreover, she has begun to have difficulty meeting court-imposed deadlines. When she moves for continuances of her cases, she often forgets to consult her clients to learn whether the new trial dates are convenient for them.

QUESTION:

51. In which of the following is Lawyer Light not subject to discipline?

A. Her offensive tactics in court.

B. Her zealous representation of her clients.

C. Her motions to continue her cases.

D. Her neglect of many of her cases.

* * *

For years, Lawyer Lopez has dealt with clients who failed to pay her the entire fee which she quoted and the client agreed to pay at the start of their lawyer-client relationship. She does not regard herself as a businesswoman, because until now she has never reacted to any client's failure to pay the fee. In other words, she had thought that when a client did not pay her fee it was somehow her fault for setting the fee too high or being too casual about collecting the fee. In addition, she did not want a reputation for being a lawyer who turned on her clients when they failed to pay her.

QUESTION:

52. Of the following, which is not an available ethical option for Lawyer Lopez when a client fails to pay her fee?

A. In a litigation context, she may seek the court's permission to withdraw from representing the client, after taking reasonable steps to protect the client's interests.

B. In a litigation context, she must seek the court's permission to withdraw from representing the client, but only after taking steps to protect her client's rights.

C. She may not ask the client to waive his right that she act with reasonable diligence or promptness.

D. She may retain her client's documents until the client pays the fee.

* * *

Lawyer Larabee advertises her services in the local phone book, on the local access channel of the cable television company, and on the front page of the local newspaper. In each of those sites, the ad content is about the same in its language, tone, and claims. After reading the following text of her media ads, decide under which of the choices is correct based on the ad's content.

"Formerly counsel for the law firm of Dewey and Howe, Lawyer Larabee is a 1995 graduate of the Harvale Law School. Because of her extensive experience in workers' compensation cases, she charges fees that are 25% lower than all other lawyers in Madison County. In representing injured workers, she has never lost a workers' compensation case in court. Call her today at Cherokee 5845. You'll be glad that you did."

QUESTION:

53. Which of the following accurately states Lawyer Larabee's ethical situation?

A. She is subject to discipline if she worked for Dewey and Howe as a runner, not as a lawyer.

B. She is not subject to discipline if the only time she has been to Harvard was when she attended and graduated from Harvard's two-week summer program for lawyers.

C. She is not subject to discipline for comparing her fees to other lawyers, even though she has no empirical support for her claim.

D. She is not subject to discipline for her claim about her success in representing injured workers, although workers' compensation cases are never resolved by a court but only through an administrative agency dedicated to workers' compensation claims.

* * *

The grand jury indicted Defendant Dogman on several counts relating the robbery and assault of a woman. Both the victim and a bystander identified Defendant Dogman in both a photo display and a line-up. Two other eyewitnesses did not see the robber in the same line-up, and a confidential informant claims that someone other than Dogman committed the crimes. Prosecutor Pincus interviewed the two who failed to identify Dogman at the line-up and concluded that neither had a good look at the perpetrator. She also interviewed the informant and concluded that she was not credible.

QUESTION:

54. Which of the following is true about Prosecutor Pincus's ethical and constitutional obligations to disclose?

A. The ethical duty but not the constitutional duty requires Prosecutor Pincus to disclose information to Defendant Dogman.

B. The constitutional duty but not the ethical duty requires Prosecutor Pincus to disclose information to Defendant Dogman.

C. Both the ethical duty and the constitutional duty require Prosecutor Pincus to disclose information to Defendant Dogman.

D. Neither the ethical duty nor the constitutional duty requires Prosecutor Pincus to disclose information to Defendant Dogman.

* * *

Judge Jerry presides over juvenile court proceedings in his hometown. His staff consists of two law clerks, a paralegal, a secretary and a deputy sheriff who maintains order in the courtroom. Because of state budget cuts, the juvenile detention and correction facilities where Judge Jerry used to send teen-aged offenders have closed. In their place, the state has delegated to juvenile judges the responsibility for identifying appropriate facilities where juvenile offenders can be placed and treated until they are ready to return to their families. After receiving bids from several local area contractors,

Judge Jerry and his staff inspected each of them and awarded the renewable three-year contract to Public Service Corrections, Inc. Within six months after that contract was awarded, whenever Judge Jerry attended a conference, he and his staff were reimbursed for their lodging, meals and mileage expenses by the owners of Public Service Corrections, plus a ten percent "appreciation bonus."

QUESTION:

55. Which of the following is true about the reimbursements to Judge Jerry and his staff and any duty of Judge Jerry to report the reimbursements on disclosure forms which must be filed periodically according to state statute?

   A. Judge Jerry may be reimbursed for the expenses, but need not report the reimbursements on the required periodic disclosure forms.

   B. Judge Jerry must report the reimbursements, which are improper.

   C. Judge Jerry must report the reimbursements, which are proper.

   D. Judge Jerry does not have to report the reimbursements which are improper.

* * *

Law clerk Lubell is in her third year of law school at the local university. She works ten hours per week for Latham and Gilman, a medium-sized firm that primarily represents persons who have suffered personal injuries from vehicular or product-related accidents. The firm has offered her a full-time position as an associate lawyer in the firm's litigation section. Besides doing research for the lawyers in the firm, her supervising lawyer Latham often sends law clerk Lubell to interview prospective witnesses likely to be called by opposing counsel.

QUESTION:

56. Which of the following best describes law clerk Lubell's ethical position as a law firm employee when she conducts the aforementioned interviews?

   A. There is no ethical prohibition as long as law clerk Lubell identifies herself and asks if the potential witness is represented by counsel.

B. There is no ethical prohibition because the law clerk Lubell is not a lawyer.

C. Lawyer Latham is subject to discipline for sending a law clerk to interview a likely witness for the opposing party, making it the unauthorized practice of law.

D. Lawyer Latham is not subject to discipline because the interviewed person is not a witness for his client.

* * *

Until two years ago, Lawyer Lubinsky was Special Counsel to the President of the United States. When the president's term ended, like her colleagues Lawyer Lubinsky received many attractive offers of employment, ranging from sitting on prestigious corporate boards to writing a book of her memoirs as Special Counsel to being affiliated with influential law firms on both the east and west coasts. After extended discussions with family members, Lawyer Lubinsky decided to do something rather unique. She became Of Counsel for two law firms: one in New York City and a separate law firm in Los Angeles. After the initial bragging rights of the two law firms subsided, Lawyer Lubinsky has encountered the reality of everyday law practice. All the lawyers of her New York City law firm recently were disqualified from representing any of the parties in a product recall by the federal government.

QUESTION:

57. What is the ethical effect of Lawyer Lubinsky's dual role as Of Counsel for two law firms on the imputed disqualification of her New York City firm?

A. The imputed disqualification of all the lawyers in the New York City firm has no effect on the Los Angeles law firm because each firm's ethical position is independent of the other.

B. The imputed disqualification of all the lawyers in the New York City firm has the effect of disqualifying all the lawyers in the Los Angeles law firm.

C. The imputed disqualification of all the lawyers in the New York City firm has no effect on the Los Angeles law firm because a lawyer cannot serve as Of Counsel for more than one law firm.

D. The imputed disqualification of all the lawyers in the New York City firm has the effect of disqualifying only the law partners in the Los Angeles law firm who completed the deal which designated Lawyer Lubinsky as Of Counsel.

* * *

Large Law Firm has represented a builder of a proposed office building for a long period of time, and includes matters relating to the financing of the building, obtaining of building permits, and zoning variances. As part of the effort to obtain the needed permits, Large Law Firm is scheduled to make presentations on behalf of the Client to the Zoning Board. Two weeks prior to that scheduled presentation to the Zoning Board, another client of the law firm in a matter unrelated to the development project, but who lives in the neighborhood of the proposed building site, learned of the zoning hearing and decided to oppose the granting of the necessary zoning variance. Unaware that the Large Law Firm represents the developer, the other client requested a firm lawyer to represent him in opposing the project. When the law firm discovered the contact by the other client, it decided that it could not represent the other client in the matter. No services were performed for and no advice was given to the other client, and the firm disclosed to the other client that it represented the developer.

QUESTION:

 58. Which of the following is **not** an acceptable solution to the Large Law Firm's continued representation of the developer in connection with the development project?

   A. Large Law Firm should withdraw from representing the developer in any aspect of the development project but it could represent the developer in other matters.

   B. Large Law Firm should withdraw from representing the developer in any litigation or administrative aspect of the development project in which there would be an adverse relationship between the developer and the other client.

   C. Large Law Firm can withdraw from representing the other client on the development project and any other matter, but continue to represent the developer.

   D. Large Law Firm can obtain an informed consent from the other client.

* * *

A corporation is a defendant in litigation. Corman, the chief executive officer of the corporation, has informed the corporation's lawyer, Lawyer Lyle, of his intent to destroy documents that are relevant to the plaintiff's claim and are subject to a judicial discovery order. Lawyer Lyle possesses copies of the documents, and Corman has told Lawyer Lyle not to produce the documents in response to the order; he also has threatened to terminate Lawyer Lyle if she does turn over the documents. In addition, Corman has requested that Lawyer Lyle return copies of those documents in her possession. The corporation is closely held but it has a board of directors to which Corman is accountable. Corman is not the sole shareholder.

QUESTION:

59. If destroying the documents would constitute a violation of law which could be imputed to the organization, and is likely to result in substantial injury to the organization, what is the first thing that Lawyer Lyle should do to address Corman's threatened conduct?

    A. She should withdraw from representing the corporation.

    B. She should consult the corporation's board of directors.

    C. She should try to talk Corman out of destroying the documents.

    D. She should give Corman the documents.

* * *

Deputy District Attorney Dickens has worked as a prosecutor for over five years. While she has acquired valuable experience prosecuting persons accused of crimes, she has decided to leave the district attorney's office and join Lawyer Edwards and Lawyer Frank to form the Dickens, Edwards & Frank law partnership which will represent criminal defendants in criminal cases brought by the district attorney's office.

QUESTION:

60. Which of the following does *not* describe the proper ethical effect of Lawyer Dickens or other lawyers in Dickens, Edwards & Frank representing criminal defendants in criminal matters?

    A. Lawyer D cannot defend clients in matters that are the same or substantially related to matters that Lawyer D handled at the district attorney's office, unless the client and the state give informed consent, confirmed in writing.

B. Lawyer D cannot defend a client on a matter that was prosecuted by other deputy district attorneys during Lawyer D's tenure in the office if Lawyer D obtained confidential information that is material to the matter, except with the informed consent of the client and the state, confirmed in writing.

C. Lawyer D's disqualification will not be imputed to the other lawyers in the DEF firm, unless Lawyer D is screened from participating in the matter.

D. Lawyer D's disqualification will be imputed to the other lawyers in the DEF firm, unless Lawyer D is screened from participating in the matter.

PROFESSIONAL RESPONSIBILITY

Exam #3—60 Problems and Questions

Lawyer Dean is a Ph.D. biologist whose law degree has given her the opportunity over time to represent many clients in environmental litigation. Five clients have consulted with her during the past month about representing them in conjunction with the release and threatened release of hazardous substances at the Tri–County Disposal site near Hartford. The possible corrective action by the United States Environmental Protection Agency may be taken under the provisions of the Comprehensive Environmental Response, Compensation and Liability Act of 1980 (CERCLA), which makes current and past owners, operators and others associated with real property responsible for removing hazardous substances from the site. Each of the five clients has been notified that it is a potentially responsible party (PRP) for the total cost of cleaning the disposal site. The five are current and former owners and operators of the disposal site, producers of the disposed hazardous substances, and transporters of the substances at the site. Milennial Industrial Services (MIS) is the largest and the wealthiest of the five PRPs. As such, it is interested in paying its own legal fees to Lawyer Dean as well as the fees of the other four PRPs.

QUESTIONS:

1. Can Lawyer Dean ethically represent the five PRPs, if each of them gives their informed consent?

   A. She can represent all five even though their interests are "directly adverse to another client."

   B. She can represent all five even though "there is a significant risk that the representation of one or more clients will be materially limited by" her responsibilities to other clients.

   C. She can represent all five if she "reasonably believes" that she "will be able to provide competent and diligent representation to each affected client."

    D.   Answers A, B, and C all are correct.

2.   Under the above facts, assuming that Lawyer Dean can represent all of the PRPs, which of the following is ***not*** part of the nature of the consent which must be acquired from each of them?

    A.   Only another lawyer can obtain the consent necessary to each client waiving Lawyer Dean's conflict of interest.

    B.   Lawyer Dean or another lawyer should provide each of them with adequate information so that each can make an informed decision about whether to consent to the concurrent representation or to seek another attorney.

    C.   Each client must consent to the representation of their conflicting interests.

    D.   Each client must consent to the disclosure of each client's confidential information to the other clients.

3.   If each of the potentially responsible parties has its own lawyer, can MIS pay Lawyer Dean's legal fees for representing all of the PRPs?

    A.   Yes, if Lawyer Dean discloses to the other PRPs that a third party is compensating the attorney for representing the client, each of whom provides informed consent to such payment.

    B.   Yes, if the payment will not interfere with Lawyer Dean's independent professional judgment or with the attorney-client relationship.

    C.   Yes, if Lawyer Dean preserves confidential information relating to the representation.

    D.   Answers A, B, and C together describe what is necessary when a third party pays a fee for someone else.

* * *

After leaving the prosecutor's office, where she worked as a trial attorney for three years bringing state criminal cases for consumer fraud and other white collar crime, Lawyer Starks joined a small firm that does an extensive amount of criminal defense work.

Lawyer Starks on several occasions heard Page talking with investigators and other assistant prosecutors about evidence in the case and litigation strategy.

QUESTIONS:

4. May Lawyer Starks represent Grace Ewald, who is under indictment by Lawyer Starks's former office for consumer fraud if the indictment was returned by a grand jury while Lawyer Starks was still at her former job when Lawyer Starks shared office space with Neil Page, the assistant prosecutor who conducted the investigation of Ewald and will try the case?

    A. No, because Lawyer Starks participated as an attorney in prosecuting Grace.

    B. No, because Lawyer Starks was sharing office space with the prosecuting attorney who investigated Grace.

    C. No, because Lawyer Starks was a prosecuting attorney for the government when Grace was indicted.

    D. No, because Lawyer Starks knew confidential government information about Grace's case.

5. Assuming that Lawyer Starks is disqualified, can her new law firm still represent Grace in defending against the criminal charge in the indictment returned while Starks was a prosecutor?

    A. Yes, but only if Lawyer Starks is properly screened and written notice is promptly given to the appropriate government agency.

    B. Yes, but only if Lawyer Starks receives no part of the fee generated by representing Grace.

    C. Yes, but only if Lawyer Starks is properly screened and she receives no part of the fee generated by representing Grace.

    D. No, because screening of a disqualified attorney is never permitted.

* * *

Lawyer Bailey believes that Lawyer Shapiro would make an excellent judge, in part because he believes that his election opponent, Judge Ito, is not smart. Lawyer Bailey wishes to assist Lawyer Shapiro in getting elected.

QUESTION:

6. Is Lawyer Bailey subject to discipline if he tells a local reporter that he supports candidate Lawyer Shapiro because he believes that Judge Ito is "not too bright"?

    A. Yes, if Lawyer Bailey practices before Judge Ito.

    B. Yes, because Lawyer Bailey is attacking a sitting judge.

    C. No, unless the reporter publishes the comment.

    D. No, because Lawyer Bailey believes that she is telling the truth.

* * *

Clinton was represented by Lawyer Perot in a lawsuit over a decade ago. Perot has not represented Clinton since then. Plaintiff Dole, who was not involved in that prior litigation with Clinton, seeks to retain Lawyer Perot to sue Clinton in another matter which, while distinct from the prior litigation, is ancillary to it and involves in part the same facts and circumstances, some of which are confidential.

QUESTION:

7. What may Lawyer Perot ethically do?

    A. Refer the matter to his law partner, Choate, who was not involved in the prior litigation and who became associated with Lawyer Perot only a year ago.

    B. Accept the representation after simply notifying Plaintiff Dole and notifying Clinton.

    C. Refer the matter to Nader, a lawyer in another firm, in exchange for a secret kickback of 10% of the fee that Nader will charge Plaintiff Dole.

    D. Decline to represent Plaintiff Dole.

* * *

After representing Farmer in a personal injury action, Lawyer Hillary settled the case. Rubin, the defendant, sends Lawyer Hillary a check for $30,000. The check is payable to the order of Lawyer Hillary. One-third of the check's amount represents Lawyer Hillary's undisputed contingent fee.

QUESTION:

8. Consistent with her ethical obligations, what can Lawyer Hillary **not** do?

   A. Deposit the check in Farmer's trust fund account, inform Farmer, and forward a $20,000 check drawn on that account to Farmer.

   B. Deposit the check in Lawyer Hillary's personal bank account and send to Farmer Lawyer Hillary's personal check for $20,000.

   C. Send the check directly to Farmer after having endorsed it, and then ask Farmer to pay the fee.

   D. Answers A, B, and C are all ethical options for Lawyer Hillary.

* * *

QUESTION:

9. In which of the following situations is the information received by the lawyer covered by **both** the lawyer-client privilege and the ethical duty to preserve the client's confidential information?

   A. Lawyer Jones is representing Smith in a boundary line dispute with Smith's neighbor. When combing through the county land records, Jones discovers that Smith's grantor apparently had no legal title to the land he purported to grant to Smith.

   B. Lawyer Jones is defending client Smith in a tax fraud case. With Smith's consent, Jones hires a tax accountant to examine Smith's records, to talk with Smith, and to prepare some worksheets for Jones to use in defending the case. The accountant turns the worksheets over to Jones.

   C. Jones is defending Smith in a first degree murder case. In the course of her investigation, Jones talks to a taxi driver who tells Jones that he remembers that on the night in question Smith rode in his taxi to an address near the scene of the murder.

   D. Jones represents Smith in an action for breach of an oral contract. When preparing the case for trial, Jones stumbles across an old newspaper clipping, reporting Smith's conviction of a felony in a distant state 15 years ago.

* * *

In complex business litigation, Client Tiger is represented by Lawyer Tony. Defendant has demanded production of all Client Tiger's records containing confidential business information. Defendant is agreeable to a protective order that prohibits it from misusing the information, and it has agreed to accept xerographic copies in lieu of the original records. Lawyer Tony's office does not have a copying machine big enough to do the job efficiently.

QUESTION:

10. In these circumstances, what may/must Lawyer Tony ethically do?

A. Lawyer Tony must do the copying job himself on his small, slow office machine.

B. Lawyer Tony must tell Client Tiger to make the copies himself, using his own facilities.

C. Lawyer Tony may select a trustworthy copying firm to do the work, provided that he is personally present to supervise the work.

D. Lawyer Tony may select a trustworthy copying firm to do the work, provided that he makes sure the firm's employees preserve the confidentiality of the records.

* * *

Judge Jane, a state trial judge, has been assigned to preside in the cases described below. Assume that the parties are not willing to waive the technical disqualification provisions of the Code of Judicial Conduct; assume, further, that even in light of the facts stated below there is no reasonable ground to doubt Judge Jane's impartiality.

QUESTION:

11. In which of the cases may she preside?

A. *People v. Erving,* a murder case in Judge Jane's family physician will testify as a witness on behalf of the prosecution.

B. *Methusala v. Union Van & Storage*, a breach of warranty action. Judge Jane's mother, age 106, lives in a nursing home and owns 100 of the three million outstanding shares of Union Van's common stock.

C. *Bernanke v. City of Air Authority*, a tort action. Judge Jane owns $2,000 worth of general obligation bonds that were issued by the City of Air Authority to fund a variety of municipal public works projects.

D. Answers A, B and C are all correct.

* * *

QUESTION:

12. In a non-litigation situation, what is a lawyer's ethical duty to withdraw?

   A. A lawyer may withdraw if the representation will result in a violation of the rules of professional conduct or other law.

   B. A lawyer must withdraw if the client has used the lawyer's services to perpetrate a crime or fraud.

   C. A lawyer must withdraw if the representation will result in an unreasonable burden on the lawyer, but only if the withdrawal can be accomplished without material adverse effect on the interest of the client.

   D. A lawyer may withdraw if the client persists in a course of action involving the lawyer's services that the lawyer reasonably believes is criminal.

QUESTION:

13. Which of the following has the inherent power to regulate the practice of law within the state?

   A. The state legislature.

   B. The state bar association.

   C. The Board of Bar Examiners.

   D. The state Supreme Court.

* * *

Attorney Alex practices with several other lawyers in a small firm. He also owns a company that collects bad checks for local businesses. The check collection business is completely unrelated to Attorney Alex's practice of law. In the check collection business, Attorney Alex was convicted of a misdemeanor violation of the applicable wage and hour law.

QUESTION:

14. Based on the foregoing fact, is Attorney Alex subject to discipline?

   A. Attorney Alex is not subject to discipline because his conduct is unrelated to the practice of law.

   B. Attorney Alex is not subject to discipline because lawyers can only be disciplined for felonious criminal acts.

   C. Attorney Alex may be subject to discipline if it is determined that he engaged in dishonesty or deceit.

   D. None of the above answers is correct.

* * *

Attorney Joe left Bates and Bates after 20 years. He soon joined Gates and Gates. While at Bates and Bates and at Gates and Gates, Joe represented Stove, Inc. in all its litigation matters. While most of that litigation involved product liability suits alleging that toasters made by Stove were defective, some litigation involved employment disputes, slip and fall cases on factory premises, and even an antitrust matter. Oven, Inc. has now requested that Bates and Bates represent it in an action against Stove and others. Oven claims that Stove and the others tortiously interfered with Oven's supply and distribution contracts. Wishbone, a lawyer with Bates and Bates, did not work with Joe on the Stove matters when Joe was with Bates and Bates but he did occasionally talk with Joe about various legal issues in the Stove cases.

QUESTION:

15. Is any lawyer in the Bates and Bates law firm subject to discipline?

   A. Any lawyer in Bates and Bates would be subject to discipline for representing Oven, an entity with interests materially adverse to a former client.

    B.   Any lawyer in Bates and Bates would not be subject to discipline for representing Oven if neither Wishbone nor any other Bates and Bates lawyer had confidential information about Stove protected by Model Rule 1.6.

    C.   Any lawyer in Bates and Bates would be subject to discipline for representing Oven if the Oven matter was substantially related to matters Joe handled while at Bates and Bates.

    D.   Any lawyer in Bates and Bates would not be subject to discipline if Wishbone and any other lawyers with confidential information about Stove were screened.

* * *

Attorney LaVar worked at the Department of Justice in Washington, D.C. LaVar represented the United States in all tax appeals in the Sixth Circuit. After two years, LaVar began working with the firm of Fine & Dart in Ohio. LaVar is a member of the firm's tax department. Fine & Dart has been asked to handle a tax appeal for Reds Corp. The Reds Corp. matter has been going on for some time but until now Reds was represented by the firm of Schott and Bowsam. While at the Department of Justice, LaVar knew that there was a Reds investigation and litigation but he had no involvement in the matter and knew nothing other than the fact of the existence of the dispute.

QUESTION:

16. Is Attorney LaVar subject to discipline?

    A.   LaVar would not be subject to discipline for representing Reds in the tax appeal.

    B.   LaVar would be subject to discipline unless the Department of Justice consents to the representation.

    C.   LaVar would be subject to discipline if he represented Reds but another lawyer at Fine & Dart could represent Reds as long as LaVar is properly screened.

    D.   LaVar and any lawyer at Fine & Dart would be subject to discipline if LaVar left the Department of Justice less than a year ago.

* * *

Draper is a law clerk for Judge Dale, a trial judge, and his one-year clerkship is almost completed. Much of their time during this year has been spent with the trial of *Sterling v. American Cigarette Corp.* Dale is the presiding judge. Sterling is represented by the firm of Dotson & Yates. American Cigarette Corp. is represented by the firm of Queeg & Constant. Draper wants to seek a job with the Queeg firm and tells Dale of this desire. Dale confides that she is considering discussing her own employment with the Queeg firm.

QUESTION:

17. Which of the following is true?

   A.   Both Dale and Draper are subject to discipline if they discuss employment with Queeg & Constant.

   B.   Dale would be subject to discipline if she discussed her employment with Queeg & Constant but Draper would not.

   C.   Neither Dale nor Draper is subject to discipline if they discuss employment with Queeg & Constant as long as they are screened from the Sterling case once they join the firm.

   D.   Neither Dale nor Draper is subject to discipline.

* * *

Attorney Monty Townes has prepared and filed his motion for summary judgment on his client's behalf. Hours before the hearing where he will argue the motion, Attorney Townes discovers several cases with dicta that are directly against his client's position. Two of the cases have holdings that by analogy are against his client's position. All of these cases are from the jurisdiction where the lawsuit was filed and where the summary judgment motion will be heard. Attorney Townes concludes that the likelihood is great that the judge would rule against his client on the summary judgment motion if she knew of these cases. Opposing counsel has not referred to these cases in his response.

QUESTION:

18. Must Attorney Townes tell the court about these cases?

   A.   No, because the cases contain dicta.

   B.   Yes, because the cases are legal authority in the controlling jurisdiction known to be directly adverse to Townes's client;

C. No, because opposing counsel overlooked the cases and it was her responsibility to uncover any relevant facts and controlling authority;

D. Yes, because Townes is an officer of the court, and the search for the truth is the objective of litigation.

* * *

Prosecutor Jack Ford has been assigned to prosecute defendant Drew for arson. Shortly after the fire was extinguished, a three-person team of arson experts was sent by the City fire department to determine the cause of the fire. The team concluded that the fire was set by a professional arsonist, and the team's report so states. Shortly before trial, Ford learned that Benson, the youngest and least experienced member of the team, had originally concluded that the fire resulted from an explosion in the furnace. Benson had tried to convince the other two team members that his conclusion was correct, but they ultimately prevailed, and Benson signed the report without dissent. Ford does not plan to offer the report in evidence at trial, and he does not plan to call any of the three team members as witnesses. Rather, he plans to use the testimony of two independent experts to establish that arson caused the fire.

QUESTION:

19. Which of the following constitutes Ford's ethical duty about the information about Benson?

A. Recommend to his superior that the charges against Drew be dismissed, since the information creates a reasonable doubt about Drew's guilt.

B. Disclose it to Drew's counsel, because it may be useful in Drew's defense.

C. Wait to see whether Drew's counsel asks for the information in the regular course of criminal discovery.

D. Do nothing about it since he does not plan to offer the report or the testimony of the team members at the trial.

* * *

The Hotel International burned to the ground, killing fifteen guests and injuring hundreds. One of the deceased's legal representatives retained Lawyer Leland to represent the interests of the deceased.

After the lawsuit was filed, Leland sent his investigator to interview the former hotel manager who was fired three months before the fire. She told him that she was fired because she had complained about the hotel's unwillingness to spend money on maintenance and an updated sprinkler system. Before the end of the interview, she gave Leland's investigator a copy of a memorandum that she had sent to her supervisor at the home office of Hotel International's owner (Hotels Are Us, Inc.) complaining about the maintenance and sprinkler issues. After Hotels Are Us found out that Leland's investigator interviewed the former manager, it filed a motion to disqualify Lawyer Leland from representing the plaintiff because of his *ex parte* contact with the former manager.

QUESTION:

20. Applying the Model Rules, will the trial court grant the motion to disqualify Lawyer Leland?

     A. Yes, because the former manager disclosed privileged and confidential information to the Leland's investigator.

     B. No, because the former manager has no lawyer.

     C. Yes, because Leland should have consulted the lawyer for Hotels Are Us, Inc.

     D. No, because the person interviewed is a former employee, her information is not privileged, and there is no indication that she misunderstood the investigator's role.

* * *

Samantha has retained Lawyer Hester to represent her in divorce proceedings instituted by her husband. Samantha has moved from the family home and is living out of town. She no longer stays in contact with her husband or children. She tells Lawyer Hester in confidence that, before the separation, she had physically abused her children. A state statute requires physicians and psychotherapists to report all suspected cases of child abuse to the police, but the statute does not mention a comparable duty for lawyers.

21. Which of the following is correct regarding whether Lawyer Hester is subject to discipline?

     A. If Hester reports the child abuse to the police, he will be subject to discipline.

B. Hester may report the child abuse to the police if he believes that the interests of justice will be served by doing so.

C. Hester must report the child abuse to the police, because the state policy favors the protection of children.

D. Hester must report the child abuse to the police, because child abuse is a crime that may result in death or serious bodily injury.

* * *

J.O. Simpson requested that Lawyer Giesel defend him on a robbery charge. Because she usually does not represent clients in criminal cases, she gave him the names of ten excellent criminal defense lawyers. As Simpson was leaving, he told Lawyer Giesel that he robbed the three victims who were not harmed. Simpson left and later hired one of the ten lawyers recommended by Lawyer Giesel. After the prosecutor learned about Simpson's remarks to Lawyer Giesel, he subpoenaed Lawyer Giesel to appear as a witness at Simpson's preliminary hearing.

QUESTION:

22. Which of the following describes the situation?

A. A lawyer-client relationship was formed between Simpson and Lawyer Giesel.

B. A lawyer-client relationship was formed between Simpson and Lawyer Giesel, but she terminated the relationship by recommending ten other lawyers.

C. The information sought by the prosecutor is protected from disclosure by Lawyer Giesel under the lawyer-client privilege.

D. The information sought by the prosecutor is not protected from disclosure by Lawyer Giesel under the lawyer-client privilege.

* * *

Judge Audra is a state trial judge whose brother is ten years older than she. He asks her to prepare a will for him, in which he wants to leave $1,000 to her and to divide the remainder of his estate equally among his grandchildren. Judge Audra told her older brother that she could not prepare the will, but she suggested that he contact Lawyer Wes who is one of the excellent estate planners in the county.

QUESTION:

23. Which of the following is *not* true?

    A. If the will names Judge Audra as executrix, she may serve as the executrix, if it will not interfere with her judicial duties.

    B. If the will names Fifth National Bank as executor and names Judge Audra as the lawyer for the estate, she may serve as the lawyer, assuming that the estate matter will not be probated in her court or one under its appellate jurisdiction.

    C. If the will leaves Judge Audra $1,000, she may accept the money.

    D. Judge Audra may prepare the will for her brother, without compensation, even though she is to receive $1,000 under the terms of the will.

* * *

Lawyer Lucy represents Plaintiff Ethel in a personal injury case arising from a vehicular accident. While the defense lawyer is visiting Lawyer Lucy's office to discuss settlement possibilities, they discuss the strengths and weaknesses of their respective cases. Lawyer Lucy tells defense counsel that she has eyewitness testimony that the defendant was speeding at the time of the accident. In reality, Lawyer Lucy has no such evidence, but she hopes to prove that the defendant was speeding through the use of circumstantial evidence.

QUESTION:

24. Is Lawyer Lucy subject to discipline?

    A. No, because Lawyer Lucy's statement is mere puffing during a negotiation session.

    B. No, because Lawyer Lucy's statement is immaterial to the litigation.

    C. Yes, because Lawyer Lucy's statement is a false statement of material fact.

  D. Yes, because Lawyer Lucy's statement is prohibited posturing during negotiation.

* * *

Clients Amanda and Alex retained Lawyer Dove to assist them in finding a child for adoption. The first court proceeding associated with the adoption is an *ex parte* proceeding in which the lawyer for the adoptive parents is responsible for presenting information to the court relating to the waiver of rights by the biological parents. All of the documents filed by Lawyer Dover with the court for the hearing to terminate parental rights pending adoption contained material misstatements. For example, the documents indicated that the biological father had waived his parental rights when Lawyer Dove knew that he had not. In addition, the documents did not mention that the child had lived with his maternal grandparents long enough to give them statutory rights to be notified about the adoption proceedings.

QUESTION:

25. Which of the following accurately describes Lawyer Dove's ethical situation?

  A. Lawyer Dove is subject to discipline, because her failure to inform the tribunal of material facts and issues in the case deprived the tribunal of the ability to make informed decisions.

  B. Lawyer Dove is subject to discipline for knowingly making a false statement of fact.

  C. Lawyer Dove is not subject to discipline because the documents do not contain affirmative false statements of fact to the court.

  D. Answers A and B are correct.

* * *

Lawyer Lemon represents Client Donaghy in a breach of contract case. When Lawyer Lemon received interrogatories from the adversary party, she forwarded them to Client Donaghy for him to answer. After he returned the interrogatory answers to her, Lawyer Lemon read them and unilaterally changed some of them before sending them back to the adversary party and filing them. All of the revised answers were true. Lawyer Lemon did not inform Client Donaghy about what she had done to his interrogatory responses.

QUESTION:

26. Which of the following best describes whether Lawyer Lemon is subject to discipline?

    A. Lawyer Lemon is subject to discipline for offering false evidence.

    B. Lawyer Lemon is subject to discipline because the filed answers were incorrect .

    C. Lawyer Lemon is not subject to discipline because the answers that were filed were true.

    D. Lawyer Lemon is not subject to discipline because she did not believe that the answers were false.

* * *

Lawyer Adkins met married her ex-husband in 1999. They separated in 2002. A year after that, Lawyer Adkins met George who was also from Cameroon. Their relationship led him to ask Lawyer Adkins to move to Massachusetts and live with him. She agreed to marry him if they could return briefly to Cameroon and go through a tribal rite of marriage there. Until 2007, they lived together during which time Lawyer Adkins gave birth to a child. In 2005, she filed for and obtained a divorce from her ex-husband. Last year, Lawyer Adkins filed for a divorce from George. In her petition, she asked for maintenance and for injunction that George no longer refuse to include her and their son on his health insurance policy. When George raised the issue that he and Lawyer Adkins had never been married by anyone other than the Cameroon tribal chieftain, Lawyer Adkins promptly withdrew her claim for maintenance and for health insurance coverage.

QUESTION:

27. Did Lawyer Adkins violate the Model Rules?

    A. Lawyer Adkins violated the Rules by making a false statement of fact to the court.

    B. Lawyer Adkins violated the Rules about false evidence already offered.

    C. Lawyer Adkins did not violate the Rules about false evidence already offered.

    D. Answers A and C are both accurate.

* * *

Client Davis was injured in a vehicular accident. Six days after the accident, he retained Lawyer Jordan to represent his interests and pursue his personal injury claim. Initially, Lawyer Jordan communicated with Client Davis frequently and assured him that he was protecting his interests. After several months, Lawyer Jordan began to communicate with Client Davis less often. Lawyer Jordan failed to file suit on behalf of his client in a timely manner. A month later, Client Davis met with Lawyer Jordan, who apologized for not filing a lawsuit on Client Davis's behalf. She told Client Davis that whatever damages Client Davis would have won would come out of her pocket.

QUESTION:

28. After Client Davis files a disciplinary complaint with the state bar association, which of the following describes Lawyer Jordan's situation?

   A. Lawyer Jordan is subject to discipline because she did not advise Client Davis in writing about the value of consulting independent counsel.

   B. Lawyer Jordan is not subject to discipline because Client Davis was her client at the time of their meeting.

   C. Lawyer Jordan is not subject to discipline because Client Davis and she did not discuss a specific dollar amount.

   D. Answers B and C are both true.

* * *

Lawyer Toner practiced in a four-person law firm for three years after law school. In his law firm, in order to derive the benefits of a small law firm, the four lawyers met every morning to discuss everyone's cases. One of the firm's clients was a small commuter airline which was being sued by several passengers who had been hurt in an airliner accident. At the end of the third year, Lawyer Toner married his high school sweetheart and moved 2,000 miles to a large town where he was hired by a large litigation firm. Within six months of his arrival, Lawyer Toner was representing one of the passengers who was now suing Lawyer Toner's old firm's client based on the same accident.

QUESTION:

29. Which of the following accurately describes Lawyer Toner's ethical situation?

A. If the old law firm moves to disqualify Lawyer Toner, the trial court will grant the motion.

B. If the commuter airlines give its oral consent to Lawyer Toner's representation of the injured passenger, he can represent that passenger's interest against the airline.

C. If Lawyer Toner's new law firm screens him from participating in the case, the trial court will grant a motion to disqualify Lawyer Toner but deny a motion to disqualify the remaining lawyers in the law firm.

D. If Lawyer Toner leaves the new law firm immediately, the trial court will deny a motion by the old firm to disqualify him and the entire new firm.

* * *

Lawyer Dennehy leaves Rose and Lind, her old law firm, which she helped to begin, in order to become a named law partner with a new law firm called Cord and Dinitz. While she was affiliated with Rose and Lind, she was the only lawyer who represented Drugs B Good, a pharmaceutical corporation that was sued often. At Cord and Dinitz, she now represents Drugs B Good in a lawsuit brought by the estate of Jones who died from ingesting pills manufactured by Drugs B Good. The estate of Jones is represented by Rose and Lind. At Rose and Lind, no lawyer had ever represented Drugs B Good for deaths caused by the specific pharmaceutical involved in the new case.

QUESTION:

30. Which of the following accurately describes the ethical obligations of the lawyers at the law firm of Rose and Lind?

A. Rose and Lind cannot represent any plaintiff in any lawsuit against Drugs B Good without written informed consent.

B. Rose and Lind cannot represent the Estate of Jones in its lawsuit against Drugs B Good.

C. Rose and Lind can represent the Estate of Jones in its lawsuit brought against Drugs B Good.

D. Answers A and B are both correct.

* * *

Lawyer Lani represents Client Convict who two years ago was convicted of one count of murder in a highly publicized trial. After he was sentenced to death, Client Convict contacted Lawyer Lani to discuss their future plans for appealing his conviction. Last week, his conviction was affirmed by the state Supreme Court in a unanimous ruling. Now that she has exhausted Client Convict's state remedies, Lawyer Lani is prepared to begin the process of petitioning a federal district court for habeas corpus relief. Client Convict has told Lawyer Lani that she should not file any further motions or claims because he wants to die for what he did to the victim. He also refuses to go along with Lawyer Lani's efforts to pursue an eleventh hour attempt to raise the question of Client Convict's competency for foregoing further appeals or post-conviction relief, despite the defendant's prior clearly expressed, longstanding and consistent desires to that effect.

QUESTION:

31. Which of the following describes Lawyer Lani's ethical situation?

    A. Lawyer Lani is subject to discipline if she seeks further relief to overturn Client Convict's conviction.

    B. Lawyer Lani is subject to discipline if she asks a court to determine Client Convict's competency.

    C. Lawyer Lani is subject to discipline if she does nothing, because in good faith she believes that Client Convict knows what he is doing.

    D. Lawyer Lani is subject to discipline if she tells Client Convict's family what he has told her, so that his family will assist her in persuading him to continue his legal challenges.

* * *

The law firm of Able, Baker and Cohen has over 300 lawyers practicing law at its six offices throughout the eastern United States. All of the firms's lawyers do not practice in each of the six states where the law firm has its offices. To keep its volume of business at a high level, the law firm is exploring options for advertising its services with a firm website on the internet.

QUESTION:

32. Which of the following options will *not* subject the law firm or its lawyer-partners to discipline under the Rules?

A. Changing the firm name to United States Lawyers.

B. Stating that all of its lawyers practice are admitted to practice everywhere in the United States.

C. Keeping the same firm name, although Baker is a United States Senator and he intends to return to practice law after he serves his term; in addition, there are no other lawyers with that name in the firm.

D. Keeping the same firm name, although Able is deceased, and there are not other lawyers with his name in the firm.

* * *

Lawyer Dudley is always looking for ways to increase her small firm's volume of business. She was dissatisfied with her firm's recent advertising campaign, because she could not figure out how to measure its benefits. Retaining a local marketing firm was not productive either, because all of its ideas were going to cost more than the risk-averse Dudley had in mind to invest in expanding her office business. She has decided to explore a more direct approach of marketing in order to gauge its success.

QUESTION:

33. Of the following ideas, which of the following is/are likely to subject Lawyer Dudley to discipline?

A. Paying her support staff to distribute her business cards.

B. Joining a non-profit lawyer referral plan by paying it for every case it refers to her.

C. Entering a reciprocal referral agreement with another law firm and she discloses the nature of the agreement to her client.

D. Answers B and C will both subject Lawyer Dudley to discipline.

* * *

Lawyer Milligan has a longstanding friendship with Lawyer Richardson, who has drinking and gambling problems. Until recently, Lawyer Richardson had been fortunate that her bad habits had not directly affected her ability to provide her clients with quality legal services. Lately, however, Lawyer Richardson has engaged in binge drinking at local bar association social events, and she has confided to her friend Lawyer Milligan that she has owes the local casino more than $20,000 in gambling debts that she currently is unable to repay. Ironically, it is Lawyer Milligan who finds herself in an ethical quandary about what to do to help her friend, especially now that Lawyer Richardson has asked Lawyer Milligan to represent her in defending a legal malpractice claim. As part of her defense to the claim, Lawyer Milligan will rely on showing Lawyer Richardson's impairment from drinking and gambling.

QUESTION:

34. Of the following, which describes Lawyer Milligan's best ethical alternative?

    A. Lawyer Milligan must report Lawyer Richardson to the appropriate professional authority.

    B. Lawyer Milligan may report Lawyer Richardson to the appropriate professional authority.

    C. Lawyer Milligan must not report Lawyer Richardson to the appropriate professional authority.

    D. Lawyer Milligan may report Lawyer Richardson to the appropriate professional authority only when her drinking or gambling has resulted in criminal charges Lawyer Richardson.

* * *

Lawyer Willard's law partner of twenty-five years recently died. The deceased lawyer, Lawyer Richards, founded the law firm forty years ago with his father. The law firm name had changed to Richards and Willard after Lawyer Willard had practiced with Lawyer Richards for almost four years. The law firm's business was primarily an office practice, meaning that it was rare that their clients pursued remedies through litigation. Although they were law partners, each of them worked on his own cases almost exclusively. At the time of his death, Lawyer Richards was still actively involved in probating several estates. Lawyer Willard is trying to figure out what he can do to identify the work that Lawyer Richards was still doing for the law firm at the time of his death. The Willard/Richards partnership agreement permits the surviving law partner to buy the practice of the deceased partner.

QUESTION:

35. Which of the following statements describes Lawyer Willard's proper course of action?

 A. Lawyer Willard cannot pay legal fees earned by Lawyer Richards to his estate.

 B. Lawyer Willard may pay legal fees earned by Lawyer Richards to his estate.

 C. Lawyer Willard must pay legal fees earned by Lawyer Richards to his widow.

 D. Lawyer Willard cannot pay Lawyer Richards's executor-widow for buying Lawyer Richards's law practice.

* * *

Judge Ice is a state judge who usually has no difficulty figuring out the applicable law for the cases on his docket. However, currently he is confused by a complicated question of law which he must decide. The briefs have been somewhat less than helpful and the case law is unclear.

QUESTION:

36. What can Judge Ice ethically do next?

 A. Consult with other judges in that area but must then inform the parties.

 B. Consult with a disinterested expert on the law if she gives advance notice to the parties about the person consulted and the substance of the advice, and also gives the parties a reasonable opportunity to respond.

 C. Not consult with other judges unless she first informs the parties.

 D. Receive additional advice only by requiring additional briefs from the parties.

* * *

Lawyer Linus is a fifth-year associate in a law firm of 75 lawyers. Client Callie spoke to him twice recently about representing her and others similarly situated in a consumer class action against a national hotel chain for covertly charging hotel guests for the use of its fitness areas. After thinking about the representation, Lawyer Linus concluded that he lacked the experience to pursue a complex case. In addition, his law firm lacked the resources to devote to a case with such a questionable likelihood of success. Lawyer Linus quickly informed Client Callie about his decision to decline the representation of her and the rest of the class. Six months later at its monthly litigation department meeting, one of the litigation partners informed the others that the same national hotel chain had been sued by a class action headed by a woman named Callie based on the same factual basis as lawyer Linus's earlier conversation with Client Callie.

QUESTION:

37. Under what circumstances, if any, can Lawyer Linus's law firm represent the national hotel chain in the class action lawsuit?

    A. Lawyer Linus's law firm can represent the national hotel chain, because Client Callie was not a client of his or the law firm.

    B. Lawyer Linus's law firm can represent the national hotel chain, if Lawyer Linus is effectively screened from the lawyers in the law firm representing that client.

    C. Lawyer Linus's law firm cannot represent the national hotel chain, even if Client Callie consents to the disclosure of the information she told to Lawyer Linus.

    D. Lawyer Linus's law firm cannot represent the national hotel chain, because Lawyer Linus's information is imputed to all others in the law firm.

* * *

Lawyer Niles was excited last year when he received an offer to change law firms and accelerate his opportunity to become a partner in his new firm. His anticipation may have encountered an obstacle, though. His new law firm represents a client which has interests that are significantly adverse to one of the clients that Niles represented at his old law firm. Because the new law firm's client is both a very old client and accounts for a hefty percentage of the billable hours for the new firm, Niles is concerned that his hopes for an accelerated road to becoming a law partner will not be realized.

QUESTION:

38. Which of the following accurately describes the ethical option for Niles to pursue?

   A. The new law firm must discontinue representing its longstanding client.

   B. Niles must resign from the new law firm.

   C. Niles and the law firm must create a screen, with the prior consent of Niles's former client.

   D. Niles and the law firm must create a screen in order for the new law firm to avoid being disqualified from representing its longstanding client.

* * *

Lawyer Nancy has practiced in her home state for more than thirty years, but she has decided to spend more time with her family and helping other people less fortunate than she. While her law partners wish her well, they are concerned that she may take some of their law business with her if she changes her mind. Lawyer Nancy is confused about what restrictions her law firm can place on her ability to practice law if she decides to resume a practice on her own or with other lawyers.

QUESTION:

39. What can Lawyer Nancy ethically do next?

   A. Lawyer Nancy may agree to restrict her right to represent current clients of her law firm.

   B. Lawyer Nancy cannot agree to restrict her right to practice law after she leaves her law firm.

   C. Lawyer Nancy may agree to restrict her right to practice if the agreement is reasonable in terms of its time and geographic scope.

   D. Lawyer Nancy may agree to restrict her right to practice as part of settling one of her large cases in which she is trying to negotiate a settlement.

* * *

QUESTION:

40. Which of the following statements comparing the work product doctrine and the lawyer-client privilege is/are accurate?

    A. Work product facts developed during trial preparation may not be privileged.

    B. The work product doctrine is broader than the lawyer-client privilege, in part because it protects legal strategies and theories developed in preparation for trial.

    C. Work product materials survive the end of the litigation, but privileged information does not.

    D. Answers A and B are correct.

* * *

Judge Chen has invited Lawyer Cochoran to his wedding. He and Lawyer Cochoran are close friends whose relationship began upon Judge Chen becoming a Judge. Lawyer Cochoran is an active litigator in Judge Chen's court. Lawyer Cochoran plans to buy Judge Chen a wedding gift costing $15.

QUESTION:

41. Can Judge Chen ethically accept this gift?

    A. No, because Lawyer Cochoran appears in Judge Chen's court often.

    B. Yes, but only if Judge Chen reports the gift as compensation.

    C. Yes, because the gift is a wedding gift.

    D. No, because the cost of the gift was more than $10.

* * *

After the conclusion of the pretrial conference in the case of *James v. Patrick*, Lawyer Penelope, who is the lawyer for the plaintiff, was about to leave the courtroom when she remembered that she had a scheduling conflict with the date that the judge had set for the next pretrial conference. Although her opposing counsel had already taken the elevator to his next scheduled appointment, Lawyer Penelope looked for and found the trial judge to discuss changing the pretrial conference date to a later time. Aware of a local court rule that allows her to discuss this matter with the judge, she assured the trial judge that she would contact her opposing counsel to make the scheduling change.

QUESTION:

42. Which of the following describes the ethical effect of what Lawyer Penelope did?

A. Lawyer Penelope is subject to discipline for having an *ex parte* conversation with the trial judge.

B. Lawyer Penelope is subject to discipline for delaying the pretrial conference.

C. Lawyer Penelope is not subject to discipline for having an *ex parte* conversation with the trial judge, if there is a local rule permitting such a conversation.

D. Lawyer Penelope is subject to discipline under the Rules for not bringing her calendar to the pretrial conference.

* * *

QUESTION:

43. The following statements compare a lawyer's duties to report corporate wrongdoing under Model Rule 1.13 and comparable duties imposed by regulations of the Securities and Exchange Commission. Which of the comparisons is *not* true?

A. The lawyer's duties under Rule 1.13 must relate to the representation of the entity; under the SEC Regulations, after a lawyer appears and practices before the SEC, she must follow the reporting procedures regardless of whether what she knows relates to her representation of her client.

B. Rule 1.13(b) requires the lawyer to "be aware" that someone is engaged in a "material violation" of federal or state (securities) law before being required to report that person; the SEC Regulation is triggered when the lawyer "knows" of evidence likely to cause substantial injury to the entity.

C. Rule 1.13 requires reporting of a violation that is likely to cause substantial injury to the entity; the SEC Regulations require the lawyer to report any "material violation" of federal or state securities law regardless of potential harm to the entity.

D. The lawyer's reporting duties under the SEC Regulations are more specific than the Rule 1.13 standards.

* * *

In her work as General Counsel for the Environmental Protection Division in his state's Attorney General's office, Lawyer Powell was not personally and substantially involved in the cases that her office was litigating. As her children approached college age, she recognized the need to bring in more income and she changed jobs. Now she is associate general counsel for a large oil company, earning four times more money than when she worked for the Attorney General. When she left the Attorney General's office, the Environmental Protection Division was litigating a case against Lawyer Powell's new employer.

QUESTION:

44. Is Lawyer Powell subject to discipline by representing her new employer in that same lawsuit brought by the Environmental Protection Division?

   A. Yes, because it is the same matter as the lawsuit that was pending when she left the Attorney General's office.

   B. Yes, because she was General Counsel with supervisory authority over the cases of her associate counsel.

   C. No, because she was not personally and substantially involved in the lawsuit when she worked at the Environmental Protection Division.

   D. No, although the lawsuit is the same matter that she was personally and substantially involved with at the Attorney General's office, she is not subject to discipline if she is properly screened from involvement in the lawsuit and another lawyer represents the oil company.

* * *

Client Carter may be 90 years old and frail but he is overjoyed with the result that Lawyer Ford has achieved for him in his breach of contract case against his former business partner. When he first went to see Lawyer Ford, his expectations were low regarding the likely outcome in his case. To him, however, Lawyer Ford's abilities were miraculous under the circumstances. Client Carter is so delighted with Lawyer Ford's work that he wants to show his appreciation to her with a special gift—the new car of her choice when the automakers introduce the new models next year. When Client Carter mentions the idea for his gift to her, Lawyer Ford thanks him and tells him that such an outpouring of gratitude is unnecessary. Nevertheless, Client Carter intends to follow through on his idea.

QUESTION:

45. Which of the following describes Lawyer Ford's ethical situation in relation to the gift idea?

    A. Lawyer Ford cannot accept a substantial gift from a client that is not directly tied to her rendering of legal services.

    B. Lawyer Ford cannot accept a substantial gift from a client if the client asks Lawyer Ford to prepare a Will in which the client bequeaths to her sufficient funds to pay for a new car of her choice.

    C. Lawyer Ford can accept a substantial gift from a client, regardless of who had the idea for the gift.

    D. Lawyer Ford can accept a substantial gift from a client, regardless of who drafts any documents relating to the gift.

* * *

Lawyer Lee represents Client Cardio in her divorce case. Before he began representing her, they had dated for six months after she separated from her husband. Before and after the lawyer-client relationship began, their relationship had included sexual relations. After he filed a petition seeking a dissolution of her marriage, in order to prepare for the custody hearings in her case, they spent even more hours together looking at medical and school records for Client Cardio's two children who are ages four and seven.

QUESTION:

46. As the time for the important custody hearing approaches, what should Lawyer Lee do?

    A. Lawyer Lee is subject to discipline for having had sexual relations with a client.

    B. Lawyer Lee is subject to discipline, unless Client Cardio signed a consent form at the beginning of their lawyer-client relationship.

    C. Lawyer Lee should consider withdrawing from his representation of Client Cardio, because his ability to represent her is materially limited by their ongoing romantic relationship.

D. Lawyer Lee is not subject to discipline, because his sexual relationship with Client Cardio predated his representation.

* * *

Lawyer Landy has worked at the local office of the Public Defender for more than ten years. Her caseload usually remains steady but in the last six months it has increased 30%. Because of budget cuts, she lacks to money to hire additional lawyers to share the caseload increase. Lawyer Landy's biggest fear is that her caseload no longer permits her to do an adequate job of representing each client.

QUESTION:

47. Does Lawyer Landy or her supervisor have an ethical problem?

   A. No, Lawyer Landy's supervisor is not subject to discipline if Lawyer Landy's caseload affects her ability to act diligently in representing her clients.

   B. Yes, because Lawyer Landy has an obligation to control her workload in order to avoid prejudice to her existing clients.

   C. No, because Lawyer Landy can ask her clients to waive the duty of diligence that she owes to her clients.

   D. No, if as the Public Defender she is the only person who can accept court appointments.

* * *

Lawyer Lana is a solo practitioner who represents anyone who comes to her office. She enjoys practicing law and meeting new people. Her positive and enthusiastic attitude toward law practice and her clients has begun to take a physical toll on her. Her doctor told her that she needs to reduce stress in her life and change her eating habits before something catastrophic happens to her in the form of a debilitating heart attack or stroke.

QUESTION:

48. Under the Model Rules, what is Lawyer Lana's ethical obligation to her current and future clients?

   A. She should write a plan to designate another lawyer to take care of her cases in the event of her death or disability.

  B. She must stop taking new cases until her health risks are controlled.

  C. She should inform the judge who presides over her clients' cases.

  D. She should purchase insurance to be sure that her clients receive the monetary relief that they deserve.

* * *

Lawyer Lawson represents the defendant in a breach of contract action which originated from a dispute about the cost of raw materials. She and her client have discussed a possible settlement for about a week. Finally, just before leaving town for a continuing legal education program at a Carribean resort, Lawyer Lawson hurriedly sent the settlement proposal in an email to the opposing party and simultaneously copied his lawyer on the email.

QUESTION:

 49. Is Lawyer Lawson subject to discipline by sending an email directly to the opposing party?

  A. Yes, if she did not have the opposing lawyer's prior consent.

  B. Yes, because a settlement offer must be in writing.

  C. No, because email is a customary method of modern communication.

  D. No, because the opposing party and his lawyer will receive the email at the same time.

* * *

Company Abner is interested in suing Company Bates for breach of contract. Company Abner asks several law firms to present its qualifications, but Company Abner does not discuss any confidential information about its proposed lawsuit with any of the law firms, including Law Partner Fisher from the Law Firm of Carey & Dyson. Company Abner decides not to retain Law Firm Carey & Dyson, which is retained by Company Bates three months later to defend Company Abner's lawsuit.

QUESTION:

 50. Which of the following best describes whether the Law Firm of Carey & Dyson can begin to represent Company Bates in the lawsuit of *Company Abner v. Company Bates*?

A. Law Partner Fisher must represent Company Bates, because she knows the basic facts about the lawsuit, even though no confidential information was acquired during the bidding process.

B. Law Partner Fisher may represent Company Bates, because no confidential information was acquired during the bidding process.

C. Law Partner Fisher may not represent Company Bates, because she knows the basic facts about the lawsuit, even though no confidential information was acquired during the bidding process.

D. Law Partner Fisher must not represent Company Bates, because she has no confidential information about the lawsuit during the bidding process.

* * *

Lawyer Long is Gotham City's Assistant City Law Director, which is analogous to being General Counsel in a corporation. In Gotham City, the position of Assistant Law Director is a part-time position, and Lawyer Long also practices law with a law firm in Gotham City. Lawyer Long's law partners often receive requests to represent defendants in criminal cases brought in Gotham City and throughout the state where Gotham City is located.

QUESTION:

51. Lawyer Long's law partners are not subject to discipline if they:

A. Represent criminal defendants in Gotham City.

B. Represent criminal defendants in Gotham City and the rest of the state.

C. Represent criminal defendants in the rest of the state.

D. Represent any criminal defendants anywhere.

* * *

Lawyer Likins, a public defender, while representing her client four years ago, developed a client file containing crime-scene and autopsy photos, third-party medical reports, victim-identification information, and psychological evaluations of her client. Some of the documents were obtained through discovery or may be subject to court-ordered restrictions on dissemination to her client. Four years after the case concluded, her client requested all of his file which contains these materials.

QUESTION:

52. Is Lawyer Likins subject to discipline if she restricts her client's access to his file?

A. Yes, if she turns over the former client's file to him.

B. No, if she gives him the material which she believes is not offensive to the victim.

C. No, if she retains information that is prohibited by law from being disclosed.

D. No, if she withholds all information that does not belong to her former client.

* * *

Client Cedric informs Lawyer Lyons that he would like to buy or sell real estate. Lawyer Lyons is willing to represent Client Cedric in the transaction and does not represent any other party in the transaction. Lawyer Lyons would, however, like to act not only as lawyer but also as a real estate agent or broker and as a mortgage broker or loan officer in the transaction.

QUESTION:

53. Is Lawyer Lyons subject to discipline if she serves in all three capacities?

A. No, because she is assuming only one role as a lawyer; the non-lawyer roles are not subject to the Model Rules.

B. Yes, because the Model Rules prohibit a lawyer from assuming multiple roles in a real estate transaction.

C. Yes, unless she obtains an informed, written consent from Client Cedric.

D. Yes, unless she obtains an informed, written consent from Client Cedric and gives him an opportunity to consult independent counsel.

* * *

The Abner, Becker & Collins law partnership is made up of three lawyers who graduated from law school and were admitted to the bar six years ago. They formed their law partnership four years ago to practice criminal defense cases. Lawyer Abner now plans to leave the partnership and go to work as a deputy district attorney for the state.

QUESTION:

54. Which of the following does *not* describe the proper ethical effect of Lawyer Abner or other lawyers in the district attorney's office prosecuting clients of the Abner, Becker & Collins law partnership?

A. Lawyer Abner cannot prosecute a person who was formerly represented by Lawyer Abner in the same or a substantially related matter, unless the former client and the state give informed consent, confirmed in writing.

B. Lawyer Abner cannot prosecute a former client of Abner, Becker & Collins about whom Lawyer Abner obtained confidential information that is material to the matter without the informed consent of Abner, Becker & Collins's former client and the state, confirmed in writing.

C. Lawyer Abner's disqualification is not imputed to the other lawyers in the district attorney's office.

D. Lawyer Abner's disqualification is imputed to the other lawyers in the district attorney's office.

* * *

Circuit Court Judge Good proposes to leave the bench and join with Lawyer Hanks and Lawyer Isaacs to form the Good, Hanks & Isaacs law partnership which intends to represent or oppose clients who had matters pending before Lawyer Good while Lawyer Good was a judge.

QUESTION:

55. Which of the following does *not* describe the proper ethical effect of Lawyer Good or other lawyers in the Good, Hanks & Isaacs law partnership representing or opposing parties who had matters pending before Lawyer Good when Lawyer Good was on the bench?

A. If Lawyer Good did not participate personally and substantially as a judge in a matter in which Lawyer Good or the Good, Hanks & Isaacs firm proposes to represent a party, neither Lawyer Good nor other lawyers in the Good, Hanks & Isaacs law firm would be prohibited from handling the matter.

B. If Lawyer Good participated personally or substantially in a matter as a judge, Lawyer Good cannot work on that matter in private practice without the informed consent of all parties, confirmed in writing.

C. If Lawyer Good participated personally or substantially in a matter as a judge, Lawyer Good cannot work on that matter in private practice if she acquired confidential information about the matter as a judge.

D. Lawyer Good's disqualification will be imputed to the other lawyers in the Good, Hanks & Isaacs firm, unless Lawyer Good is screened from participating in the matter.

* * *

Aaron & Boone LLP is a limited liability partnership. Five of the seven lawyers in the firm represent labor unions and union benefit plans. The remaining two lawyers represent claimants in workers' compensation, social security disability, and plaintiffs' personal injury cases. Charles & Dolly, P.C. is a professional corporation consisting of four lawyers, three of whom attorneys represent plaintiffs in personal injury cases, with the fourth lawyer representing claimants in workers' compensation matters. The two partnerships and eleven lawyers intend to form a new partnership known as Aaron, Boone, Charles & Dolly. The lawyers and support staff who will be performing work for the new firm ABCD will be on the Aaron & Boone, LLP payroll. Their salaries and expenses will be charged to the new firm as an internal accounting matter. The new law firm will take over the pending workers' compensation and social security disability cases of both predecessor firms, as well as all of the personal injury cases of both partnerships. Aaron & Boone, LLP will continue to separately represent labor unions and union benefit plans.

QUESTION:

56. Which of the following statements is accurate?

A. An ongoing conflicts check is necessary for the Aaron, Boone, Charles & Dolly's clients only.

B. The conflict of interest of any member of any of either law firm becomes the conflict of interest of all the members of both law firms.

C. Client confidentiality is unnecessary by each law firm to obtain a client's or potential client's informed consent to do the required conflict of interest check.

D. Aaron, Boone, Charles & Dolly has no concern about the two predecessor law firms' past clients.

* * *

The law firm is hired to form an investment fund (the "Client") and to represent the Client and on some occasions the general partner and investment manager of the Client, presumably with respect to Client matters. As specifically delineated in the investment documentation, neither the Client nor the lawyers represent investors in the Client. The Client is obligated to indemnify the managers, general partner and their affiliates, employees and agents against the claims of third parties, which parties include fund investors. The indemnification extends to claims which include and are related to misrepresentation. It is the intention to either specifically name the lawyers as indemnified persons or include them within the definition of "agents."

QUESTION:

57. Can the lawyers in the law firm contract with a client (by inclusion in the engagement letter) for indemnification against non-client third-party claims arising from the representation? (The indemnification would not extend to a suit by the Client itself against the lawyers.)

A. No, because the Rules permit the parties to limit their liability.

B. No, because a law firm cannot ask a client to hold their lawyers harmless.

C. Yes, if the Rule requirements for a business transaction with a client are followed.

D. Yes, as long as the indemnification also extends to future suits by the client against the lawyers.

* * *

Lawyer Lang is defense counsel for Client Calhoun who was the driver of a car involved in a one-vehicle accident in which her husband and one son were injured and another son killed. Client Calhoun's husband has instituted suit against her. Client Calhoun is said to have $25,000/50,000 (per claim and in the aggregate, respectively) in liability insurance limits. Client Calhoun is the sole defendant and Lawyer Lang believes that there are no liability defenses. Client Calhoun has expressly instructed Lawyer Lang not to "vigorously defend against my family's injuries" and not to hire expert witnesses. At the same time, Lawyer Lang is concerned because the insurance policy obligates her to defend the Client Calhoun.

QUESTION:

58. What is the extent of the defense that Lawyer Lang owes to Client Calhoun?

   A. Lawyer Lang must follow Client Calhoun's directions.

   B. Lawyer Lang may follow Client Calhoun's directions.

   C. Lawyer Lang must not Client Calhoun's directions.

   D. Lawyer Lang must follow the liability insurer's directions.

* * *

The law firm of Samuel, Shelton & Williams has consulted several marketing strategists to increase the firm's business. Some have suggested increased advertising; some have suggested putting the firm lawyers' pictures on the cover of the local telephone book, and some have suggested that each lawyer's image should be displayed on a prominent billboard that borders the interstate highways in the area. Finally, with less money than it thought was available for a marketing campaign, the law firm settled on a two-part plan for increasing the incentives for its staff and current clients to identify and refer new clients to the law firm. In the first plan, the law firm employee would receive a percentage of fees collected from the referred client or a progressively larger lump sum dollar amount for the referral. In the second plan, the firm's current clients would receive a discount for referring other clients to the firm.

QUESTION:

59. Does either of the two plans for nonlawyer firm staff or current clients who refer clients violate the Rules?

   A. Both plans are acceptable under the Rules.

B. The firm can pay its employees for referrals but not reduce its fees to its current clients for referring new clients.

C. The firm can reduce its fees to its current clients for referring new clients but not pay its employees for referrals.

D. Neither plan is acceptable under the Rules.

* * *

Lawyer Linker represents Client Cox who is the plaintiff in a personal injury case. Lawyer Linker and opposing counsel learned during a conference call with the judge that Client Cox had written to the judge to confirm the dates of both the pretrial conference and the trial. Following that conference call, the judge's secretary faxed Lawyer Linker the letter and its enclosures. Client Cox's letter attempted to persuade the judge of the value of the case, and enclosed some pleadings and some confidential lawyer-client correspondence between Lawyer Linker and Client Cox. When Lawyer Linker requested a hearing before the judge to discuss Client Cox's possible and uninformed waiver of the lawyer-client privilege, Lawyer Linker learned that her client had also delivered his medical records to the judge's chambers. The judge did not read the records and ordered everything returned to Client Cox. Lawyer Linker has yet to reach her client to discuss what has happened.

QUESTION:

60. Does Lawyer Linker have a duty to disclose the content of Client Cox's letter to opposing counsel, and/or does she have to disclose the enclosures which included privileged lawyer-client communications?

A. Lawyer Linker has a duty to disclose both the content of Client Cox's letter and his enclosures that he sent to the judge.

B. Lawyer Linker has a duty to disclose the content of Client Cox's letter but not his enclosures to the judge.

C. Lawyer Linker has a duty to inform opposing counsel about Client Cox's enclosures to the judge but not the content of the letter.

D. Lawyer Linker must not disclose either the content of Client Cox's letter or his enclosures that he sent to the judge.

PROFESSIONAL RESPONSIBILITY

Answer Key for Exam #1—Answers and Explanations

PROBLEM #1. ANSWER A IS THE BEST ANSWER.

When a client discloses information to a lawyer about its past conduct, generally that information cannot be disclosed by the lawyer without the client's consent. Model Rule of Professional Conduct 1.6(a). Rule 1.6(a) requires a lawyer to maintain inviolate information relating to the representation of a client. Here, the CEO did not give permission to Lawyer Maris to disclose information about the acquisition possibility. He clearly told Lawyer Maris *not* to disclose the information to anyone. Thus, Lawyer Maris violated the duty of confidentiality owed by an attorney to the client.

Answer B is incorrect because it is the opposite of answer A. **C is incorrect** because Lawyer Maris had a duty of confidentiality to the client, which is the organization. **D is incorrect** because there is no distinction made between the types of information learned about or from the client. Under the Model Rules, any information relating to the representation of a client is confidential, regardless of whether it was obtained from the client directly or it was obtained from others and pertains to the client.

PROBLEM #2. ANSWER C IS THE BEST ANSWER.

Answer C describes both of the conditions necessary for Lawyer Larry to represent LaVerne in discussions with Shirley. Under Rule 1.9(a), a lawyer who has previously represented a client must not represent another person in the same or a substantially related matter in which that person's interests are materially adverse to the interests of the prior client. In addition, under Rule 1.9(c), a lawyer cannot use information relating to the former representation for the disadvantage of the former client. Lawyer Larry represented the college's compliance officer two years ago in her divorce. Because

LaVerne is asking Lawyer Larry to discuss her job situation with Shirley, there does not appear to be any possibility that the current representation relates to the same or a substantially related matter under Rule 1.9(a) as Shirley's divorce action. On the other hand, Lawyer Larry may be aware of confidential information about Shirley or her divorce action that he may want to raise with Shirley in his discussions with Shirley about LaVerne's problem. Rule 1.9(c) prohibits him from using any information he obtained about Shirley during that representation to her disadvantage, regardless of whether he learned it from Shirley or others, unless that information is generally known. **Answers A and B are incorrect**, because they are too narrow insofar as each describes the conditions under which Lawyer Larry can represent LaVerne. **Answer D** is incorrect. The prohibition on successive representation is not a function of the time since the most recent representation of the now "adverse" client.

PROBLEM #3. ANSWER D IS THE BEST ANSWER.

Under Rule 3.3(a)(2), an attorney must "disclose to the tribunal legal authority in the controlling jurisdiction known to the lawyer to be directly adverse to the position of the client and not disclosed by opposing counsel." **Answer A is incorrect**. Although a lawyer believes that the language in the case is dicta, a court may disagree and believe instead that the dicta is important to consider in deciding the case. **B is incorrect**, because Lawyer Schurman should have disclosed the cases to the court either in his response to the opponent's summary judgment motion or no later than his oral argument at the pretrial conference. **C is incorrect**, because Lawyer Schurman's obligation is to disclose the cases; he does not have to elaborate on the adverse implications of the cases for his client, and he instead may argue that the adverse cases were decided incorrectly or are distinguishable on their facts.

PROBLEM #4. ANSWER C IS THE BEST ANSWER.

If a lawyer learns before the conclusion of the proceedings that a piece of evidence he offered was false when admitted, he must take reasonable remedial measures. Rule 3.3(a)(3). Although a deposition is not conducted in open court, it is part of a judicial proceeding. Because Lawyer Schurman realizes that the Jones's deposition testimony concerned an important fact, he must take "reasonable remedial measures" such as try to persuade Jones to tell the truth. If Jones is unwilling to tell the truth, Lawyer Schurman must disclose the nature and extent of Jones's misleading testimony to the court. Because C is correct, it should be apparent A, B and D are incorrect.

PROBLEM #5. ANSWER B IS THE BEST ANSWER.

In order for Lawyer Travis to be disqualified when he will be a witness, he also must be acting as an advocate in the case. Lawyer Travis is prohibited from acting as an advocate *and* witness. Because Travis likely will be a witness in the case, he will be disqualified under Rule 3.7. The Rules also deal with the imputed disqualification consequences of the lawyer as witness. Even if Travis is a witness under Rule 3.7(a), Smith and Jones still could represent First Bank under Rule 3.7(b) as long as there is no conflict of interest under Rule 1.7 or 1.9. Rule 1.7 does not appear relevant, because it is phrased in the present tense, and Smith and Jones currently does not represent Sims in any matters. Rule 1.7(b)'s proscription relating to conflicts involving lawyers' personal interests is an issue if a Smith and Jones attorney, current or past, has been involved with Sims on his deals, or he was a "friend of the firm" or a referral source. **Answer A is incorrect**, because it would suggest a per se disqualification of the whole firm when one of its attorneys is a witness in a case in which the firm is also counsel of record. **Answer C is incorrect**; Rule 1.9 is not relevant here because Lawyer Travis was not an attorney at the time he worked as a loan officer and therefore was not in a position to have received confidential information from Sims. **Answer D is incorrect**, because the imputed disqualification consequences apply to any lawyer other than the person who will be a witness, not just to the named partners.

PROBLEM #6. ANSWER A IS THE BEST ANSWER.

Per Rule 3.1, when a lawyer, like Lawyer Smith, agrees to be the advocate for a client, she may present any nonfrivolous interpretation of the law that favors her client. She cannot present frivolous claims, defenses, or motions. She does not have to make a complete factual or legal investigation before asserting a claim, defense or motion, but she is acting frivolously when as here she knowingly puts forth a position unsupported by the facts and the law. **B is incorrect**; Rule 3.1 is applicable regardless of whether Lawyer Smith has earned any part of his fee at the time she filed the suit for Prosperous Perot. **C is incorrect**; similar to answer B, Rule 3.1 applies regardless of whether Lawyer Smith has advised Prosperous Perot about the lawsuit's baselessness prior to any fee payment. **D is incorrect**; again, the reasonableness of the lawyer's fee is irrelevant to the frivolousness of the lawsuit that is filed.

PROBLEM #7. ANSWER D IS THE BEST ANSWER.

Under the authority of Rule 6.2, there are types of cases which a lawyer *must* decline, such as when she is too busy, or when the case is frivolous or is brought to harass another. The lawyer should *not* decline just because the client or his cause is unpopular. She should not refuse a court appointment in a *pro bono* case except for "compelling reasons" or for "good cause." One example of good cause occurs if the representation "is likely to result in a violation of the Rules ... or other law," such as a conflict of interest with another client. Another category of good cause that justifies turning down a court appointment is when "the cause is so repugnant to the lawyer" so as to impair the lawyer-client relationship or the quality of the representation. Rule 6.2(c). Lawyer Ballantine may decline the representation if her feelings are so strong that she could not do a competent job. **A is incorrect**; the lawyer's belief about his client's probable guilt is not equivalent to the client's cause being so repugnant so as to justify turning down the court appointment. **B is incorrect**; as already mentioned, a lawyer should not decline a case because representing the client will hurt his reputation. **C is incorrect**; the identity or influence of the adversary is irrelevant to the lawyer's general duty as an officer of the court to accept court appointments.

PROBLEM #8. ANSWER B IS THE BEST ANSWER.

A judge disqualified under CJC Rule 2.11 may disclose on the record the basis for her disqualification and may ask the parties and their lawyers to waive any disqualifying grounds, except for personal bias or prejudice. CJC Rule 2.11(C). Here, the trial judge was justified in seeking a waiver under CJC Rule 2.11(A) because the trial judge held more than a *de minimis* interest in Pfeezer, Inc. that could be substantially affected by the proceeding. Without a waiver by the lawyers, the judge would have to recuse herself from the case. The problem here is that the attempted waiver by counsel in the case was improper. Under the facts, the judge addressed the lawyers about the possibility of waiver, but the judge's remarks and the lawyers' agreement did not appear to include concern for or the participation of the parties. In addition, it is not clear that the judge was absent during the lawyers' discussion about waiver. CJC Rule 2.11(C) **A is incorrect**, because as mentioned a judge can seek a waiver of disqualification of an economic interest (i.e., any basis other than personal bias or prejudice) under CJC 2.11(C). **C is incorrect**; as mentioned above, the attempt at waiver of the disqualification was improper under the language of CJC 2.11(C). **D is incorrect**, because as mentioned without waiver by the parties the judge would have had to recuse himself. He held more 10,000 shares of the stock of Pfeezer, Inc. worth $1,900,000. The Terminology section of the Code of Judicial Conduct defines a *de minimis* interest as "an insignificant interest that could not raise a reasonable question regarding the judge's impartiality." The trial judge was subject to being disqualified because he held more than a *de minimis* interest in Pfeezer, Inc.

PROBLEM #9. ANSWER B IS THE BEST ANSWER.

Under Rule 5.5, a lawyer may have disciplinary problems with the unauthorized practice rules, either by practicing in a state where she is not admitted or by helping a lay person like Sarducci engage in unauthorized practice such as writing a threatening letter on a lawyer's letterhead. (Besides lawyer discipline, Corleone's complicity in Sarducci's unauthorized practice is remedied by criminal penalties, injunctive relief, or holding the offender in contempt.) **A is incorrect.** Besides aiding the unauthorized practice by Sarducci, Corleone personally can write a letter to a person stating that a lawsuit will be filed within a period of time if a settlement is not forthcoming from that person. **C is incorrect**; the essence of Corleone's misconduct is not the threat but instead is using Sarducci to write a letter knowing that Sarducci is not authorized to act as a lawyer. **D is incorrect**; even if Sarducci is authorized to act as Corleone's agent it is the conduct Sarducci engages in that constitutes unethical behavior by Corleone (facilitating unauthorized practice) and Sarducci (engaging in unauthorized practice).

PROBLEM #10. ANSWER C IS THE BEST ANSWER.

Under Rule 1.8(g), in representing multiple clients, a lawyer may negotiate an aggregate settlement of their civil claims. An "aggregate settlement" occurs when two or more clients consent to have their matters resolved together. In aggregate settlement situations, a lawyer may be tempted not to investigate the cases individually and may be tempted to close the cases too soon. Each client therefore must consent in writing after consultation; that disclosure must include "disclosure of the existence and nature of all the claims involved and of the participation of each person in the settlement." Rule 1.8(g). Because of the importance of what the client is doing, this writing requirement is more demanding than the general conflict of interest Rules. The following information must be disclosed: (1) the total amount of the aggregate settlement or the result of the aggregate agreement, (2) details of every client's participation in the aggregate settlement of agreement, (3) the total fees and costs to be paid to the lawyer as a result of the aggregate settlement, if they are to be paid from the settlement's proceeds or by an opposing party, (4) the method by which costs are to be apportioned among the clients, and (5) the existence and nature of all claims, defenses, or pleas involved in the aggregate settlement. ABA Formal Opinion 06–438.

A is incorrect. Unlike their predecessor standards, the Model Rules do not provide ethical aspirations. Rule 1.8(g), for example, contains imperative standards rather than mere "guidance" about how a lawyer should proceed when she has multiple clients. While it may be ideal for each client to have her own lawyer, Rule 1.8(g) describes the process of an aggregate settlement covering multiple clients. The information necessary for each client to assess whether to settle a case places a priority on the individual client, despite the fact that her lawyer has multiple clients involved the situation. **B is incorrect**; the purpose of Rule 1.8(g) is for each of Bushkin's clients to be aware of the nature of the proposed settlement with every other Bushkin client. True, sharing that information may upset the goal of settling the case, but Rule 1.8(g) places a priority on full disclosure by the lawyer to all clients to ensure that each client's claim is handled fairly and is not being sacrificed for the good of claims of any or all other client claims. **D is incorrect**. When Bushkin represents more than one client in the same matter, as here, the joint client exception to the lawyer-client privilege applies, meaning that the lawyer-client privilege does not apply among Bushkin's joint clients.

PROBLEM #11. ANSWER D IS THE BEST ANSWER.

Pursuant to Rule 1.5(d), because none of the choices is correct. A lawyer cannot ethically use a contingent fee in a domestic relations matter. In divorce cases, contingent fees are forbidden because a lawyer might be tempted to prevent reconciliation of the married couple in order to recover her fee. Rule 1.5, Comment 6 states: "Paragraph (d) prohibits a lawyer from charging a contingent fee in a domestic relations matter when payment is contingent upon the securing of a divorce or upon the amount of alimony or support or property settlement to be obtained. This provision does not preclude a contract for a contingent fee for legal representation in connection with the recovery of post-judgment balances due under support, alimony or other financial orders because such contracts do not implicate the same policy concerns." **A is incorrect** because as just mentioned, it is too broad a statement. **B is incorrect**. Under Rule 1.8(a), lawyers can enter into business transactions under specific circumstances, but Rule 1.5(d) mandates that a particular type of "transaction" (a contingent fee transaction) is impermissible in a particular type of case. **C is incorrect**. Rule 1.8(i) prohibits a lawyer from acquiring a proprietary interest in a case, except that except that she "may acquire a lien authorized by law to secure the lawyer's fee or expenses; and contract with a client for a reasonable contingent fee in a civil case." A lawyer cannot acquire this type of interest in this type of case.

PROBLEM #12. ANSWER D IS THE BEST ANSWER.

All three of the answers are incorrect. **Answer A is incorrect**. A state may regulate a lawyer's in-person solicitation for private gain without a showing of harm, due to the misleading, deceptive and overbearing conduct. Such regulation protects the public, as long as the regulations are reasonable and present no danger to the public. *Ohralik v. Ohio State Bar*, 436 U.S. 447 (1978). In that case, the lawyer solicited an accident victim who was in traction in a hospital and who was "especially incapable of making informed judgments or of assessing and protecting their own interests." **B is incorrect**. *Shapero v. Kentucky Bar Association*, 486 U.S. 466 (1988) struck down state prohibitions against lawyers sending any targeted direct mail advertising. The mailed letters sent to people facing specific legal problems were truthful and not misleading. Because of the nature of the solicitation, there was no pressure on the recipient for an immediate response. The Court ruled that the mere potential for abuse does not justify a blanket prohibition. **C is incorrect**. The Court has prohibited correspondence sent too soon after the event which raised the need for legal representation. In *Florida Bar v. Went for It, Inc.*, 515 U.S. 618 (1995), the Court held that a state may ban targeted mailings for thirty days after the event. The Court, however, did uphold the lawyer's right to send untargeted letters to the general public.

PROBLEM #13. ANSWER D IS THE BEST ANSWER.

None of the answers in A, B, or C is correct. **A is incorrect**. A lawyer may take a type of case with which she is unfamiliar, per Rule 1.1. That makes sense, because everybody has a first case of a particular kind. Otherwise, how would a lawyer become experienced in any type of case? By studying or talking to other lawyers, a lawyer becomes knowledgeable even if she lacked the requisite knowledge when she began the representation. Through her knowledge, she also becomes thorough and prepared to represent her clients. **B is incorrect**. Lawyers in different firms may divide fees only under specified conditions. First, the division must either be divided in proportion to the services performed by each lawyer or have each of them assume joint financial and ethical responsibility for the case. Second, Chris Client must agree in writing to the division, including the share for each lawyer. Finally, the total fee must be reasonable. If Lawyer Lyle does no work on the case, he is not entitled to any fee. **C is incorrect**, because a divided fee may be proportional to the work done, *or* it may be divided if each lawyer has assumed joint financial and ethical responsibility for the case.

PROBLEM #14. ANSWER C IS THE BEST ANSWER.

Pro bono work by lawyers refers to legal services provided without a fee being charged or the expectation of a normal fee. Rule 6.1 encourages lawyers to engage in *pro bono* activities by rendering at least (50) hours of pro bono legal services per year. Each state is free to specify a different number of hours, but no state has adopted a mandatory *pro bono* requirement. If the hours are unmet through legal representation, lobbying, or mentoring people of limited means, a lawyer can do *pro bono* work for groups or individuals seeking to protect their civil or public rights or you can perform *pro bono* work for charitable, religious, or bar organizations. Because C is correct, **B is incorrect**. Rule 6.1 encourages but does not require lawyers to do *pro bono* work. **A is incorrect**. Although the United States Supreme Court has stated that courts have the power to compel lawyers to accept appointments to cases before the court, it has not decided the extent (if any) to which lawyers may be required to take such appointments with little or no compensation. Besides, issues of *pro bono* work are likely regarded as matters of state law rather than federal constitutional law.

D is incorrect. A lawyer should not refuse a court appointment in a *pro bono* case except for "compelling reasons" or for "good cause." One example of good cause occurs if the representation "is likely to result in a violation of the Rules ... or other law," such as a conflict of interest with another client. A second type of good cause occurs when accepting the appointment would result in "an unreasonable financial burden." Rule 6.2(b). For example, if a lawyer has recently accepted several court appointments, she may decline the current appointment because of the need to earn money from paying clients in order to pay bills and to support dependents. The third category of good cause that justifies turning down a court appointment is when "the cause is so repugnant to the lawyer" so as to impair the lawyer-client relationship or the quality of representation. Rule 6.2(c).

PROBLEM #15. ANSWER D IS THE BEST ANSWER.

A lawyer must include the name and office address of at least one lawyer or her law firm responsible for the content of any such communication. Rule 7.2(c). **A is incorrect.** Generally, in-person, live telephone, and real-time electronic (as with chat rooms or instant messaging) solicitations of a prospective client are prohibited when the lawyer's significant motive is her own compensation. However, there are exceptions. A lawyer may solicit another lawyer for business. Rule 7.3(a)(1). She also can contact family members who are in need of legal services, as well as people with whom she has a close personal relationship. Both of these groups know about the lawyer's competence and that she is not going to take advantage of them. Rule 7.3(a)(2). A lawyer can always contact former clients, who know whether they were satisfied with her previous work. Rule 7.3(a)(2). **B is incorrect**. A lawyer cannot solicit professional employment from a prospective client in person or through any form of communication (e.g., a targeted mailing), either when that person has made known to the lawyer the prospective client's desire not to be solicited by the lawyer or when the solicitation involves coercion, duress, or harassment. Rule 7.3(b)(1)-(2). (The Rule does not include the thirty-day restriction allowed by the Supreme Court in *Florida Bar v. Went for It, Inc.*) **C is incorrect**, because it is stated too broadly. Lawyers may compare their services with those of other lawyers. However, if a lawyer's ad provides an unsubstantiated comparison of her legal services to others, the ad may be misleading if it is "presented with such specificity as would lead a reasonable person to conclude that the comparison can be substantiated." Rule 7.1, Comment 3.

PROBLEM #16. ANSWER C IS THE BEST ANSWER.

A is incorrect; discipline may be imposed for crimes that reflect "adversely on the lawyer's honesty, trustworthiness or fitness as a lawyer." Rule 8.4(b). Discipline is inappropriate for personal morality offensess such as adultery. Rule 8.4, Comment 2. Therefore, a lawyer's conviction for any felony does not justify discipline, unless that misconduct reflects "adversely on the lawyer's honesty, trustworthiness or fitness as a lawyer." **B is incorrect**. A lawyer has a general obligation to report information about another lawyer's serious disciplinary violation, and the lawyer's failure to report such misconduct may subject her to discipline. However, B is incorrect because the scope of the duty to report misconduct does not include a duty to report any and all misconduct; the obligation to report requires that the lawyer report only those violations that raise "a substantial question" about the other lawyer's "honesty, trustworthiness or fitness" as a lawyer. Rule 8.3(a). "Substantial" refers to the "seriousness of the possible offense." The duty includes the exercise of judgment about the seriousness of the violation. From this discussion, it is clear that **C is the correct answer**. Rule 8.3(a) requires a lawyer to report any violation of the Rules when she knows that the violation raises a substantial question about the other lawyer's honesty, trustworthiness or fitness. Answer C goes on to note in the second sentence, though, that the duty imposed by Rule 8.3(a) is superseded by the duty of confidentiality under Rule 1.6, as when a lawyer's client tells her that another lawyer has engaged in serious misconduct, or she represents a lawyer who has himself committed serious misconduct. **D is incorrect**, because C is correct.

PROBLEM #17. ANSWER C IS THE BEST ANSWER.

A lawyer *may* disclose confidential information if she reasonably believes that disclosure is necessary to sue her client for an unpaid fee, or to defend a malpractice, disciplinary, or criminal charge. Rule 1.6(b)(5). The purpose of this exception is to prevent the client, who benefits from the fiduciary relationship, from taking advantage of the relationship to his lawyer's detriment. As with all of the discretionary disclosure provisions, a lawyer may reveal client confidences only when it is "reasonably necessary." Here, Attorney has the discretion to disclose confidential information to establish that her client owes her a fee, as well as the amount of the fee. If her client fails to pay her after she has rendered services for him, she may sue him for the fee he still owes and disclose confidential information if he defends the fee action by attacking her representation. Or, she may reveal confidential information to establish that she has the assets to pay you. A lawyer's discretion to disclose is subject to two qualifications. If it is practical, before disclosing Attorney should give her client a chance to avoid the need for her disclosure. In case that attempt fails, she should limit the scope of disclosure or dissemination. Rule 1.6, Comments 14 and 17.

A is incorrect, because a lawyer's threat to disclose confidential information to her client's detriment in order to receive her fee is not a reasonably necessary disclosure. Rule 1.6, Comment 10. **B is incorrect**. While a lawyer does not like to sue her (former) client to collect her fee, she is as entitled as anyone to use the legal system to collect debts owed to her. Attorney is not subject to discipline for bringing a civil suit to collect a fee. **D is incorrect**. As mentioned with answer A, Attorney's letter was not proper. In addition, a lawyer is not required to settle fee disputes amicably, in part because the lawyer as a party lacks control over how the opposing party (now former client) may behave in resisting the lawyer's attempt to recover her fee.

PROBLEM #18. ANSWER B IS THE BEST ANSWER.

Rule 1.13(a) states that a lawyer for an organization represents the "organization" as an entity rather than the individuals who act or work for the organization. Part of a lawyer's responsibility in representing an entity is to act in its best interests. Rule 1.13(b) describes how a lawyer determines what the entity wants to do, how high up the corporate ladder the lawyer is required to go, and what happens when the lawyer reaches the top of the ladder and the lawyer is still unsatisfied. A lawyer has a special duty to protect the entity when she knows that someone affiliated with her entity client is acting in a manner that is reasonably certain to directly or indirectly cause substantial harm to the client. This duty exists because organizational clients can act only through their duly authorized (but non-client) representatives such as managers. A lawyer must monitor those decisions when they threaten substantial injury to an entity client.

> If a lawyer for an organization knows that an officer, employee or other person associated with the organization is engaged in action, intends to act or refuses to act in a matter related to the representation that is a violation of a legal obligation to the organization, or a violation of law which reasonably might be imputed to the organization, and that is likely to result in substantial injury to the organization, then the lawyer shall proceed as is reasonably necessary in the best interest of the organization.

Rule 1.13(b). Because Miles does all of Coffee Inc.'s legal work, he always has a duty to prevent harm to his client. His first duty is to use the entity's internal remedies and seek assistance of those in the chain of authority who can influence the decision of the person who is acting contrary to the best interests of the entity. How best to proceed up the chain of command depends on the motives of the people involved, the seriousness of the violation, and the manner in which the entity has treated such issues in the past. If the entity's internal remedies prove to be ineffective, the lawyer must refer the issue to a higher authority in the entity, including the highest authority like a Board of Directors that legally can act on behalf of the entity.

A is incorrect. As mentioned, Miles's first course of action is to follow Coffee Inc.'s internal remedies which do not include informing Coffee Inc.'s shareholders. If Miles's efforts to go up the chain of authority fail, he then may reveal information to persons outside the entity if it is a clear violation of law, and he still "reasonably believe[s] that the violation is reasonably certain to result in substantial injury to the organization." Rule 1.13(c)(2). **D is incorrect**. Rule 1.13(c) prescribes possible disclosure by Miles to persons or agencies outside the corporate governance structure only as an option *after* efforts to go up the corporate chain of command has failed. **C is incorrect**, because to do nothing would violate Miles's duty as lawyer for the corporation to act in the corporation's best interests.

PROBLEM #19. ANSWER C IS THE BEST ANSWER.

The Rule 1.7 analysis for concurrent conflicts applies to lawyers who are married to each other and who are on opposite sides of the same case. Inadvertent disclosure of confidential information is the primary concern, such as voice mail messages on the answering machine used by both lawyers. The related counsel must disclose the existence and the implications of the relationship between them before each lawyer agrees to the representation. Both clients should consent before the lawyer-spouses represent them. Because of the personal nature of the conflict, however, their conflict is not imputed to others in either of their law firms. Rule 1.7, Comment 11. **A is incorrect,** because the personal nature of Betty's and Don's marriage relationship is not imputed to other lawyers in either of their law firms. **B is incorrect**, because Roger's representation of Dropsy, Inc. is not automatically materially limited by practicing in the same law firm with Don Draper. There may be something about the situation that could materially limit Roger's ability to represent the client, but the facts here do not present that concern. **D is incorrect.** In the context of conflicts of interest, concerns about a lawyer not sharing a fee arise in cases where one lawyer in a firm has a conflict which is imputed to other lawyers in the firm but screening the conflicted lawyer is allowed. In that situation, the conflicted lawyer cannot share in the fee arrangement for the firm's representation of the client. As already noted, however, there is not imputation of the conflict here to others in Don's law firm.

PROBLEM #20. ANSWER A IS THE BEST ANSWER.

Rule 1.8(i) states that "[a] lawyer shall not acquire a proprietary interest in the cause of action or subject matter of litigation the lawyer is conducting for a client." If a lawyer acquires a financial interest in her client's litigation, there is a risk that her independent professional judgment will be affected by her interest. The lawyer's client may believe that her lawyer is more objective about the transaction than she really is, and she may be tempted to use the client's confidential information to the client's disadvantage. Therefore, a lawyer cannot acquire a proprietary interest in a claim for relief or the subject matter of a litigation. (The Rule is inapplicable to a pre-existing interest held by you before the representation begins, but Rule 1.7 would apply.) Here, the prosecutor would be subject to discipline by buying the subject matter of the prosecution before the case is resolved. After the case concludes, the prosecutor would not be subject to discipline for buying the ring. Thus, **B is incorrect**. **C is incorrect**. Even if Michael, the defendant, "clarifies" that he is not making a claim to ownership of the ring, the prosecutor is still attempting to purchase the subject matter of the case. Michael's statement is irrelevant to the prosecutor's potential for being disciplined, although Michael's statement may compromise his own defense to the theft charge. **D is incorrect**. Regardless of whether Michael consents (even assuming that he had the right to consent) to the prosecutor's purchase, the prosecutor ethical problem here still relates to his attempt to acquire a proprietary interest in the subject matter of the prosecution.

PROBLEM #21. ANSWER D IS THE BEST ANSWER.

Under Rule 1.16(b)(2), a lawyer may withdraw if her client persists in a course of action that she reasonably believes is criminal or fraudulent. **A is incorrect**. The language in the answer describes a basis for *mandatory* withdrawal under Rule 1.16(a)—if her continued employment in the matter would result in violating the ethical rules or other law. **B is incorrect**. The language describes a Rule 1.16 standard for permissive withdrawal, not for mandatory withdrawal—if her client has used her services to perpetrate a crime or fraud. **C is incorrect**. Although the language at the beginning of answer C states another basis for permissive withdrawal in Rule 1.16(b)—that the lawyer's representation will result in an unreasonable financial burden upon her—the qualification thereafter is not part of the Rules. However, regardless of the reason a lawyer resigns, she must make reasonable efforts to protect the client's interests, e.g., turning over the client's papers and property. Rule 1.16(d).

PROBLEM #22. ANSWER D IS THE BEST ANSWER.

A "lawyer must not allow the tribunal to be misled by false statements of law or fact or evidence that the lawyer knows to be false." Rule 3.3, Comment 2. To prevent the tribunal from being misled, she must correct any statement of fact that she learns was both false and material to the proceeding. Rule 3.3(a)(1). Significantly, the "failure to make a disclosure is the equivalent of an affirmative misrepresentation." Rule 3.3, Comment 3. When Attorney Cranfill realizes that Andrew is lying to the tribunal, she *must* take action to correct that fraud/perjury. First, she is supposed to attempt to persuade her client to correct the fraud. Second, if that attempt fails, she must disclose the fraud to the court regardless of whether Rule 1.6 permits her to disclose. Rule 3.3. Thus, even though the information from Andrew about his criminal record is protected by the lawyer-client privilege and the information from her own inquiry generally is protected by the ethical duty of confidentiality, Attorney Cranfill here must disclose that information to prevent Andrew from misleading the court by confirming the erroneous information in the pre-sentence investigation.

A is incorrect. True, if Attorney Cranfill corrected the record by disclosing the truth about Andrew's criminal record, he could be violating the ethical standards regarding confidentiality. As mentioned, though, to prevent a fraud from being perpetrated on the tribunal, the Rules require Attorney Cranfill to violate the duty of confidentiality to Andrew. Rule 3.3(c). **B is incorrect**. Even if Andrew's statement constitutes perjury, it cannot be imputed to his lawyer, Attorney Cranfill. However, Attorney Cranfill is required to correct the record even though that requires disclosure of information otherwise protected by Rule 1.6. **C is incorrect**. A lawyer has an ethical obligation to correct any statement of fact that she learns was false and material to the proceeding, even if it was made by her client. Thus, if Andrew made a false statement to the court, Attorney Cranfill thereafter has a duty to the court to correct that misrepresentation.

PROBLEM #23. ANSWER D IS THE BEST ANSWER.

The lawyer's obligation to preserve her client's confidential information generally survives the end of her lawyer-client relationship with the client. Rules 1.6, Comment 18; 1.9(c)(2). The confidential information cannot be disclosed by the lawyer without the client's consent. That duty also survives the death of the lawyer's client. **A is incorrect**. The principle about the durability of the privilege applies regardless of whether there is a statute of limitations for a particular crime. Thus, without Hyman's consent, Lawyer Simon must not reveal Burlingame's information to the police. **B is incorrect**. Evasion of the law is not a specifically defined offense like bail jumping which arguably has a past component (failing to appear for a court date) and a future component (continuing to fail to comply with the obligation to appear). In addition, even if evasion of the law was a crime with a future component, disclosure about such misconduct is permissive, not mandatory as answer B indicates. **C is incorrect**. The only way that this information could be disclosed by Lawyer Simon would be if there was consent by Burlingame to disclose, or the information from her was not confidential. The information from Burlingame is confidential, because Hyman's commission of the murder relates to the representation of Burlingame in the child custody matter against Burlingame's ex-husband. Burlingame's consent is necessary to Lawyer Simon's disclosure of that information. Hyman would not have to consent to the disclosure, even though it obviously related to Hyman's criminal liability. When Lawyer Simon learned about the murder from Burlingame, Lawyer Simon no longer represented Hyman.

PROBLEM #24. ANSWER C IS THE BEST ANSWER.

Being admitted to practice in one state does not automatically entitle a lawyer to practice in another state where he has not been admitted. Each state has its own rules for admission to practice, and failure to comply with them constitutes unauthorized practice in the state. A lawyer cannot open a law office in a state where he is not admitted. Rule 5.5(b). Under certain circumstances, a lawyer can offer temporary legal services in another jurisdiction from where he is admitted. He may associate himself with local counsel who actively participates in any representation of his clients. Rule 5.5(c)(1).

A is incorrect, because it fails to recognize that there are four exceptions to the general prohibition on practicing in a state where the lawyer is not admitted. Besides the exception mentioned in the previous paragraph, a lawyer may be admitted by a court to practice one case *pro hac vice*, and may work in the other state in anticipation of such an admission. Rules 5.5(b); 5.5(c)(2). The third exception allows a lawyer to participate in an alternative dispute resolution proceeding in the other state if it is reasonably related to or arises out of a representation in the place where he is admitted to practice. Rule 5.5(c)(3). Finally, as a catch-all, a lawyer may represent a client in a matter in the other state when that matter is closely related to the lawyer's representation of a client in the state where he is admitted. Rule 5.5(c)(4). **B is incorrect**, because even a person like Clarence has the option to practice outside the state where he is admitted on a temporary basis. **D is incorrect**, because a national license to practice law does not exist. The multijurisdictional practice exceptions do not constitute such a national license.

PROBLEM #25. ANSWER D IS THE BEST ANSWER.

Both **A and B are incorrect**, because they are both true. Answer A is accurate. If a lawyer is admitted in New Jersey, he is subject to discipline there, even if his misconduct occurs outside New Jersey. Because the purpose of lawyer discipline is to determine fitness for legal practice, any misconduct (no matter where it occurs) reflects on his ability to practice in New Jersey. Thus, New Jersey has the authority to discipline Clarence for unprofessional conduct; he cannot avoid discipline by carefully avoiding the commission of any offending act within the boundaries of New Jersey. Answer B also is accurate. If Clarence is not admitted to practice in Mississippi, he is nevertheless subject to discipline in Mississippi if he provides or offers to provide legal services there. Rule 8.5(a). **Answer C is incorrect**, because it is the opposite of Answer A.

PROBLEM #26. ANSWER A IS THE BEST ANSWER.

Lawyer Lanier is subject to discipline because her omission of any reference to the later will constitutes a misrepresentation under Rule 3.3. By presenting only the second will for probate, Lawyer

Lanier in effect is falsely stating that this will 1) is the only will prepared by Client Cal's sister, and 2) if there were more than will that she wrote, this is the most recent will. **B is incorrect.** People sometimes have written more than one will. It is the lawyer's obligation to present as many of the wills from a deceased that can be located so that the Probate Judge can sort them out to decide which is the will that meets all legal requirements. **C is incorrect.** Lawyer Lanier is subject to discipline, both for not presenting to the court the most recent will and not presenting to the probate court all the wills endorsed by Client Cal's sister. **D is incorrect**, because neither B nor C is true.

PROBLEM #27. ANSWER C IS THE BEST ANSWER.

Rule 5.6 generally prohibits agreements that restrict a lawyer's right to practice after leaving his law firm. A lawyer cannot offer or make a contract restricting his right to practice law after the termination of the relationship created by a partnership, operating, shareholder, or employment agreement. Rule 5.6(a). It also is clear from the case law that Osborne and Glick cannot bind departing lawyers like Lawyer Lackey to leave clients behind. Similarly, Lawyer Lackey cannot promise their firms not to take clients along when he leaves. Clients do not belong to a lawyer who does most or all of their legal representation or to the lawyer's law firm. The decision about who will represent a client when Lawyer Lackey leaves Osborne and Glick belongs *exclusively* to each client. Each client may choose to be represented by Lawyer Lackey, Osborne and Glick, neither, or both. Similarly, client files and property must be retained or transferred in accord with the client's dictates. ABA Formal Opinion 99–414. For the foregoing reasons, **A, B and D** are incorrect.

PROBLEM #28. ANSWER C IS THE BEST ANSWER.

ABA Formal Opinion 99–414 stated that a departing lawyer like Lawyer Lackey has a duty of notification if he is responsible for a client's representation or plays a "principal" role in the delivery of services in a current matter. The impending departure of Lawyer Lackey creates a duty of communication that must be conveyed under Rule 1.4(a)(3), which imposes a duty to "keep the client reasonably informed about the status of the matter." The status of a representation includes whether the lawyer who has been representing the client is moving from his current office to another affiliation. Lawyer Lackey's notice should convey sufficient information to enable the client to decide whether her legal work will remain with Osborne and Glick or will be transferred to him in his new professional association. The client also should be advised that it has the sole right to decide who will complete or continue matters—the departing lawyer, the firm, or another lawyer altogether. In his notice, Lawyer Lackey should not disparage the Osborne and Glick firm. ABA Formal Opinion 99–414. **A is incorrect**. Lawyer Lackey has the duty to contact current clients for whom is doing work; his obligation is mandatory not permissive. **B is incorrect**. While Lawyer Lackey may contact former clients under Rule 7.3(a)(2), Rule 7.3 prohibits him (even when he is moving offices) from pursuing in-person, live telephone, and real-time electronic (as with chat rooms or instant messaging) solicitations of a prospective client when his significant motive is his own compensation. All the clients of the firm are not Lackey's former clients, although some may be. **D is incorrect**, only because of the mandatory nature of that option. However, ABA Formal Opinion 99–414 permits targeted mailings of any client of the former firm by Lawyer Lackey.

PROBLEM #29. ANSWER C IS THE BEST ANSWER.

If Lawyer Little leaves her law firm without knowing any confidential information about Coan Industries, Inc., she would not be disqualified from representing Jaye Corporation, the adversary of Coan Industries, Inc., at her new firm. Her representation of Jaye Corporation does not breach any expectation of loyalty from her old firm. Because she is not disqualified, neither Lawyer Rodes nor anyone else in her new firm is disqualified. Rule 1.9(b). Disqualification here would unduly restrict mobility in the legal profession. **A is incorrect**. The motion to disqualify Lawyer Little and Lawyer Rodes would be granted only if Coan Industries, Inc. was a client of Pernick and Hinerfeld while Lawyer Little was there and she had acquired confidential information about Coan Industries, Inc. If that were true, then Lawyer Rodes and any other lawyer at Barber and Richmond also would be disqualified based on imputed disqualification. **B is incorrect.** What matters for disqualification here is the acquisition by Lawyer Little of Coan Industries, Inc.'s confidential information, not whether Lawyer Little socialized with its CEO. **D is incorrect**. If Lawyer Little were disqualified, everyone else at Barber and Richmond would also be disqualified. (Screening may suffice to remove the imputation of disqualification, by walling off the disqualified lawyer and permitting her colleagues to proceed with the representation. While some case law and some state disciplinary codes permit the use of screening if this type of conflict of interest exists, under the Model Rules, screening Lawyer Little from the case is not permitted.)

PROBLEM #30. ANSWER D IS THE BEST ANSWER.

The only way for a client to participate effectively in being represented by a lawyer is for the lawyer to keep the client informed about what is going on. When clients complain about lawyers neglecting their case, their complaint is usually about the failure to keep them reasonably informed about the progress of the case. A lawyer's obligation to her client includes the obligation to "keep the client reasonably informed about the status of the matter." Rule 1.4(a)(3). Unless he has told his lawyer not to communicate such information, a lawyer should inform her about what she and the opposition have done in his case, judicial rulings and, consistent with Rule 1.2, settlement offers from the opposing party. **Answer A is correct**. Because the interrogtories in this fact pattern call for detailed information, it is unlikely that she would be able to answer them based on what is in her office files about Client Charlie's case. **Answer B is correct.** If she waits until her return from a four-week vacation to send the interrogatories to Client Charlie, there will be only two days left before the deadline has expired. Because of the nature of the information being sought by the other side, Lawyer Harriet cannot delay forwarding the interrogatories to him. **Answer C is correct**. It is unreasonable for Lawyer Harriet to fail to communicate with Client Charlie by sending the interrogatories to him when she knows that the information in her office files cannot satisfactorily comply with the information sought by those interrogatories.

PROBLEM #31. ANSWER D IS THE BEST ANSWER.

Answers A and C are both true. **A is incorrect** but accurate. If a lawyer receives a document relating to a representation and the lawyer knows or reasonably should know that the document was delivered to him inadvertently, he must inform the sender *promptly*. Rule 4.4(b). Lawyer Ben's duty to maintain confidentiality extends to accidental or inadvertent disclosure of confidential information, as when Lawyer Ben accidentally sends a misdirected fax to Lawyer Brandon. The Rules require that the lawyer take "reasonable efforts" to protect the other lawyer's client's information. Rule 1.6, Comment 17. Either the receiving lawyer or the sending lawyer thereafter may file motions in court and leave it to the judge to decide what should happen next. Lawyer Ben may wish to obtain a protective order so that Client Daniels does not lose the protection of the lawyer-client privilege. ABA Formal Opinion 05–437 states that "Rule 4.4(b) ... does not require the receiving lawyer either to refrain from examining the materials or to abide by the instructions of the sending lawyer." If a court decides that the fax did not waive the privilege, Lawyer Brandon cannot take advantage of Lawyer Ben's mistake. But if the court concludes that the fax's disclosure effectively waived the privilege, Client Brandon can take advantage of Client Ben's mistake without concern that Client Brandon is violating the Rules. **Answer B is incorrect**. Comment 3 to Rule 4.4(b) leaves it to the recipient's professional judgment to determine whether to return the document unread. **Answer C is incorrect** but true. The duty imposed by Rule 4.4(b) upon Lawyer Brandon when he receives a misdirected fax is to notify Lawyer Ben rather than to forward the documents.

PROBLEM #32. ANSWER D IS THE BEST ANSWER.

Answers A, B and C are all true. **A is incorrect** but true. Lawyer Lewis knew that Client Turpin was impaired and she had a duty to maintain a normal client-lawyer relationship with Client Turpin, meaning a duty to abide by her estate planning objectives as far as reasonably possible. Lawyer Lewis violated Rule 1.14(a) when she failed to implement Client Turpin's estate plan. **Answer B is incorrect** but true. Rule 1.15(d) provides that a lawyer must promptly deliver to her client any funds or other property that the client is entitled to receive and shall promptly render a full accounting regarding the property. Because Lawyer Lewis failed to deliver to the estate of Client Turpin $1,995 that the estate was entitled to receive, Lawyer Lewis violated Rule 1.15(d). **C is incorrect but true**. Rule 1.16(d) provides that upon termination of representation, a lawyer shall take steps to the extent reasonably practicable to protect a client's interests. Those steps include "refunding any payments of fees or expenses that have not been earned or incurred." Because Lawyer Lewis failed to timely refund the $1,995 in attorney fees to Client Turpin's estate, he violated Rule 16(d). Because all three statements are true, answer D is correct.

PROBLEM #33. ANSWER D IS THE BEST ANSWER.

Lawyer Kramer will not be subject to discipline for stating that she is a specialist as a result of her membership in a ABA-accredited group and stating the name of the certifying group in her ad. If a state has a system for certifying specialists in specific areas of the law, you can publicize your certification as a specialist from a state-approved or ABA-accredited group. The name of the certifying organization must appear clearly in the communication about her services. Rule 7.4(d)(1)-(2). **A is incorrect**. She will be subject to discipline for claiming to be a family adoption specialist and a child custody specialist because the latter is not true, thereby violating Rule 7.1. **B is incorrect**. She will be subject to discipline for advertising that she is a family adoption specialist and a patent law specialist for the same reason. Even though the Rules recognize historic specialties in admiralty law and patent law, the claim of being a specialist in that form of practice still must be truthful under Rule 7.1. **C is incorrect**. The state where she advertises does not have to recognize certified types of specialization before she can advertise that she is a specialist. Generally, under the Rules a lawyer may call herself a specialist in a particular field or fields of law under limited circumstances as long as her claim is truthful and not false or misleading.

PROBLEM #34. ANSWER D IS THE BEST ANSWER.

All the answers are true. All in-person, live telephone, and real-time electronic (as with chat rooms or instant messaging) solicitations of a prospective client are prohibited when your significant motive is your own compensation. Defining prohibited solicitations also requires enumeration of permitted solicitations, such as the examples offered in the three statements. **Answer A is incorrect but true**, because lawyers can solicit other lawyers for new business. Rule 7.3(a)(1). **Answer B is incorrect but true**, because a lawyer may contact family members who are in need of legal services, as well as people with whom she has a close personal relationship. Both of these groups know about the lawyer's competence and that she is not going to take advantage of them. Rule 7.3(a)(2). **Answer C is incorrect but true**. The general prohibition on solicitation of new clients does not apply to a lawyer's participation in a prepaid or group legal services plan that she does not own or direct, when the lawyer's in-person or telephonic solicitation is for membership in the plan for people not known by her to need legal services in a particular matter. Rule 7.3(d).

PROBLEM #35. ANSWER B IS THE BEST ANSWER.

Through Rule 5.7(a), a lawyer may provide "law-related services," which are "services that might reasonably be performed in conjunction with and in substance are related to the provision of legal services, and that are not prohibited as unauthorized practice of law when provided by a nonlawyer." Rule 5.7(b). Specifically, law related services include "title insurance, financial planning, accounting, trust services, real estate counseling, legislative lobbying, economic analysis, social work, psychological counseling, tax return preparation, and patent, medical or environmental consulting." Rule 5.7, Comment 9. Lawyers may offer those services directly from their law offices or from a different location. Rule 5.7(a). **A is incorrect**. Providing law-related service subjects a lawyer to the requirements of Rule 1.8(a) for business transactions with a client, which requires disclosure of factual information and the opportunity for your client to consult with independent counsel. Before a lawyer contracts for law-related services in a manner that is distinct from her law practice, she must disclose to her client that those law-related services do not constitute law practice. Under those circumstances, she is not subject to the Rules that apply to lawyers who are acting as lawyers, such as conflicts of interest, advertising, or confidentiality. Regardless of whether she provides those services separately or as part of her law practice, she is subject to the Rules that apply to lawyers without regard to whether she is acting in her capacity as a lawyer. **C is incorrect.** When Lawyer Dee's legal services and the financial investment advisory service are intertwined, she must follow Rule 5.3's requirement that she supervise the non-lawyers in the delivery of those services. **D is incorrect.** As mentioned, Rule 5.7 enables Lawyer Dee to offer law-related services such as financial investment advice, in addition to her legal services for assisting Client Corrine in obtaining a divorce.

PROBLEM #36. ANSWER A IS THE BEST ANSWER.

Rule 4.1 creates a duty to disclose information to third parties in order to avoid assisting a client's fraudulent act. A lawyer's obligations under Rule 4.1 are limited by her duty of confidentiality under Rule 1.6, but those limits are not absolute. The Rules permit a lawyer to disclose confidential information about past, present, or future client fraud or client crime that has caused or is reasonably certain to cause financial harm to another person. The lawyer *may* reveal information reasonably necessary to prevent her client from carrying out a plan to commit a crime or fraud that is reasonably certain to cause substantial injury to another person's financial interests or property *and* which involved her client's use of your services. Rule 1.6(b)(2). This discretionary disclosure provision was adopted by the ABA in 2003, in response to the Enron scandals. The lawyer's right to disclose this category of confidential client communication is based on the client's breach of duty to the lawyer not to use her services in this manner. A lawyer also *may* reveal information to prevent, mitigate or rectify substantial injury to another person's financial interests or property that is reasonably certain to result or already *has resulted* from her client's commission of a crime or fraud *and* which involved her client's use of your services. Rule 1.6(b)(3). Under this provision, a lawyer can reveal client confidences *after* the criminal or fraudulent behavior but before its effects are complete. The lawyer's disclosure is intended to prevent further conduct, or mitigate or rectify the conduct which has already occurred. Without her client's past or current use of her services to commit a fraud or crime, a lawyer has no discretion to disclose under either Rule 1.6(b)(2) or (b)(3). If a lawyer's client uses her services to further her "criminal or fraudulent conduct," she must withdraw. Rule 1.6, Comment 7; Rule 1.16(a)(1). That withdrawal may effectively constitute a disclosure of her client's communications. As described above, Rules 1.6(b)(2) and (b)(3) give a lawyer the authority to deal with her client who involves her in his fraud.

To summarize, unless prohibited by the Rule on confidentiality, a lawyer cannot knowingly fail to disclose a material fact to a third person when such disclosure is necessary to avoid assisting a criminal or fraudulent act by her client. Rule 4.1(b). Disclosure of material facts under Rule 4.1(b) is mandatory. When combined with Rule 4.1(b), the permissive disclosure provisions of Rules 1.6(b)(2)-(3) become mandatory provisions. Thus, disclosure to third persons is mandatory for financial crimes likely to cause substantial injury. If a lawyer fails to make the disclosure, she is participating in the fraud or crime by her client. If she realizes that her client is committing a crime or fraud against another person, she must inform her client that she cannot participate further. Rule 1.2(d). If the fraud or crime is ongoing and a lawyer has provided legal services connected with the crime or fraud, she must withdraw if her client refuses to change his conduct, Rule 1.16(a), informing the opposing party of her withdrawal and disaffirming any false documents such as the demand letter in this case. **B is incorrect** because the Lawyer Lotz's duty is mandatory, not permissive. **C is incorrect** because Lawyer Lotz has a duty to disclose Client Clore's fraud. **D is incorrect** because A is correct.

PROBLEM #37. ANSWER C IS THE BEST ANSWER.

A lawyer cannot have a sexual relationship with a client, unless that consensual relationship already existed prior to the beginning of the lawyer-client relationship. Rule 1.8(j). A lawyer's fiduciary obligations require that he not take unfair advantage of his client. Sexual relations with a client create an ethical problem for a lawyer because of his potential undue influence and the client's emotional vulnerability, both of which affect the lawyer's independent personal judgment and rebut the client's meaningful consent. ABA Formal Opinion 92–364. If a lawyer's conflict with a client relates to having sexual relations with her client since the start of the lawyer-client relationship, she still can send that client to your law partner to handle the client's case. **A and B are incorrect**; Rule 1.8(j) does not indicate that a client's consent can validate the continued lawyer-client relationship between lovers, regardless of whether another lawyer's advice is sought prior to the consent. **D is incorrect**. Rule 1.8(j) prohibits the lawyer from having sexual relations with a client regardless of whether the relationship is consensual and regardless of the absence of prejudice to the client. Rule 1.8, Comment 17.

PROBLEM #38. ANSWER C IS THE BEST ANSWER.

A lawyer cannot acquire the literary rights to his client's case while she is still working for him on that case. Rule 1.8(d). The Rule protects both the client from the lawyer's potential overreaching and the judicial system from being used for her benefit. Lawyer Phillips should not be tempted to practice her case in a manner that increases the publicity value of the media rights. For example, she should not reject a plea offer ending her client's case to his benefit because going to trial instead would increase the market value of a book or movie about his case. *After* the representation concludes, Client Phillips would have no advantage over a literary agent in obtaining the rights to her (possibly now former) client's story. If he still owes her fee, at that time Client Justin and Lawyer Phillips could agree on forgiving that debt in exchange for publication rights. **A is incorrect**, because the Rule does not exempt a situation when the client still owes the fee to his lawyer during the representation. **B is incorrect**. The publication deal is being negotiated while Lawyer Phillips still represents Client Justin in the wrongful death case, regardless of what the focus of the book would be. **D is incorrect**. This Rule 1.8 conflict between Lawyer Phillips and Client Justin is imputed to other lawyers in her firm. Rule 1.8(k).

PROBLEM #39. ANSWER C IS THE BEST ANSWER.

A lawyer cannot support his client financially by giving her money for her living expenses or medical bills. That type of assistance could produce an improper level of zealousness. Lawyer Lonnie is likely to do a better job as Client Taylor's lawyer if he is not also her creditor. A lawyer may advance or even guarantee a client's litigation expenses and court costs without the client being ultimately responsible for paying them. Rule 1.8(e). (Litigation expenses include payments for expert witnesses or expenditures for your client to travel to a deposition. Court costs include filing fees and copying costs. If a client is not indigent, a lawyer must incorporate any advance of those expenses in the fee agreement, providing that they must be paid from the proceeds of any recovery. If a client is indigent, a lawyer is allowed to pay them and not make them payable from any proceeds.) **A and B are incorrect**, because of the prohibition on a lawyer financially supporting a client while representing the client, as discussed above. **D is incorrect**. The Rules do not qualify the standard against financial support based on a lawyer's sympathy for the client.

PROBLEM #40. ANSWER D IS THE BEST ANSWER.

In order to obtain advice about her compliance with the Rules, a lawyer *may* reveal information relating to the representation of her client. Rule 1.6(b)(4). Bar associations offer services to lawyers for the purpose of obtaining advice from other members of the bar about their ethical conduct. ABA Formal Opinion 98–411 acknowledged that such consultations, made typically without a fee and without intending to create an additional lawyer-client relationship, are often useful and in the interest of the client. The Opinion cautions lawyers to (1) consult in hypothetical terms, (2) to obtain permission from your client if the consultation might put her at risk, (3) not to consult a lawyer who might represent the adverse party, and (4) to obtain assurances of confidentiality for the information. **A is incorrect**. Although the ABA Opinion just discussed mentions consent as a precaution, the Rules permit a discretionary disclosure without first obtaining the consent of the client. **B is incorrect**, because the Rules explicitly allow discretionary disclosure of confidential information in order to obtain ethical compliance with the Rules. **C is incorrect**. The Rules do not restrict the discretionary disclosures to a conversation with someone who works with an ethics hotline service. Presumably, the disclosures can be made to a broader group.

PROBLEM #41. ANSWER B IS THE BEST ANSWER.

A lawyer "may reveal information relating to the representation of a client to the extent the lawyer reasonably believes necessary" to "prevent reasonably certain death or substantial bodily harm." Rule 1.6(b)(1). The provision is discretionary, not mandatory. The disclosure is intended to address future death or bodily harm. (A lawyer cannot disclose client information that she already has killed or has caused serious harm to someone. That information is protected by your duty of confidentiality.) The reference to "certain" death or substantial bodily harm includes imminent, lingering, and delayed death or bodily harm. Lawyer Fitzgerald may reveal that her client's environmental practices and legal violations will likely cause death to people. Rule 1.6. Comment 6. The reference to "substantial" means that disclosure of information to prevent serious bodily harm is proper. **A is incorrect**. The Rules rarely impose a duty to disclose confidential information. Rule 1.6(b)(1) is permissive, not mandatory. **C is incorrect**, as discussed above, regarding the permissive disclosure of confidential information. **D is incorrect.** Although there may be discretionary disclosures of confidential information to prevent future harm, the goal of such disclosures is restricted to the certain death or bodily harm, not financial harm.

PROBLEM #42. ANSWER D IS THE BEST ANSWER.

A positional conflict exists when a lawyer represents a client in one matter seeking a particular result, and at the same time she represents another client in a different case in which she is taking a contrary *legal* position. Lawyer Willa may advocate antagonistic legal positions in different cases, as long as the positional conflict does not materially limit her representation of one of her clients. Rule 1.7(b). Relevant factors include "where the cases are pending, whether the issue is substantive or procedural, the temporal relationship between the matters, the significance of the issue to the immediate and long term interests of the clients involved, and the clients' reasonable expectations in retaining the lawyer." Rule 1.7, Comment 24. **A is incorrect**. As the prior discussion suggested, positional conflicts may be unethical but they are not *per se* unethical. Analysis of the situational facts is necessary to make the *ad hoc* determination about the ethics of taking both sides of basically the same legal issue. **B is incorrect**. A positional conflict may exist in a nonlitigation setting. **C is incorrect**, because it misstates the application of the relevant standards. In either of Lawyer Willa's representations, both unions and the corporation would have to consent to the conflict of interest.

PROBLEM #43. ANSWER B IS THE BEST ANSWER.

B is the correct answer. Waiving the evidentiary privilege does not waive the ethical duty of confidentiality. As for the lawyer-client privilege, Lawyer Sarah cannot claim the privilege and refuse to reveal Client Sam's admission. The privilege belongs to Client Sam, who has lost it by revealing the information about the representation to others. If Lawyer Sarah attempts to resist disclosure by asserting the privilege, the court can order her to disclose matters not falling within the evidentiary privilege. Even if Client Sam loses the evidentiary privilege, Lawyer Sarah still has an ethical obligation to maintain Client Sam's confidential information. If Lawyer Sarah is called to testify about Client Sam's admission, she must assert her ethical duty of confidentiality but the court may order her to disclose the information. Because of the aforementioned conclusions about the lawyer-client privilege and the ethical duty of confidentiality, **A, C and D are incorrect**.

PROBLEM #44. ANSWER D IS THE BEST ANSWER.

D is the correct answer. A lawyer who is not diligent in her representation may be liable for monetary damages to a former client for malpractice committed by her or by her employee. Several legal theories may be the basis of a malpractice allegation:(1) breach of contract, for violating an agreement with the client to use her skill to protect the client's interests, (2) breach of fiduciary duty, for having violated her duties of loyalty, confidentiality, and honesty, (3) intentional tort liability for claims such as fraud, abuse of process, or conversion, and (4) unintentional tort liability for negligence in violating her duty of care toward her client. Negligence is the most common civil claim brought by former clients against their lawyers. Because former clients frequently bring legal malpractice claims, many lawyers carry legal malpractice insurance.

Answer A is incorrect but true. A lawyer is competent if she has "the legal knowledge, skill, thoroughness and preparation reasonably necessary for the representation." Rule 1.1. Her skills must include the ability to research, write, advocate, and negotiate. Her failure to provide competent representation may result in discipline, malpractice liability, or an ineffective assistance of counsel claim. A lawyer like Lawyer Lana may take a type of case with which she is unfamiliar. Rule 1.1, Comment 2. That makes sense, because everybody has a first case of a particular kind. By studying or talking to other lawyers, she can become knowledgeable even if she lacked the requisite knowledge when she began the representation. Rule 1.1, Comment 2. Through her knowledge, she also becomes thorough and prepared to represent her clients. Under the tort of negligence, a lawyer may be liable for either a single instance of neglect or a pattern of negligent activities. To recover damages for malpractice, the former client must prove that (1) the lawyer owed him a duty of care, (2) the lawyer breached that duty, (3) the breach caused injury to him in the form of damages, and (4) without the lawyer's negligence he would have been more successful in the underlying matter. The standard of care she owes is a level of diligence and competence to be exercised by a reasonable lawyer in similar circumstances. As a lawyer, Lawyer Lana owes a duty of care to Client Cross to sue based upon law which offers the best opportunity of success. If as the facts indicate any reasonably competent general practitioner would have discovered a more favorable body of parallel federal law as the basis for a lawsuit on behalf of Client Cross, then Lawyer Leonard has breached that duty of care to Client Cross. **Answers B and C are incorrect** but true. Lawyer Ames as the supervising lawyer and Lawyer Lana's employer is responsible for her misconduct. Rule 5.1(c)(2). Lawyer Bean also is liable for malpractice because she has "managerial authority" over Lawyer Lana and must make reasonable efforts to assure that all lawyers in their firm comply with the Rules. Rule 5.1(a).

PROBLEM #45. ANSWER B IS THE BEST ANSWER.

A is incorrect because it is not true. From time to time, the United States Supreme Court has identified a Due Process issue in the context of judicial disqualification. For example, *In re Murchison*, 349 U.S. 133 (1955) was a Due Process case in which the Court reversed a contempt conviction when the same judge who acted as a "one-judge grand jury" in bringing contempt charges also presided over the contempt hearing. Three decades later, the Court found a Due Process violation when an Alabama Supreme Court Justice cast the deciding vote in a case involving the same issue which he personally was litigating in a trial court. *Aetna Life Ins. Co. v. Lavoie*, 475 U.S. 813 (1986). Most recently, the Court identified a

Due Process violation in *Caperton v. A. T. Massey Coal Co.*, ___ U.S. ___, 129 S.Ct. 2252 (2009), when a party-defendant had spent over $3 million in support of a West Virginia Supreme Court Justice's successful election bid and the Justice had refused to recuse himself from the contributor's appeal. Answer **C is incorrect** because it is untrue. Regardless of whether a judge is aware of the grounds for her disqualification, a later motion to disqualify the judge can result in the judge's earlier rulings retroactively being set aside because the conflict existed when the judge's ruling was made. If a judge is aware of a disqualifying conflict of interest, she is supposed to recuse herself from a case or in most circumstances she can ask the lawyers in the case if they are willing to waive the conflict. But even is she does neither of the foregoing when she is aware of grounds for recusal, a lawyer for a party may later seek her disqualification. While a judge is supposed to keep informed about her personal and fiduciary economic interests and while she is supposed to make a reasonable effort to keep informed about the personal economic interests of her spouse or domestic partner and minor children residing in her household, she may not realize that grounds for recusal exist. **Answer D is incorrect**, because only answer B is correct.

PROBLEM #46. ANSWER B IS THE BEST ANSWER.

Rule 4.2 prohibits lawyers from directly contacting a person the lawyer knows is represented by an attorney. Lawyer Dewey has violated Rule 4.2 because she knew that Lawyer Cheatham represented Adversary Abner before sending Investigator Ike to meet with Adversary Abner. Lawyer Dewey is also responsible under Rule 5.3 if Investigator Ike tries to do what Lawyer Dewey, i.e., contact a represented person with Lawyer Dewey's knowledge or consent. ABA Formal Opinion 95–396 states that a lawyer cannot direct an investigator to communicate with a represented person when the lawyer herself would be prohibited from doing so. **A is incorrect** because it is the opposite of B. **C is incorrect**. Rule 4.4(a) prohibits a lawyer from using "methods of obtaining evidence that violate the legal rights of such a person." Rule 4.4, Comment 1 states that a lawyer cannot use methods of gathering evidence that involve "unwarranted intrusions into privileged relationships, such as the client-lawyer relationship." Lawyer Dewey would violate Rule 4.4(a) for sending Investigator Ike to solicit privileged information from Adversary Abner during the interview with Adversary Abner. As the prior discussion indicated, **D is incorrect** because sending Investigator Ike to talk to Adversary Abner is an ethical violation, regardless of whether Investigator Ike learns any privileged information during the interview.

PROBLEM #47. ANSWER D IS THE BEST ANSWER.

While Rule 1.8(c) prohibits Lawyer Lark from drafting an instrument which bequeaths a substantial gift to her, and Rule 1.8(k) states that Lawyer Lark's law partner cannot draft such an instrument either, a lawyer whose practice is not affiliated with Lawyer Lark's may draft such an instrument. Answers A and B address two exceptions to Rule 1.8(c). **A is incorrect** because it will subject Lawyer Lark to discipline. Lawyer Lark cannot draft an instrument making a substantial gift to herself. If she cannot draft an instrument making a substantial gift to herself, she also cannot draft an instrument making a substantial gift to anyone related to her, unless Lawyer Lark or her daughter is related to the client. Rule 1.8(c). "Related persons include a spouse, child, grandchild, parent, grandparent or other relative or individual with whom" a lawyer or her client "maintains a close, familial relationship." Rule 1.8(c). The facts state the at the client came to town last year not knowing anyone. **B is incorrect**, because it will subject Lawyer Lark to discipline. Although Rule 1.8(c) does not prohibit Lawyer Lark from seeking an appointment as executrix of her client's estate, Rule 1.8, Comment 8, the combined fee for acting as fiduciary and as lawyer must be reasonable under Rule 1.5(a). ABA Formal Opinion 02–426. The stated facts indicate that the fee alone that is prescribed in the will for being the executrix of the client's estate would exceed what is reasonable for being both the executrix and the lawyer for the client's estate. **C is incorrect**. Because of the operation of Rule 1.8(k), Lawyer Lark's conflict of interest is imputed to her law partners. When she cannot draft an instrument providing a substantial gift to herself, neither can her law partner draft such an instrument.

PROBLEM #48. ANSWER C IS THE BEST ANSWER.

C is the only one of the offered answers that does not describe ethical conduct by a criminal defense lawyer representing an accused. Answers A, B, and D are ethical courses of conduct. A criminal defense lawyer during trial may allude only to matters that she reasonably believes are relevant or admissible. For example, she cannot ask a clearly prohibited question, or assert her personal opinion or personal knowledge about the facts. Rule 3.4(e). **A is incorrect**. A criminal defense lawyer may ask the court's permission to violate its order of document disclosure because the documents are privileged. Rule 3.4(c). **B is incorrect**. A defense lawyer may advise her client and certain nonclients not to volunteer any information to the prosecutor, without obstructing the prosecutor's ability to gather evidence. Rule 3.4(a). **D is incorrect**. A criminal defense lawyer may review documents before turning them over in order to avoid accidental waivers of privileged information. The criminal defense lawyer may request that an unrepresented nonclient refuse to volunteer information *if* he is the lawyer's relative, employee or agent and that nonclient's interests will not be adversely affected if the request is honored. Rule 3.4(f).

PROBLEM #49. ANSWER D IS THE BEST ANSWER.

A, B, and C are correct statements of a prosecutor's ethical duty under Rule 3.8(b), (c), and (g). D is an inaccurate statement of a prosecutor's ethical responsibilities regarding subpoenaing defense counsel. A prosecutor is limited in the circumstances in which a lawyer can be subpoenaed. If the prosecutor "reasonably believes" that no privilege applies, the evidence the prosecutor has is "essential" to the success of her investigation or prosecution, and she has no "feasible alternative" of obtaining the evidence she seeks from the lawyer, she can be subpoenaed. Rule 3.8(e). **A is incorrect** though true. A prosecutor must provide a defendant a reasonable opportunity to obtain counsel by informing the defendant of the right to have his own lawyer. Rule 3.8(b). **B is incorrect** though true. If a defendant proceeds *pro se*, the prosecutor must negotiate directly with him, but she cannot urge a *pro se* defendant to waive pretrial rights, e.g., the right to a preliminary hearing. Rule 3.8(c). **C is incorrect** though true. A prosecutor must promptly disclose to both the court and the convicted defendant any "new, credible and material evidence creating a reasonable likelihood" that he did not commit the crime for which he was convicted. In addition, the prosecutor must investigate the matter further. Rule 3.8(g).

PROBLEM #50. ANSWER C IS THE BEST ANSWER.

A lawyer may limit the scope of her representation if the limitation is reasonable and the client gives the lawyer his informed consent. Rule 1.2(c). Before he can give informed consent, the lawyer must explain the risks of limited representation and any available alternatives to such limitations. Rule 1.0(e). Even though it often is the client and not the lawyer who places limitations on the scope of the representation, the lawyer must still explain the risks and document his informed consent in writing. **A is incorrect**. As mentioned, the scope of the representation does not have to be dictated by only the lawyer or only the client. The scope and objectives of a lawyer's representation of a client may be defined by the lawyer's agreement to represent him. Without such a descriptive or limiting agreement, a lawyer has a duty to use available legal methods to pursue the client's objectives. When a lawyer and her client disagree about what she should do to accomplish the client's objectives, the Rules encourage clients to defer to the lawyer's expertise, especially on "technical, legal, and tactical matters." On the other hand, the lawyer should defer to the client's decisions which involve added expense or harm to others. Rule 1.2, Comment 2. Although the Rules do not prescribe how to resolve such disagreements, a fundamental disagreement may permit or require you to withdraw, per Rule 1.16. **B is incorrect**. For the same reasons just mentioned, the client does not have the exclusive right to decide the scope of the representation. As long as a lawyer does not assist a client in criminal or fraudulent conduct, the lawyer can explain to the client the consequences of possible actions. Rule 1.2(d). A lawyer also may help the client to determine whether specific conduct is criminal or fraudulent under applicable law. A lawyer must withdraw from representing a client if her continued representation will violate this Rule (or any Rule). Rule 1.16. **D is incorrect**, because C is correct.

PROBLEM #51. ANSWER A IS THE BEST ANSWER.

A third-party neutral does not represent either party to a dispute, but is seeking to promote the resolution of that dispute through the use of alternative dispute resolution (ADR) proceedings. Mediators are examples of third-party neutrals under the Rules. If a lawyer acts as a third-party neutral, she must disclose to unrepresented parties that she is not representing them to remove potential confusion about her role. Rule 2.4(b). She must explain the differences between her role as a third-party neutral and her role when she represents a client. The disclosure is comparable to her duties when she represents a client against a party who has no counsel, although the third-party neutral is not acting in a representational capacity. **B is incorrect**. While she is serving as a third-party neutral, she cannot discuss future employment with either a party or lawyer representing a party in the matter. Rule 1.12(b). **C is incorrect**. A party to the mediation may ask the third-party neutral to represent him in a future proceeding related to the proceeding of the ADR process. The lawyer-as-mediator cannot represent a party in the same matter in which she "participated personally and substantially" as a third-party neutral, unless all of the parties to that proceeding give their informed consent, confirmed in writing. Rule 1.12(a). **D is incorrect**. When the lawyer-as-mediator is disqualified from later representing one of the parties due to her prior status as a third-party neutral, no one in her law firm can represent any of the parties either, unless (1) she is screened in a timely manner from later representation in the matter, (2) she receives no part of the fee from the later representation, and (3) the parties and "any appropriate tribunal" receive notice in writing about the screen so that they can decide whether the first two requirements are being followed. Rule 1.12(c).

PROBLEM #52. ANSWER A IS THE BEST ANSWER.

Lawyer Lincoln violated Rule 3.3(a)(1) by making a false statement of fact to the court as the basis for seeking and obtaining the continuance of the trial. Having made such a false statement, Lawyer Lincoln had a duty to correct that false statement of fact. Any factual assertions to the tribunal ("my client is ill") must be based on the lawyer's knowledge that he knows are true or believe to be true on the basis of a reasonably diligent inquiry. Rule 3.3, Comment 3. **Answers B, C, and D are incorrect**. Once it is established that Lawyer Lincoln has committed an ethical violation, it must be determined whether any of his supervisors is subject to discipline for failing to correct the false statements made by Lawyer Lincoln. In this case, both Partner Peters and Lawyer Lyons are subject to discipline, albeit under different Rules. Partners in a law firm must make reasonable efforts to assure that all the lawyers in their firm comply with the Rules. Rule 5.1(a). Even though Partner Peters does not work in the same department as Lawyer Lincoln and has nothing to do with the specific matter, Partner Peters still must ensure that the other lawyers in the law firm comply with the Rules. Lawyer Lyons likewise is subject to discipline. Even if she is not a partner in a firm, as a senior associate Lawyer Lyons has supervisory authority over Lawyer Lincoln in the litigation matter. Her responsibilities are the same as a partner in order to assure compliance with ethics standards by the junior associate lawyers such as Lawyer Lincoln working under her authority, but her responsibilities relate only to those associate lawyers. Those responsibilities extend to the performance and quality of those lawyers' work, and includes being available to answer their questions. Rule 5.1(b). Because both Partner Peters is subject to discipline under Rule 5.1(a) and Lawyer Lyons is subject to discipline under Rule 5.1(b), they are both subject to discipline for their inaction.

PROBLEM #53. ANSWER B IS THE BEST ANSWER.

A judge must disqualify or recuse herself "in a proceeding in which the judge's impartiality might reasonably be questioned." Code of Judicial Conduct, Rule 2.11(A). This general standard is applicable when the Code does not specifically describe a situation where the judge's partiality is presumed. CJC Rule 2.11(A)(1)-(6) lists the specific situations in which he judge's partiality is presumed, e.g., when the judge has a personal bias or prejudice about a party or her lawyer. Judge Jackson was not allowed to preside over Prosecutor Paul's cases when they were married because of the concern that she would have a personal bias in favor of her spouse. After their marriage ended, she may still have a personal bias, except that it would be *against* the party whom her ex-spouse represented. **A is**

incorrect. As mentioned, the Code of Judicial Conduct does list several situations where the challenged judge's partiality is presumed, but it does not explicitly recognize presiding over a case in which the judge's ex-spouse is counsel of record as one of those presumptively disqualifying situations. **C is incorrect**. As indicated, even when the Code does not recognize a situation as being presumptively disqualifying, the phrase "the judge's partiality might reasonably be questioned" functions as a residual clause by which all other factual contexts are evaluated to decide whether recusal is necessary. **D is incorrect.** There is no duty to sit. At one time, the prevailing view was that judges have a duty to sit, meaning that if the judge herself subjectively believed that she could be impartial in the case, she not only could sit in the case but *had* to sit in the case. The objective standard of deciding whether the judge's impartiality might *reasonably* be questioned abrogated the duty to sit. Now, if a reasonable person might question the judge's impartiality, the judge is required, *sua sponte*, to recuse herself, regardless of her own opinion about her impartiality.

PROBLEM #54. ANSWER A IS THE BEST ANSWER.

Rule 7.6 prohibits a lawyer or her law firm (which includes a "political action committee owned or controlled by" the lawyer) from accepting a governmental "legal engagement" or a judicial appointment if she made or solicited such political campaign contributions for the purpose of obtaining or being considered for that type of engagement or appointment. It is said that the Rule prohibits "pay-to-play contributions." The prohibition applies only to contributions that would not have been made but for the lawyer's desire to the political or judicial appointment. If the motive for Lawyer King's contributions simply was to be on the winning side, her acceptance of the guardian appointments would not support an inference of impropriety, especially when the amount of her contribution was average compared to the contributions from others. Similarly, judicial appointments made on a rotating basis from a list compiled without regard to the fact or amount of a campaign contribution are excluded from the Rule's application. On the other hand, if Lawyer King's latest contribution was motivated by her need to become the only guardian in Judge Pfeiffer's court, Lawyer King has violated Rule 7.6. The scope of discipline applies both to the lawyer and her law firm, which is unique among the Rules. The Rule applies only when she accepts the appointment she sought. **B is incorrect**. The size or legality of the Lawyer King's contribution is irrelevant to her exposure to discipline under Rule 7.6. **C is incorrect**. As already noted, it is the motive rather than the size of the contribution that is determinative. **D is incorrect**. Mixed motives do not absolve a lawyer from discipline under Rule 7.6, as long as one "purpose" for making the political contribution is to obtain or be considered for a judicial appointment.

PROBLEM #55. ANSWER B IS THE BEST ANSWER.

A lawyer may disclose confidential information in order "to comply with other law or a court order." Rule 1.6(b)(6). If a state law, such as a child abuse reporting requirement, requires that a lawyer disclose confidential client information, Rule 1.6(b)(6) overrides the general confidentiality requirement. Rule 1.6, Comment 12 states, "When disclosure of information relating to the representation appears to be required by law, the lawyer must discuss the matter with the client to the extent required by Rule 1.4. If, however, the other law supersedes this Rule and requires disclosure, paragraph (b)(6) permits the lawyer to make such disclosures as are necessary to comply with the law." If a court orders a lawyer to disclose information that she believes is protected by the lawyer-client privilege, she may either reveal it or challenge the court's order. She is not required to be held in contempt before obeying the court's order to disclose. The lawyer may comply with the court's order and disclose, without first violating the order and risk being held in contempt. **A is incorrect**. As written, Rule 1.6(b)(6) gives the lawyer discretion to disclose information required by law; the Rule permits disclosure of otherwise confidential information rather than mandating it. **C is incorrect**. Rule 1.6(b)(6) is a discretionary exception to the ordinary requirement that a lawyer must not disclose confidential information from the client without the client's consent. **D is incorrect**. As the prior discussion indicated, a lawyer has the discretion to disclose information relating to the client's representation which the law requires to be reported.

PROBLEM #56. ANSWER C IS THE BEST ANSWER.

Clients have the authority to waive their lawyer's conflict of interest in advance. Rule 1.7, Comment 22. A prospective waiver means the same as the phrase "informed consent" in the Rules. Such a waiver is more likely to be effective if it relates to a future conflict that is unrelated to the subject matter of the current representation. An effective disclosure depends on the lawyer's ability to explain all important risks connected to the future conflict. For a consent to be "informed," a lawyer must explain to her client the "material risks" and "reasonably available alternatives" of going forward with or without her as counsel. Rule 1.0(e). **A is incorrect**, because consent to a future conflict of interest under Rule 1.7 must be in writing, and the foregoing discussion describes the additional information that must be included as part of that writing. **B is incorrect**, because

Rule 1.0(e) clearly describes that the Rules require an informed consent to be in writing. **D is incorrect**. ABA Formal Opinion 05–436 stated that a waiver of a future conflict may be valid even though it is very general.

PROBLEM #57. ANSWER B IS THE BEST ANSWER.

B is the only statement that would not subject Lawyer Lotz to discipline. True, a lawyer has an obligation to disclose all material facts, adverse or otherwise, at an *ex parte* hearing under Rule 3.3(d). However, information about statewide spouse abuse s not material to whether in her case the court should grant a restraining order against Client Catherine's husband to prevent him from abusing her in the future. **A is incorrect.** When a lawyer agrees to be the advocate for a client, the lawyer may present any nonfrivolous interpretation of the law that favors the client. A lawyer cannot present frivolous claims, defenses, or motions. Rule 3.1. The lawyer does not have to make a complete factual or legal investigation before asserting a claim, defense, or motion, but the lawyer is acting frivolously by knowingly putting forth a position unsupported by the facts and the law. This answer is incorrect, because as answer D's explanation will point out, at an ex parte hearing a lawyer must disclose all material facts, adverse or otherwise, so that it can make an informed decision. **C is incorrect.** A lawyer cannot knowingly make false statements of fact to a tribunal, and the lawyer must correct any statement of fact that the lawyer learns was both false and material to the proceeding. Rule 3.3(a)(1). A lawyer must not offer evidence that the lawyer knows is false. Rule 3.3(a)(3). As an officer of the court, a lawyer cannot participate in misleading the court even when the client insists. If Lawyer Lucky knew that presenting evidence that Client Catherine never abused her husband was presenting false evidence, there is an ethical violation. **D is incorrect**. In an *ex parte* proceeding, a lawyer must disclose *all* material facts, adverse or otherwise, and all applicable law to the tribunal so that it can make an informed decision. Rule 3.3(d). Lawyer Lucky's increased duty of disclosure is necessary to offset the absence of an adversary position presented by the other side. Rule 3.3, Comment 14. An example of an *ex parte* proceeding would be an applications to a court for a temporary restraining order.

PROBLEM #58. ANSWER D IS THE BEST ANSWER.

When Lawyer Samuels from another firm retains Lawyer Leslie, the latter may have a conflict of interest if they concurrently represent clients who are adverse to each other in separate cases. Despite that concurrent conflict, Lawyer Leslie may represent Lawyer Samuels if she "reasonably believes that [she] will be able to provide competent and diligent representation" to him and to her divorce clients and each of her clients gives "informed consent, confirmed in writing." Rule 1.7(b)(1), (b)(4). Informed consent by all of her affected clients is possible if Lawyer Leslie insists that Lawyer Samuels make a full disclosure to his clients. See Rule 1.7, Comment 14. **A is incorrect**. Lawyer Leslie is subject to discipline, because she is "directly adverse" to her lawyer-client (Lawyer Samuels) if she attacks his credibility in the cases where they both have clients. Rule 1.7(a)(1). **B is incorrect**. A risk also exists that Lawyer Leslie may temper her advocacy on behalf of her clients in the other cases so as not to alienate Lawyer Samuels whose representation she wants to maintain. **C is incorrect**. Lawyer Leslie's representation of Lawyer Samuels under these circumstances may also violate Rule 1.7(a)(2). The importance of the case to Lawyer Samuels, the relative size of Lawyer Leslie's fee for representing Lawyer Samuels, and the relative importance of the two cases are factors which may "materially" limit Lawyer Leslie's relationship with Lawyer Samuels. ABA Formal Opinion 97–406. If her fee to represent Lawyer Samuels is quite large compared to the fee she is charging the divorce clients in the cases where she and Lawyer Samuels are on opposite sides of the cases, there is a strong argument that representing her divorce clients is materially limited by her responsibilities to another current client, Lawyer Samuels. If they were aware of the size of Lawyer Leslie's fee for representing Lawyer Samuels, her divorce clients may believe that she has more loyalty to her client's spouse's lawyer than to her own divorce clients.

PROBLEM #59. ANSWER B IS THE BEST ANSWER.

If a lawyer represents a corporation, she may be asked to serve on its board of directors. At times, her corporate client may not understand whether she is giving business advice in her role as director or legal advice as lawyer for the corporation. She must "determine whether the responsibilities of the two roles may conflict," and she should not serve in this dual capacity if "there is a material risk that the dual role will compromise" her independent professional judgment. "Consideration should be given to the frequency with which such situations may arise, the potential intensity of the conflict, the effect of the lawyer's resignation from the board and the possibility of the corporation's obtaining legal advice from another lawyer in such situations." Rule 1.7, Comment 35. If her obligations in the dual role are "materially adverse" to each other, she must withdraw from representation unless her corporate client consents. In the absence of the corporate client's consent, she should not continue to serve in the dual capacity and should resign the position either as the corporation's lawyer or as a member of the corporate board. Rule 1.7, Comment 35. **A is incorrect** for two reasons. First, the nature of

Lawyer Landers's choice is ethical, not financial. Second, as the previous discussion confirms, Lawyer Landers has more than one choice; if her roles are "materially adverse," her alternatives are to remain on the board or to remain as the lawyer for the corporation. **C is incorrect**. As indicated, Lawyer Landers's "materially adverse" and conflicting obligations do not require her to resign from both positions of trust; instead she may choose one of the roles. **D is incorrect**. Comment 35 also indicates a different type of advice for Lawyer Landers to offer than is stated is answer D. She should tell the rest of the board "that in some circumstances matters discussed at board meetings while the lawyer is present in the capacity of director might not be protected by the attorney-client privilege and that conflict of interest considerations might require the [her] recusal as a director or might require [her] to decline representation of the corporation in a matter." Rule 1.7, Comment 35.

PROBLEM #60. ANSWER C IS THE BEST ANSWER.

When harmful confidential information from Company Abner is shared with Law Partner Fisher, Law Partner Fisher cannot represent Company Bates in the later lawsuit of *Company Abner v. Company Bates*. Even if Law Partner Fisher from Law Firm Carey & Dyson is prohibited from representing Company Bates in a substantially related matter, Law Firm Carey & Dyson may still be able to represent Company Bates in that lawsuit. Generally, a conflict which prohibits an individual lawyer from representing a client is imputed to other lawyers working at the law firm, creating a presumption of disqualification of every attorney at the firm. Rule 1.18(c) provides: "If a lawyer is disqualified from representation ... no lawyer in a firm with which that lawyer is associated may knowingly undertake or continue representation in such a matter...." Rule 1.18(d) explicitly recognizes the use of screens to rebut the imputation of the conflict of interest in the case of a prospective client: "[w]hen the lawyer has received disqualifying information ... representation is permissible if ... the lawyer who received the information took reasonable measures to avoid exposure to more disqualifying information than was reasonably necessary to determine whether to represent the prospective client; and the disqualified lawyer is timely screened from any participation in the matter and is apportioned no part of the fee therefrom; and written notice is promptly given to the prospective client." In assessing whether a law firm has effectively screened a personally prohibited lawyer from the rest of the firm, enabling the firm to represent a client with materially adverse interests to the prospective client in a substantially related matter, courts evaluate a number of factors: the timeliness of the firm's implementation of the screen, the size of the screening firm, the proximity of the disqualified lawyer from those lawyers at the firm who will represent the client, affidavits from the lawyer attesting to no confidential information disclosures, and whether the disqualified lawyer works on other cases with the lawyers representing the client. **A, B, and D are incorrect** for the same reasons that C is correct.

PROFESSIONAL RESPONSIBILITY

Answer Key for Exam #2—Answers and Explanations

PROBLEM #1. ANSWER D IS THE BEST ANSWER.

Lawyer Arthur has discretion under Rule 1.6(b)(1) to disclose such intent by Jones if Lawyer Arthur reasonably believes that giving the information to the police would prevent Jones from committing a criminal act that the lawyer believes is likely to result in reasonably certain death or substantial bodily harm to the area's teenagers. This discretionary disclosure is contingent on Jones using Lawyer Arthur's services to promote his criminal conduct.

A is incorrect, because there is no distinction made between the types of information learned about or from the client. Under the Model Rules, any information relating to the representation of a client is confidential, regardless of whether it was obtained from the client or merely about the client. **B is incorrect**, because although Model Rule 1.6 prohibits an attorney from revealing Jones's *past* criminal activities, Rule 1.6(b) does permit discretionary disclosure of some types of information. **C is incorrect**, because discretionary disclosures of future criminal conduct are limited to specific types of conduct, e.g., conduct that the lawyer reasonably believes necessary to "prevent reasonably certain death or substantial bodily harm." Such a provision is discretionary, not mandatory, and is intended to address *future* death or bodily harm but not all future criminal conduct. (Lawyer Arthur would have to assess whether Jones intends to continue committing the crime and whether the crime of cocaine trafficking would cause reasonably certain death or substantially bodily harm. For example, if Lawyer Arthur knows that people die or become seriously ill from ingesting cocaine, reporting Jones's activities can prevent others from experiencing death or substantial bodily harm.)

PROBLEM #2. ANSWER C IS THE BEST ANSWER.

Smith and Jones cannot be disqualified under imputed disqualification. Imputed disqualification is relevant because Lawyer Travis recently went to work for Smith and Jones after practicing at Wilson and Craig. Rule 1.10 prescribes standards by which an entire firm can be disqualified due to a conflict of interest attributable to one lawyer in that firm. However, no Smith and Jones lawyer is disqualifiable under Rule 1.10(a). Smith and Jones would have been disqualified from representing First National Bank if Wilson and Craig represented Sims (while Lawyer Travis was at Wilson and Craig) on the same or a substantially related matter as the current case, and during that time Lawyer Travis acquired confidential information that is material to the *First National Bank* case.

Answer A is incorrect; information about the fee misunderstanding hardly would appear to qualify as information which could be used to Sims's disadvantage, especially if Smith never suspected Sims of any breach of fiduciary duty (a likely issue in *First National Bank v. Sims*) in Sims's role as executor. Rule 1.9(b) mandates that an attorney not use information relating to a prior representation to the disadvantage of the former client, without the consent of the former client. Smith and Jones represented Sims in the estate matter. **Answer B is incorrect**. The firm of Smith and Jones cannot be disqualified under Rule 1.9, because the current representation against Sims and the prior representation of Sims are not the same matter under Rule 1.9. Under Rule 1.9(a), an attorney who formerly represented a client in a matter cannot thereafter represent another person in the same or a substantially related matter where the current client's interests are materially adverse to the former client's interests, unless the former client consents after consultation. The only direct representation by Smith and Jones of Sims occurred when Sims was executor of the Dale estate. Even conceding that Smith and Jones represented Sims and not the estate itself, the prior administration of an estate is not factually identical or substantially the same matter as the fraud case brought by First National. **Answer D is incorrect**. The only information Smith learned from Sims that did not end up in papers filed in court was a fee misunderstanding mediated by Smith.

PROBLEM #3. ANSWER D IS THE BEST ANSWER.

Lawyer Travis acquired no confidential information whatsoever about Sims's breach of contract case while at Wilson and Craig, much less any information which would be material to the *First National Bank* case. Because there does not appear to be any violation of Rule 1.9, Smith and Jones may continue to represent First National Bank in its lawsuit against Sims. **Answer A is incorrect**; one dispute is a 2009 breach of contract case between Sims and his business partner. The *First National Bank* case deals with defrauding the bank in 2008. The two matters are not factually the same or even substantially related. **Answer B is incorrect**; while Lawyer Travis worked at Wilson and Craig, he did no work on on any matter where Sims was involved, as a bank officer or personally, but he does recall Sims's representation by Wilson and Craig in a dispute between Sims and Sims's business partner. **Answer C is incorrect**. Even if the two cases were substantially related, Travis's general recollections are irrelevant. Rule 1.9(b)(2) requires that a lawyer must "not ... knowingly represent a person in the same or a substantially related matter in which a firm with which the lawyer formerly was associated had previously represented a client ... about whom the lawyer had acquired [confidential] information ... that is material to the matter, unless the former client gives informed consent.... "

PROBLEM #4. ANSWER A IS THE BEST ANSWER.

The earlier representation of Minutia related to a completely different matter, Lawyer Kussy is not violating Rule 1.9. In addition, nothing during that prior time of collecting delinquent accounts would have revealed any confidential information about his then client. **Answer B is incorrect.** Lawyer Kussy *is* subject to discipline for violating Rule 3.3(a)(1), which states that an attorney cannot make false statements relating to a witness's availability to testify. Rule 3.3(a)(1) prohibits an attorney from knowingly making a false statement of fact to a tribunal. In his interrogatory answer, Lawyer Kussy stated that Dr. Doan would be testifying for his client at trial. Dr. Doan and a corroborating witness clearly testified that Dr. Doan never agreed to serve as an expert witness for Lawyer Kussy. **C is incorrect.** Lawyer Kussy also is subject to discipline under Rule 3.4(c), which states that an attorney shall not knowingly "disobey an obligation under the rules of a tribunal." Because this jurisdiction has a local rule which requires a litigant to answer interrogatories fairly and not falsely or in a manner calculated to mislead, Lawyer Kussy failed to obey this rule's requirement to provide truthful disclosures when he signed the interrogatory response knowing that it falsely stated that Dr. Doan would be an expert witness in the case. By violating the local rule, Lawyer Kussy also violated Rule 3.4(c) and therefore answer C is incorrect. **Answer D is incorrect.** Under Rule 3.4(d), an attorney must make a reasonably diligent effort to comply with a legally proper discovery request by an opposing party. When counsel for Minutia sent an interrogatory to Lawyer Kussy seeking information about expert witnesses for trial, Lawyer Kussy had an obligation to comply with that request. Instead, the hearing testimony established that Lawyer Kussy failed to make a diligent effort to determine if Dr. Doan had agreed to be his expert, as well as a failure to make diligent efforts to determine the content of Dr. Doan's purported testimony if he were called as Lawyer Kussy's expert witness.

PROBLEM #5. ANSWER A IS THE BEST ANSWER.

Under Rule 1.15, a lawyer can deposit the cash proceeds belonging to the client in her trust account only for a brief period until payment to the client can be made. The rule requires a lawyer to hold the property of a client that is in her possession in connection with a representation separate from her own property in a separate account. Complete records of those funds must be kept by the attorney. Rule 1.15(c) states that when, as a result of representing a client, a lawyer possesses property in which she and the client both claim interests, the property is to be kept separate by the attorney until there is an accounting and severance of their interests. When a dispute arises about the respective interests of the attorney and the client, the amount in dispute must be kept separate by the attorney until the dispute is resolved. It was proper for Lawyer Jones to put the $250,000 check in her trust account but only for a brief period. That account exists for (1) any sum belonging to the client until payment to the client can be made, and (2) any sum that is disputed. The initial deposit in the account was permissible, but the $150,000 (60% of the $250,00 corpus) to which the client was clearly entitled should have been paid the client promptly, and the attorney should have withdrawn her $62,500 which the client conceded was due. $37,500 is in dispute here, and the remainder cannot be held hostage in the dispute. **Answer B is incorrect.** Lawyer Jones may not withdraw the $37,500, regardless of whether she thinks the client is wrong on the contract. Under Rules 1.15(a) and (c), Lawyer Jones must deposit the $250,000 check in her trust account, but must immediately pay the client the undisputed part of the fee. She also must promptly withdrawn her undisputed part of the fee. She cannot withdraw the disputed part of the fee.

Answers C and D also are incorrect. Under Rule 1.15, a lawyer who is in possession of property in which a client has an interest must promptly notify the client and deliver the property to the client. Rule 1.15(a) requires a lawyer to hold the property of a client that is in her possession in connection with a representation separate from her own property. Under Rule 1.15(b), when a lawyer receives property in which her client has an interest, she must promptly notify her client. Unless otherwise agreed with the client, the lawyer must promptly deliver the property which the client is entitled to receive to the client. In this case, non-cash property like the necklace must be safeguarded in a safe deposit box or other secure location. When Jones wore the necklace, she was neither safeguarding it nor returning it to the rightful owner—her client.

She was treating the client's property as her own, in effect commingling the client's property with her own. Under Rules 1.15(a) and (b), upon receiving the necklace to which her client is entitled, Lawyer Jones must immediately notify her client about the necklace and deliver it to the client. She is commingling her client's property with her own if she wears the necklace. The necklace belongs to her client, and Lawyer Jones cannot keep it as leverage to use in connection with her unresolved monetary disagreements with her client.

PROBLEM #6. ANSWER A IS THE BEST ANSWER.

Under Rule 8.4(b), discipline may be imposed for crimes that reflect "adversely on the lawyer's honesty, trustworthiness or fitness as a lawyer." Having a defective tail light does not reflect adversely on the lawyer's fitness to practice law. **B is incorrect**; Lawyer Simson's fitness to practice law may be based upon his conduct regardless of whether he is acting in his professional capacity at the time. **C is incorrect**; lack of respect for the law is not the standard used by the Model Rules; the standard is honesty, trustworthiness or fitness as a lawyer. **D is incorrect**, because A is correct.

PROBLEM #7. ANSWER D IS THE BEST ANSWER.

Rule 8.4(c) prohibits lawyers from engaging in "dishonesty, fraud, deceit, or misrepresentation." By contrast, issues of "personal morality, such as adultery" lack a specific connection to a person's fitness to practice law. **A is incorrect**. Rule 8.4(c)'s prohibition applies regardless of whether the lawyer's misconduct occurs while is his acting in his capacity as a lawyer. **B is incorrect**; the misconduct occurs upon submission of the fraudulent claim, regardless of any kickback received by Lawyer Cowell. **C is incorrect**; as with answer A, the prohibition against "dishonesty, fraud, deceit, or misrepresentation" is applicable without an accompanying conflict of interest.

PROBLEM #8. ANSWER B IS THE BEST ANSWER.

Under Rule 8.3(a), the scope of the lawyer's duty to report misconduct does not include a duty to report any and all misconduct. The obligation to report requires that a lawyer know that another lawyer has violated the Rules. A reasonable belief about the violation does not trigger the obligation. The Rule focuses on conduct that raises a "substantial question" about the other lawyer's "honesty, trustworthiness or fitness as a lawyer." "Substantial" refers to the seriousness of the possible offense. The duty includes the exercise of judgment about the seriousness of the violation. Knowledge of the theft from the client would trigger the lawyer's duty to disclose. However, the Rule 8.3(a) duty to report is extinguished or super-seded by the duty of confidentiality under Rule 1.6, as here when Lawyer Dardeen's client tells Lawyer Dardeen that another lawyer (Lark) has engaged in serious misconduct. **A is incorrect**; without the exception previously mentioned, A would be the right answer under the general proposition of Rule 8.3(a). **C is incorrect**, because the Rule 8.3(a) duty does not have a threshold amount that triggers the duty to report. **D is incorrect**, because the motive for reporting Lark's misconduct is irrelevant to the duty to report Lark.

PROBLEM #9. ANSWER D IS THE BEST ANSWER.

Pursuant to Rule 1.5(d), all three of the preceding fee arrangements are ethical alternatives. Because the facts indicate that none of the fee arrangements discussed involves a criminal case, Rule 1.5(d)(2) does not render any of them unreasonable *per se*. That Rule prohibits any arrangement for charging or collecting a contingent fee for representing a defendant in a criminal case. **Answer A** is a reasonable fee, which provides that a fee is earned when it is paid, before any work is begun. When someone pays a lawyer in advance, the lawyer charges her fee against the advance payment as she earns it. The lawyer should deposit the advance fee in her client trust account until she earns it. Typically, if she does not earn the entire amount of the advance fee, she must return the unearned portion to her client, but here the nonrefundable aspect of the retainer is properly part of the fee agreement. **Answer B** is correct, because it is a reasonable fee, which may depend on whether it was fixed or contingent on the outcome of the representation. Contingent fees may appear large in retrospect, but not if the client considers that the lawyer risked earning nothing in the matter. **Answer C** provides for a reasonable fee arrangement, even though the nature of the fee is a hybrid—part fixed and part contingent.

PROBLEM #10. ANSWER D IS THE BEST ANSWER.

One example of a concurrent client conflict exists under Rule 1.7(a)(1), which prohibits a lawyer from representing a client if that representation "will be directly adverse to another client." The nature of the conflict is between two current clients. The Rule is based on the lawyer's obligation of loyalty to the lawyer's current clients, who expects that the lawyer will not represent someone whose interests are "directly adverse" to theirs. Suing a current client like Gore, even on an unrelated matter, is a directly adverse conflict. A second example of a concurrent client conflict occurs under Rule 1.7(a)(2), which prohibits representation if there is a significant risk that the representation will be "materially limited" by the lawyer's responsibilities to another, whether that client is a current client, a former client, a third person, or even the lawyer herself. "Materially limited" conflicts focus on client harm, implicating significant risks that the lawyer's ability to represent a current client is limited by the lawyer's other obligations. In other words, there is a "significant risk" exists that the representation of one client will affect the lawyer's obligations to other clients or to herself.

To resolve the Rule 1.7(a) conflicts of interest, Rule 1.7(b) has four requirements. A lawyer must independently decide whether she can competently and diligently represent all the affected clients, and not represent one client against another client "in the same litigation." Each of the affected clients must give the lawyer "informed consent, confirmed in writing." There are situations when a conflict cannot be saved by client consent. A lawyer cannot continue a conflicted representation unless she "reasonably believe[s]" that she can provide competent, diligent representation to those clients whose circumstances present the lawyer's conflict. Under Rule 1.7(b)(3), in any case before a tribunal, a lawyer cannot represent two or more clients who are asserting claims against each other. The general rule is that a lawyer cannot sue a client like Gore on behalf of a client like Kemp, while representing Gore on an unrelated matter. Even though the cases are unrelated and create no danger of using the confidential information from one case to assist the representation in the other case, the lawyer breached the duty of loyalty to Gore by accepting Kemp's case. The rule exists to prevent either an actual or apparent conflict in loyalties or a reduction in the zeal of the representation.

A is incorrect; under Rule 1.10 on imputed disqualification, if Choate is disqualified from representing Kemp, anyone associated with Choate is also disqualified from representing Kemp. **B is incorrect**. Although it is plausible for Choate to refer Kemp to another lawyer when Choate is disqualified from representing Kemp, the use of a referral fee is unethical because Choate would be receiving a fee for something he was not ethically permitted to do, i.e., represent Kemp. Even if Choate were permitted to represent Kemp but decided to refer the case to another law firm the nature of fee sharing arrangement here is improper. Lawyers in different firms may divide fees only under specified conditions. First, the division must either be divided in proportion to the services performed by each lawyer or have each of them assume joint financial and ethical responsibility for the case. Second, Kemp would have to agree in writing to the division, including the share for Choate and the other law firm. Rule 1.5, Comment 7. Finally, as with all fees, the total fee must be reasonable. Rule 1.5(e)(1)-(3). **C is incorrect**.

As discussed in the previous paragraph, Choate's conflict of interest cannot be saved by Kemp's consent. The general rule is that a lawyer cannot sue a client like Gore on behalf of a client like Kemp, while representing Gore on an unrelated matter. Rule 1.7(b)(3).

PROBLEM #11. ANSWER A IS THE BEST ANSWER.

Rule 7.3 states that in-person, live telephone, and real-time electronic (as with chat rooms or instant messaging) solicitations of a prospective client are prohibited when the lawyer's significant motive is her own compensation. Defining prohibited solicitations requires enumeration of permitted solicitations. One of those permitted solicitations is with former clients. **B is incorrect**. Even if Bert's motive in informing Ernie about how Ernie's legal situation may have changed is to secure further employment by Ernie, the choice in retaining Bert in this matter is Ernie's. The purpose of the Rule is to ensure that a former client's legal rights are not adversely affected by a change in the law. **C is incorrect**; as mentioned, the purpose of this exception is to protect the rights of the former client even if the former client chooses not to renew the lawyer-client relationship with Bert. **D is incorrect**. Solicitations of former clients function as an exception to the general rules against client solicitation. Rule 7.3(a)(2).

PROBLEM #12. ANSWER C IS THE BEST ANSWER.

Recusal is required under CJC 2.11(A) when the judge or a person within the third degree of relationship or that person's spouse or domestic partner has more than a *de minimis* interest that could be substantially affected by the proceeding. CJC 2.11(A)(2)(c). In answer C, the interest of the minor child is equal to three one-thousandth of a percent, which is not "more than a *de minimis* interest." CJC Rule 2.11(A) requires judicial recusal when the judge knows that she, her spouse or her domestic partner, or a person within the third degree of relationship to either of them, or the spouse or domestic partner of such a person is a lawyer in the proceeding (**answer A**, per CJC 2.11(A)(2)(b)); has personal knowledge about the disputed facts in the proceeding (**answer B**, per CJC 2.11(A)(1)) and is likely to be a material witness in the case (**answer D**, per CJC 2.11(A)(2)(d)). Thus, in answers A, B and D, the judge is required to disqualify himself.

PROBLEM #13. ANSWER D IS THE BEST ANSWER.

Under CJC Rule 2.4(B), a judge cannot permit her family interests or relationships (e.g., her husband's political candidacy) to influence her judicial conduct. **Answer A is incorrect** because, 1) CJC Rule

4.1(A)(4), prohibits a judge from soliciting funds for a candidate for public office, 2) CJC Rule 4.1(A)(3) prohibits a judge from publicly endorsing a candidate for public office, and 3) CJC Rule 4.1(A)(5) prohibits a judge from attending events sponsored by a candidate for public office. **Answer B is incorrect** because, under CJC Rule 3.1(E), a judge must not make use of her stationery to engage in prohibited extrajudicial activities. **Answer C is incorrect**. CJC Rule 4.1(A)(5) a judge is prohibited from attending events sponsored by a candidate for public office.

PROBLEM #14. ANSWER D IS THE BEST ANSWER.

Under Rule 1.8(a), as a fiduciary of her client, a lawyer has duties regarding relationships with her client that fall outside the lawyer-client relationship. The focus of the Rules is on whether a transaction by a lawyer with her client is fair and reasonable to the client, i.e., that the lawyer does not abuse her position of trust. Under Rule 1.8(a), a lawyer may knowingly enter into a business transaction with a client only if: (1) the transaction is fair and reasonable to the client, including the lawyer's role, (2) the terms of the transaction are given by the lawyer to her in writing in clear language so that she can understand the terms, (3) she is advised in writing that she can consult another lawyer, and (4) she gives informed consent in writing. **D is correct** because Mary Ann failed to present the loan proposal to her client Ginger in writing. **Answer A is incorrect**, because the Rules do not create a complete ban on business transactions with clients. Such transactions are permitted, as long as the aforementioned steps are followed. **B is incorrect**. Because Ginger was Mary Ann's client when Mary Ann sought the loan, the provisions of Rule 1.8(a) apply. **C is incorrect**, because the client's level of sophistication is irrelevant; no matter whether a client is a sophisticated consumer of legal services, the Rule 1.8 requirements must be followed.

PROBLEM #15. ANSWER C IS THE BEST ANSWER.

Rule 1.9(c) states a lawyer like Rubble cannot disclose information relating to a former client's representation (regardless of whether he learned it from Fred or others) unless the Rules permit or require disclosure or unless that information has become generally known. A is incorrect. The Rules use the phrase "directly adverse" to apply to conflicts between two current clients. The facts here describe a situation of successive, not simultaneous, representation, where Attorney Rubble in 2010 seeks to represent a client in a lawsuit against Fred, whom he represented in 2008. In cases of successive representation, Rule 1.9 imposes duties on lawyers to their former clients. **Answer A is incorrect**. Rule 1.9 does permit lawyers to represent others against their former clients under limited circumstances. **B is incorrect**. The Rules about successive representation apply regardless of whether the lawyer with the potential conflict of interest has a prior professional relationship with the new client. **D is incorrect**. Attorney Rubble may be subject to discipline, although the malpractice claim in 2008 is not the same or substantially related to the product liability case in 2010. For the aforementioned reasons relating to the use of a former client's confidential information to his disadvantage, Attorney Rubble may be subject to discipline if he uses confidential information he learned while representing Fred inn 2008 against Fred while representing Dino in a different case during 2010.

PROBLEM #16. ANSWER D IS THE BEST ANSWER.

Under Rules 1.7(a) and 1.10, Attorney Brian would be subject to discipline for representing Fruit Truck because screening of a disqualified lawyer like Attorney Blinky is not permitted in order that Attorney Brian can represent Fruit Truck. Attorney Brian would be subject to discipline if he represented Fruit Truck. **A is incorrect**. Rule 1.7(a) prohibits representation of Fruit Truck by Attorney Blinky if there is a significant risk that the representation will be "materially limited" by Attorney Blinky's current or former responsibilities to another client such as World Bank. "Materially limited" conflicts focus on client harm, implicating significant risks that Attorney Blinky's ability to represent Fruit Truck is limited by her obligations to World Bank. If Attorney Blinky were to be disqualified from representing Fruit Truck due to Rule 1.7(a), the question then becomes whether Brian also is disqualified because Brian is Attorney Blinky's associate. When a lawyer is disqualified from representing a client, generally none of the lawyers with whom she is affiliated can represent that client either. Rule 1.10(a). The rationale is that a lawyer uses all the resources of his firm in representing a client, including sharing confidential information with her colleagues. All lawyers with whom she is affiliated owe a duty of loyalty to their clients. A client like World Bank that is affected by imputed disqualification principles may waive its protections by giving informed consent confirmed in writing, if the otherwise disqualified lawyer like Brian reasonably believes that he will be able to provide competent and diligent representation for Fruit Truck. Rule 1.10(c).

B is incorrect, because screening is not approved generally in the Rules. (True, a screen may suffice to remove the imputation of disqualification, by walling off the disqualified lawyer and permitting his colleagues to proceed with the representation. Screening "denotes the isolation of a lawyer from any participation in a matter through the timely imposition of procedures within a firm that are reasonably adequate under the circumstances to protect information that the isolated lawyer is obligated to protect under these Rules or other law." Rule 1.0(k).) While screening has been approved in the case law, in some state disciplinary codes, in the Restatement, and in specific conflict of interest Rules such as Rules 1.11, 1.12, and 1.18, it is not approved as an alternative approach to the general imputed disqualification. **C is incorrect** for many of the aforementioned reasons that A and B are incorrect. Neither Attorney Blinky nor Attorney Brian could represent Fruit Truck without threat of discipline. Attorney Blinky cannot represent Fruit Truck because her ability to do so would be materially limited by her current or former responsibilities to World Bank. Even if that were not the case, her belief that she would be able to to provide competent and diligent representation to Fruit Truck is not reasonable. Even if her belief was reasonable, it is unlikely that World Bank would give an informed consent for Attorney Blinky to represent Fruit Truck.

PROBLEM #17. ANSWER A IS THE BEST ANSWER.

If a lawyer represents a client and knows that another person is represented by his own lawyer, the lawyer cannot communicate with that person about that matter, unless the other lawyer consents or the contact is authorized by law or court order. Rule 4.2. The rationale for the Rule is to prevent a lawyer from unduly influencing the other person. The represented person does not have to be a party or be adverse to the lawyer's client. The Rule refers to communications relating only to the matter in which the person is represented. Woodrow's knowledge that the bookkeeper is represented by counsel "may be inferred from the circumstances." Rule 4.2, Comment 8. Here, having filed suit against CBE and Wayne, Woodrow knows that CBE has its own lawyer, because CBE answered the complaint through its lawyer, Thus, Woodrow was obligated by Rule 4.2 to obtain the consent of CBE's lawyer prior to interviewing one of its current employees. **B is incorrect**, because Rule 4.2 applies not only to the party but also to its employees such as the bookkeeper. **C is incorrect**, because it was necessary to obtain the consent of CBE only. Because the bookkeeper is employed by CBE and not by Wayne, only CBE's lawyer's consent was necessary prior to Woodrow ethically being able to speak to any of CBE's employees. CBE's lawyer's consent is necessary only if the assistant bookkeeper is an important part of the CBE decision-making personnel. Rule 4.2, Comment 7. **D is incorrect**. Rule 4.2 applies to any employee of a party, not just to those who have significant responsibilities within the party-organization. The standard stated in answer D is relevant to the scope of the lawyer-client privilege in a corporate setting; some jurisdictions follow the "control group" test and others follows the "subject matter" test.

PROBLEM #18. ANSWER D IS THE BEST ANSWER.

There are various reasons for a lawyer to possess her client's property, e.g., a settlement check which she owes to her client. The Rules seek to protect the property of others in a lawyer's possession and to maintain both the fact and appearance of her honesty. Lawyers must keep separate identifiable trust fund accounts of clients' funds and they must not be commingled with her money. Rule 1.15(a). The lawyer's duty includes safeguarding legal fees and expenses which have been paid in advance until they have been earned or incurred. Rule 1.15(c). The proper procedure is to withdraw funds from the client's account when a lawyer is entitled to do so, place it in her account, and then write a check on her account for that amount. After a lawyer receives funds belonging in a trust fund account, she must promptly notify the client or non-client third party. She also must promptly pay or deliver to the client any trust funds or property to which she is entitled. Thus, even if it is in the best interest of the client, a lawyer cannot withhold notice or payment, unless she has a prior agreement with her client. If a lawyer and her client have a dispute about trust fund property, she cannot withdraw the disputed portion of the fee until the dispute is resolved. Rule 1.15(e). The lawyer must distribute the undisputed portion promptly. She must not coerce her client to give up her claim by refusing to deliver money that belongs to the client. As the foregoing indicates, answers **A, B, and C are incorrect**.

PROBLEM #19. ANSWER A IS THE BEST ANSWER.

A lawyer cannot knowingly make false statements of fact to a tribunal. Rule 3.3(a)(1). While she does not testify to a tribunal under oath, any factual assertions to the tribunal ("my client is ill") must be based on her knowledge that she knows is true or believes to be true on the basis of a reasonably diligent inquiry. The "failure to make a disclosure is the equivalent of an affirmative misrepresentation." Rule 3.3, Comment 3. **B is incorrect**. Since 2002, the Rule 3.3(a)(1) prohibition against making false factual statements is not dependent upon the falsely made fact being "material." **C is incorrect**. Having knowingly made a false statement of fact to the court, his intent to deceive the court is irrelevant. **D is incorrect**. When a trial judge asks a lawyer a question, the lawyer is not under oath when he answers the question. Thus, no perjury was committed when Lawyer Luke lied to the judge about Client Callie's location.

PROBLEM #20. ANSWER C IS THE BEST ANSWER.

As with any lawyer-client relationship, Lawyer Len is free to offer advice to Client Redd about how Client Redd is spending his money.

A lawyer who is concerned about a client's ability to act in his own interest may want to take action to protect her client. A lawyer like Lawyer Len may do so, but only under the circumstances described in Rule 1.14(b), which requires that the lawyer "reasonably believe[] that the client has diminished capacity, is at risk of substantial physical, financial or other harm unless action is taken, and cannot adequately act in the client's own interest." As a preliminary matter, the lawyer must make an assessment of the client's capacity. Rule 1.14, Comment 6 lists factors to be considered by a lawyer in assessing the nature and extent of her client's diminished capacity. If Lawyer Len has determined that protective action is permitted under the Rule 1.14(b) criteria, only reasonably necessary measures that constitute the "least restrictive action under the circumstances" may be imposed. ABA Formal Opinion 96–404. **A and B are both incorrect**. Here, neither Lawyer Len's disagreement with Client Redd's position nor Lawyer Len's belief that Client Redd is acting unwisely suffices to justify "protective action." ABA Formal Opinion 96–404. In other words, a lawyer cannot act under Rule 1.14 when she has an imprudent but competent client. **D is also incorrect**. Under certain circumstances Lawyer Len may seek appointment of a guardian for a client with diminished capacity if he has decided that less drastic measures will be inadequate to protect Client Redd's interests. However, here the premise for taking that action is missing, i.e., Client Redd is not demonstrating a diminished capacity that should lead to appointment of a guardian.

PROBLEM #21. ANSWER D IS THE BEST ANSWER.

A lawyer must not offer evidence that she knows is false. Rule 3.3(a)(3). As an officer of the court, a lawyer cannot participate in misleading the court even when the client insists. If other law requires a lawyer to keep silent or permits the lawyer's client to present false testimony through a narrative approach, that law supersedes the Rules. Rule 3.3, Comment 7. The facts here do not refer to a narrative approach. If Lawyer Powell learns before the conclusion of the proceedings that a piece of "material evidence" she offered was false when admitted, she must take reasonable remedial measures. Rule 3.3(a)(3). Her first attempt should be to convince Client Jones to correct the false testimony. If her efforts are not successful, she must consider withdrawing from the representation. Her duty to take reasonable remedial measures supersedes any duty of confidentiality to Client Jones under Rule 1.6. If withdrawal is not possible or if it will not reverse the effect of the false evidence, Lawyer Powell must disclose the false information to the tribunal which then must decide how to proceed—to inform the factfinder, to declare a mistrial, or to do nothing. Rule 3.3, Comment 10.

A is incorrect. If Client Jones tells Lawyer Powell that his sister will testify falsely, Lawyer Powell's duty of candor requires that she not call that witness. If a lawyer reasonably believes but does not "know" that a piece of evidence is false, she may refuse to offer it. **B is incorrect.** If Client Jones wants Lawyer Powell to present the false evidence, Lawyer Powell or Client Jones may prefer to terminate the lawyer-client relationship. For cases already before a tribunal, the court's permission to withdraw as counsel is necessary. Rule 1.16(a). However, Rule 1.16(c) indicates that a trial judge may deny a motion by a lawyer to withdraw and order a lawyer to "continue representation notwithstanding good cause for terminating the representation." **C is incorrect.** The Supreme Court has held that there is no constitutional right for a party to lie or for a lawyer to assist in that perjury. *Nix v. Whiteside*, 475 U.S. 157 (1986). Lawyer Powell may refuse to call Client Jones as a witness, although in criminal cases he has a constitutional right to testify (but not falsely). Court rules may allow Client Jones to testify in some narrative form but not permit Lawyer Powell to elicit any testimony from Client Jones.

PROBLEM #22. ANSWER A IS THE BEST ANSWER.

Rule 3.3(b) states: "A lawyer who represents a client in an adjudicative proceeding and who knows that a person intends to engage, is engaging or has engaged in … fraudulent conduct related to the proceeding shall take reasonable remedial measures, including, if necessary, disclosure to the tribunal." In this case, the "person" who engaged in fraudulent conduct was Client Clyde. Lawyer Cahill failed to reveal to the court the reduction of the marital assets which caused the court to continue to divide the couple's property based on the false premise that the IRA account still existed. In discussing the steps Lawyer Cahill must take before disclosing fraud to the court, Rule 3.3, Comment 10 states:

> Having offered material evidence in the belief that it was true, a lawyer may subsequently come to know that the evidence is false. Or, a lawyer may be surprised when the lawyer's client, or another witness called by the lawyer, offers testimony the lawyer knows to be false, either during the lawyer's direct examination or in response to cross-examination by the opposing lawyer. In such situations or if the lawyer knows of the falsity of testimony elicited from the client during a deposition, the lawyer must take reasonable remedial measures. In such situations, the advocate's proper course is to remonstrate with the client confidentially, advise the client of the lawyer's duty of candor to the tribunal and seek the client's cooperation with respect to the withdrawal or correction of the false statements

or evidence. If that fails, the advocate must take further remedial action. If withdrawal from the representation is not permitted or will not undo the effect of the false evidence, the advocate must make such disclosure to the tribunal as is reasonably necessary to remedy the situation, even if doing so requires the lawyer to reveal information that otherwise would be protected by Rule 1.6. It is for the tribunal then to determine what should be done—making a statement about the matter to the trier of fact, ordering a mistrial or perhaps nothing.

B is incorrect, because as noted Lawyer Cahill must first call upon her client to rectify the situation before considering disclosure to the court. **C is incorrect**. This answer is taken from DR 7–102(B) of the ABA Model Code of Professional Responsibility, which described a lawyer's duty to reveal a client's fraud on the court but which also created an exception for the duty to report where as here the information was confidential. **D is incorrect**. Under Rule 1.16(b), Lawyer Cahill had the discretion to withdraw because Client Clyde was using Lawyer Cahill's services to perpetrate a crime or fraud. Instead of withdrawing, however, Lawyer Cahill proceeded to facilitate Client Clyde's misleading of the court which is not an acceptable option to withdrawal.

PROBLEM #23. ANSWER C IS THE BEST ANSWER.

Rule 3.3(b) states: "A lawyer who represents a client in an adjudicative proceeding and who knows that a person intends to engage, is engaging or has engaged in ... fraudulent conduct related to the proceeding shall take reasonable remedial measures, including, if necessary, disclosure to the tribunal." This Rule applies to the facts here, because Lawyer Linda has represented Client Hamilton who is a preferred creditor in the estate of Simione. The confidential information Client Hamilton has told Lawyer Linda pertains to the manner in which Abner as executor for the Simione estate has stolen from that estate. Under Rule 3.3(b), because the "person" who engages in fraudulent or criminal conduct does not have to be the lawyer's client or the client's witness, Lawyer Linda had a duty to disclose Abner's fraudulent conduct. Because Lawyer Linda had represented Client Hamilton in prior matters, she had a reason to trust the credibility of what he told her, albeit in confidence, and therefore it can be said that Lawyer Linda "knows" that Abner has engaged in fraudulent or criminal conduct. What creates a discipline problem for lawyer Linda, however, is the scope of the disclosure she has made about Abner's misconduct. Rule 3.3(b) is clear that she has a duty to make the disclosure to the probate judge, and any further disclosure is beyond the scope of her duty under that Rule. When she sent the memorandum to the public officials (other than the probate judge) and to the local newspaper, she has violated both Rule 1.6 and Rule 3.3(b). A is incorrect, because as mentioned, even if Lawyer Linda did have a duty to report the misconduct by Abner, her disclosure went beyond the Rule required her to do. **B is incorrect** as well, because Lawyer Linda has a duty to disclose rather than the discretion to disclose. **D is incorrect** because neither A nor B is a correct answer.

PROBLEM #24. ANSWER D IS THE BEST ANSWER.

Rule 1.8(h)(1) prohibits a lawyer from making an agreement prospectively limiting the lawyer's liability regarding future services, unless a client has independent representation. Courts and bar association ethics opinions generally agree that placing a binding arbitration clause in a retainer agreement does not violate the Rule 1.8(h)(1) prohibition. Accord, Rule 1.8, Comment 14. As answer D suggests, a binding arbitration clause does not limit a lawyer's prospective liability, but instead simply uses an arbitration panel instead of a court to resolve the malpractice claim. ABA Formal Ethics Opinion 02–425 requires that a client: 1) be advised about the advantages and disadvantages of arbitration, such as waiver of jury trial and waiver of appeal, 2) give informed consent, and 3) not be prevented from suing his lawyer which he has a right to pursue under existing law. Under those circumstances, a lawyer may include an arbitration clause in a fee agreement without violating her fiduciary duties. For the reasons just stated, **A is incorrect**, because an arbitration clause in a fee agreement is not regarded as a limitation on a prospective malpractice claim by the client. **B and C are incorrect**, with each stating the same incorrect proposition—that another lawyer must be consulted before an arbitration clause will be upheld. Consultation with a lawyer is relevant under Rule 1.8(h)(1) only if a lawyer does attempt to limit her future malpractice liability.

PROBLEM #25. ANSWER D IS THE BEST ANSWER.

A lawyer for an entity represents the entity, and has an ethical obligation to act on her knowledge about an entity's agent's activities which are likely to result in substantial injury to the entity. Rule 1.13(a) requires an lawyer representing an entity to understand that the entity, acting through its officers and others, is the client. **Answer A is incorrect**. When *any* lawyer such as the Associate General Counsel who represents the entity knows that an agent of the entity has acted or intends to act in a manner which is likely to result in substantial injury to the entity, Rule 1.13 states that she must proceed to act in a way which appears reasonably necessary to be in the best interest of the entity. Here, Jordan represents

Continental Towing as the Associate General Counsel. She has knowledge about the General Counsel's intentions relating to the acquisition. Her awareness suggests that it is reasonably necessary to act in the best interest of the entity and speak to the CEO.

Answer B is incorrect. According to Rule 1.13(b), once the lawyer *knows* about the likelihood of substantial injury (not just any injury) to the entity by its agent, her possible actions include: 1) talking to the person whose conduct has produced the ethical dilemma, and urging him to reconsider its likely consequences for the entity; or 2) referring the matter to a higher authority in the organization, including referral to the highest internal authority such as a Chief Executive Officer. To speak directly to the General Counsel here appears futile, given her awareness of his previous conduct in trying to promote his own interest at the risk of harming the entity. The General Counsel may discharge Jordan immediately for her knowledge about his activities and/or her questioning of his authority. **Answer C is incorrect**. Jordan is not limited to speaking to the General Counsel, although speaking first to the CEO may yield the same result in getting Jordan fired. If the CEO does not address Jordan's concerns, she may address the entity's highest authority, probably the Board of Directors, in an effort to protect the interests of the entity. If, despite her best efforts to comply with Rule 1.13(b), Jordan believes that the CEO and the Board are not addressing her concerns about the entity, Rule 1.13(c) permits her as lawyer for the entity to reveal information relating to her acquisition concerns if she reasonably believes that disclosure is necessary to prevent substantial injury to the entity.

PROBLEM #26. ANSWER C IS THE BEST ANSWER.

A lawyer who sells his law practice cannot disclose to a potential buyer confidential information about his clients, their cases, or their files. Once there is an agreement about a sale, Tipton's clients have a reasonable chance to consent or withhold consent before confidences are revealed to Tipton's nephews. Each client must receive written notice of the proposed sale, the right to retain other counsel, and the right to take possession of her file. Rule 1.17(c)(1)-(3). Consent to disclosure is presumed if a client does not object or respond within ninety days. Rule 1.17(c)(3). If a client cannot be given notice, the buyer must obtain a court order authorizing the transfer, and the court decides whether reasonable efforts to locate and notify the client have occurred. **A is incorrect.** Rule 1.17 permits a lawyer like Tipton to sell either his entire practice *or* an entire area of practice to one or more lawyers or law firms. In other words, as to the sale of an area of your practice, a lawyer cannot sell some cases of one type but keep other cases of the same type. Several collateral restrictions on the sale of a law practice accompany the sale. **B is incorrect.** Tipton can practice law even after selling his law practice. Becoming in-house counsel, working for the government, or working for a legal services entity does not constitute a return to private law practice. Rule 1.17, Comment 3. **D is incorrect**. Tipton's nephew, as the buyer of the law practice cannot increase the fee charged to Tipton's former clients. Rule 1.17(d).

PROBLEM #27. ANSWER C IS THE BEST ANSWER.

Rule 6.5 applies to a lawyer's participation in a short-term legal services program sponsored by a nonprofit organization or a court, as when the lawyer has no expectation of a continuing lawyer-client relationship. Under the circumstance of a short-term legal services program, the current client or former client conflict Rules (1.7 and 1.9) do not apply unless the lawyer is aware of a conflict of interest at the time. Rule 6.5(a)(1). If Lawyer Lori is aware of a conflict, she cannot represent the Wills Clinic client even in a short-term context. Here, answer C states that Lawyer Lori is aware that one of her current clients has a property dispute about title to a piece of property. If Lawyer Lori were unaware of such a conflict of interest, she may form a lawyer-client relation with a Wills Clinic client and give short-term legal advice. **A is incorrect**, because the previous discussion notes the potential for discipline under Rule 6.5, even when a lawyer is generous enough to donate her professional time to a project like a Wills Clinic for senior citizens. **B is incorrect** because it states the opposite of C, which is correct. **D is incorrect**, because imputed disqualification under Rule 1.10 applies only if Lawyer Lori knows that one of her Wills Clinic clients has a current or former client conflict with another lawyer in her law firm. Rule 6.5(a)(2).

PROBLEM #28. ANSWER B IS THE BEST ANSWER.

If a lawyer appears before a policy-making entity like a Congressional subcommittee or government agency to testify, she must disclose whether she is there in a representative capacity. Rule 3.9. Moreover, when a lawyer knows that the interests of her client may be significantly benefitted by a law reform decision in which she participates, such as testifying, she has an obligation to disclose that fact even though she does not have to identify her client. Rule 6.4, Comment 1. The purpose of the disclosure is to preclude any suspicion that the lawyer is using improper influence to promote her client's interests. **A is incorrect.** A lawyer may serve as an officer, director, or member of a law reform organization, even though the law reform may affect her client's interests. **C is incorrect**. When a lawyer knows that her client's interests may be materially benefitted by a decision in which she participates in that law reform organization, she must disclose that fact but she does not have to identify her client. Rule 6.4. **D is incorrect**. A lawyer such as Lawyer Stephanie who is serving on a law reform committee usually does not have a client-lawyer relationship with the organization. Otherwise, a lawyer could not serve in a law reform program that might indirectly affect a client.

PROBLEM #29. ANSWER C IS THE BEST ANSWER.

Lawyer Lynn cannot knowingly participate in a decision of action of the organization if her participation would be inconsistent with the obligations she owes to her current client or could have a "material adverse effect" on the organization's client. Rule 6.3(a)-(b). Ordering that Legal Aid no longer sue some of her private practice clients would violate this ethical obligation. **A is incorrect**. Subject to the requirements of Rule 6.3, there is no ethical violation for simultaneously serving on the governing body of a legal services organization like a Legal Aid Society and the Executive Committee of her own law firm. **B is incorrect**. A lawyer in a law firm also may serve as an officer or director of a legal services organization, even if the organization's clients have interests adverse to her client. Rule 6.3. **D is incorrect**. As a board member of such an organization while she represents a client adverse to the client of the organization, she should be screened from the decision-making process of the organization.

PROBLEM #30. ANSWER D IS THE BEST ANSWER.

Generally, a lawyer has the authority to make decisions on issues that do not either affect the merits of his client's case or substantially prejudice the client's rights. Lawyer Frank may agree unilaterally to extensions of time for the trial date, unless that is contrary to the client's express wishes. Otherwise, the client has the exclusive authority to make decisions. As the agent for the client, Lawyer Frank must follow his client's "decisions concerning the objectives of representation," but he also can act on his client's behalf in a manner which is "impliedly authorized to carry out the representation." Rule 1.2(a). For example, Lawyr Frank's client can delegate her settlement authority to Lawyer Frank by saying, "You do not have to contact me if the other side offers less than $100,000." Additionally, his client is not bound by a settlement that she has not authorized his lawyer to make. The Rules also offer examples about decision-making authority between client and lawyer. Lawyer Frank's client decides whether to accept a settlement offer, to plead guilty, to waive a jury trial, testify in her own defense in a criminal case, or to appeal. Rule 1.2(a). Under these facts, **A is incorrect**, because the client already has implicitly authorized him to reject any offer of less than $100,000. The motion for a continuance of the trial date is a procedural matter that Lawyer Frank can agree to without consent from his client, especially when the parties each have sought continuances. **B is incorrect**, because his client already has implicitly authorized Lawyer Frank to rejct any offer of settlement less than $100,000. **C is incorrect**, because the motion for a continuance is not usually a matter that will prejudice the client's rights.

PROBLEM #31. ANSWER B IS THE BEST ANSWER.

Often, the client's own lawyer has the most information about the client-defendant's ability to understand the proceedings and to consult with her. The lawyer may be called upon to testify about her client's competency to meet her burden of showing an objective and reasonable basis for believing that the client cannot act in his own interest. The majority rule is that lawyers may testify about their observations, opinions and perceptions about the client's competency *if* they do not disclose the substance of any lawyer-client communications. For that reason, B is correct and **C is incorrect**. Lawyer Harris may testify about Client Moran's physical appearances that have led her to a concern about her client's competence, but she cannot testify about their lawyer-client communications even if they relate to her concern about competence. **A is incorrect.** If Lawyer Harris has a good faith doubt about Client Moran's competency, she has a duty to raise the issues with the trial court and ask the court to determine Client Moran's competency. Rule 1.14(b) states: "When the lawyer reasonably believes that the client has diminished capacity, is at risk of substantial physical, financial or other harm unless action is taken and cannot adequately act in the client's own interest, the lawyer may take reasonably necessary protective action, including consulting with individuals or entities that have the ability to take action to protect the client.... " In *Drope v. Missouri*, 420 U.S. 162 (1975), the Supreme Court stated that "evidence of a defendant's irrational behavior, his demeanor at trial, and any prior medical opinion on competence to stand trial are all relevant in determining whether further inquiry is required, but [ ] one of these factors standing alone may, in some circumstances, be sufficient." For the same reason, **D is incorrect** as the opposite of answer A. Lawyer Harris will be subject to discipline if she fails to do anything about the competency concerns she has after hearing and observing Client Moran.

PROBLEM #32. ANSWER B IS THE BEST ANSWER.

The Rules forbid any communications by anyone that "will have a substantial likelihood of materially prejudicing an adjudicative proceeding in the matter." Rule 3.6(a). Anything a lawyer such as a prosecutor says about a witness's identity, likely testimony, credibility or prior criminal record, pretrial statements or the absence of such statements, or opinion about the defendant's guilt are examples of potentially prejudicial statements. The perspective for examining that standard is from the view of the reasonable lawyer making the statement, rather than the reasonable person. The statement in question must be one which the lawyer knows or reasonably should know will be publicly disseminated, due to its possible influence on the fact-finder. Prosecutor Peters's statement may be less prejudicial if the fact-finder is a judge instead of a jury. Despite the foregoing standard, a prosecutor may make certain extrajudicial statements: information in a public record, a request for assistance in obtaining evidence, a warning of the danger about an individual if there is reason to believe such danger exists, scheduling or steps in the litigation, general scope of the investigation, and the identities of the accused as well as that of the arresting and investigating officers. Rule 3.6(b). A prosecutor also may make statements that a reasonable lawyer would believe are required to protect a client from the "substantial undue prejudicial effect of recent publicity not initiated by" him or his client. Such statements must be limited to information that is necessary to mitigate that adverse publicity. Rule 3.6(c). **A is incorrect**, because as the examples just discussed indicate, some statements such as those about prior convictions "will have a substantial likelihood of materially prejudicing an adjudicative proceeding in the matter" and other statements such as seeking community assistance to solve criminal activity do not. **C is incorrect** for the opposite reasons that B is correct. **D is incorrect**. The truth of an extrajudicial statement does not prevent a lawyer from discipline. The Rules are clear that lawyers cannot make some statements that will be disseminated to the press if they "will have a substantial likelihood of materially prejudicing an adjudicative proceeding in the matter."

PROBLEM #33. ANSWER C IS THE BEST ANSWER.

Rule 1.18 explicitly recognizes a duty to a prospective client, even though a lawyer may not talk to him for very long or in much depth about his case and even if she ends up not representing him. A "prospective client" is a "person who discusses with a lawyer the possibility of forming a client-lawyer relationship with respect to a matter." Rule 1.18(a). Comment 2 limits this broad definition. Unilaterally giving information to the lawyer does not guarantee that there is a client-lawyer relationship. Instead, it is the lawyer's willingness to discuss the possibility of forming a client-lawyer relationship that determines whether the client has a "reasonable expectation" of becoming a client. Lawyer Lennox has a duty of confidentiality to Client Cal as a prospective client while deciding whether to represent him, no matter how brief was their initial conference. Rule 1.18(b). The confidential information obtained from him cannot be disclosed unless he agrees in writing that the content of the conversations are not to be treated as confidential. If the representation goes no further, the Rules treat her as a former client regarding the confidential information he disclosed to her, and she cannot use that information to his disadvantage. Rule 1.9; Rule 1.18. The exception to that standard applies when the information becomes generally known or if a Rule like 1.6 or 3.3 requires disclosure. Rule 1.9. **A is incorrect**, because a fee arrangement is unnecessary to the formation of a lawyer-client relationship, e.g., a legal services client or an indigent criminal defendant does not pay or discuss fees but there is still a lawyer-client relationship. **B is incorrect**. As discussed above, Lawyer Lennox owes a duty of confidentiality to a prospective client such as Client Cal, even though she did not talk to him for very long or in much depth about his case and even if she ends up not representing him. **D is incorrect**. As a result of his conversation with Lawyer Lennox, Client Cal had a reasonable expectation of becoming her client when he talked to her about his case, and even when Lawyer Lennox abruptly ended their conversation. Because of his reasonable expectation, there was a lawyer-client relationship between them which Lawyer Lennox has a duty to protect, including the duty to maintain the confidentiality of their conversation.

PROBLEM #34. ANSWER D IS THE BEST ANSWER.

Both answers B and C are correct. **Answer A is incorrect**. A lawyer cannot escape her responsibility for ethical misconduct by claiming that she was just following orders. Rule 5.2(a). However, if the existence of an ethical violation is not clear, she can defer to the judgment of her supervising lawyer when she followed the "reasonable resolution of an arguable question of professional duty." Rule 5.2(b). **Answer B is incorrect but true**. Lawyers have brought wrongful discharge claims against their law firms or their clients when they have been fired for their refusal to engage in unethical activity. The typical case relates to being fired for not following the supervising lawyer's unethical directive. Rule 5.2(a). **Answer C is incorrect but true**. As the opposite of Answer A, Lawyer Kim is ethically responsible for her own actions, regardless of the directives issued by the lawyers she works for.

PROBLEM #35. ANSWER C IS THE BEST ANSWER.

Because a lawyer has a duty to instruct her nonlawyer employees about the ethical aspects of their employment, she must exercise "reasonable care" to prevent them from violating confidentiality norms. Rule 5.3, Comment 1. She may have periodic discussions about the duties of lawyers, such as the duty of confidentiality. The essence of the disciplinary violation is Lawyer Kuric's failure to supervise Paralegal Delk, even if Paralegal Delk improperly discloses no confidential information. Because A is the opposite of answer C, **A is incorrect**. **B is incorrect**. Even though they are both employees of the law firm, Lawyer Kuric has an ethical obligation to instruct the law firm employees she supervises about the ethical aspects of their jobs with the firm. Rule 5.3(a) applies to any law partner, lawyers with managerial authority, and lawyers who supervise nonlawyer employees or independent contractors such as law clerks. **D is incorrect**. If Paralegal Delk improperly discloses confidential information about firm clients, Lawyer Kuric has no ethical responsibility if she adequately supervised him. The nonlawyer support staff is expected to treat confidential information in the same manner as the lawyers. The lawyer has a duty to her client to reasonably supervise the staff who learn about confidential client information through the course of doing their job, in order to prevent them from disclosing confidential client communications. Rule 5.3.

PROBLEM #36. ANSWER D IS THE BEST ANSWER.

Because A and C are both true, D is correct. After a jury is discharged, a lawyer cannot communicate with them under several circumstances. **A is incorrect** but true. Juror contact is prohibited if the "the law prohibits such contact." **C is incorrect** but true. Juror contact by Lawyer Laurie is forbidden if her conversation with the jurors involves "misrepresentation, coercion, duress or harassment." Rule 3.5(c). **Answer B is incorrect**. A lawyer cannot speak to the jurors if they ave requested that no one communicate with them.

PROBLEM #37. ANSWER A IS THE BEST ANSWER.

Rule 3.8 describes the special responsibilities of a prosecutor. If an accused like Donald Dorchester elects to represent himself and proceed *pro se*, a prosecutor like Prosecutor Petrie must negotiate directly with Dorchester. **B is incorrect**. If Dorchester chooses to represent himself, one of his motivations for proceeding *pro se* is that he can communicate directly with the prosecutor. **C is incorrect**. A prosecutor cannot urge an unrepresented person like Dorchester to waive important pretrial rights such as the right to a preliminary hearing. Rule 3.8(c). **D is incorrect**. Dorchester's right to proceed *pro se* does not require that he have a standby counsel, especially for matters occurring outside the courtroom.

PROBLEM #38. ANSWER D IS THE BEST ANSWER.

Prosecutor Painter is limited in the circumstances in which she can have a lawyer subpoenaed. If she "reasonably believes" that no privilege applies, the evidence is "essential" to the success of her investigation or prosecution, and she has no "feasible alternative" of obtaining the evidence she seeks from Lawyer Jacobs, he can be subpoenaed. Rule 3.8(e). **A, B and C are incorrect**, or more precisely each is only partially correct, because the requirements in Rule 3.8(e) are cumulative.

PROBLEM #39. ANSWER D IS THE BEST ANSWER.

Like other lawyers, prosecutors are subject to Rules 5.1 and 5.3, which relate to responsibilities regarding lawyers and nonlawyers who work for or are associated with the lawyer's office. Rule 3.8(f) reminds the prosecutor of the importance of these obligations in connection with the unique dangers of improper extrajudicial statements in a criminal case. In addition, Rule 3.8(f) requires a prosecutor to exercise reasonable care to prevent persons assisting or associated with the prosecutor from making improper extrajudicial statements, even when such persons are not under the direct supervision of the prosecutor. Ordinarily, the reasonable care standard will be satisfied if the prosecutor issues the appropriate cautions to law-enforcement personnel and other relevant individuals. **A is incorrect**. As mentioned Prosecutor Alston is not subject to discipline if she exercised reasonable care in training her spokesperson about what he could say to the press. **B is incorrect**. Even though the spokesperson's statements may affect the criminal charges against the defendant, the issue of disciplinary proceedings against Prosecutor Alston is a separate matter. **C is incorrect**. As the previous discussion suggested, Prosecutor Alston is subject to discipline if she failed to exercise reasonable care in training her spokesperson about the propriety of the statements he makes to the press.

PROBLEM #40. ANSWER D IS THE BEST ANSWER.

If an entity such as a corporation is the lawyer's client, the lawyer may disclose client confidential information when corporate action or inaction would involve a clear violation of the law that is reasonably likely to result in substantial injury to the entity. For such disclosure to be permitted, it is not necessary that the lawyer's services be used in furtherance of the violation. Rule 1.13, Comment 6. However, it is required that the matter be related to the lawyer's representation of the organization. The comment also notes that Rule 1.13(c) supplements Rule 1.6 by providing an additional basis upon which a lawyer is permitted to reveal client confidences, but it does not "modify, restrict, or limit" the exceptions to client confidentiality listed in Rule 1.6. The Rule does not specify to whom he should reveal that information, but his disclosure must be confined to information necessary to prevent substantial injury to the entity, and disclosure may be made regardless of whether the Rule 1.6 confidentiality standard permits disclosure to protect the entity. **A is incorrect**. Rule 1.16 requires a lawyer to withdraw from representation in three instances, none of which is applicable: "the representation will result in violation of the rules of professional conduct or other law; the lawyer's physical or mental condition materially impairs the lawyer's ability to represent the client; or the lawyer is discharged." The facts do not suggest that Lawyer Edward will be violating the Rules if he remains as general counsel. His course of action to disclose to outside authorities is discretionary, not mandatory. **B is incorrect**. As the previous discussion indicates, although what Lawyer Edward knows about the corporate wrongdoing is regarded as confidential, the Rules still permit him to disclose it to an outside authority. **C is incorrect** for two reasons. The previous discussion notes that Lawyer Edward's disclosure is discretionary not mandatory. In addition, the Rules allowing him to make a discretionary disclosure does not specify to whom he should reveal the information.

PROBLEM #41. ANSWER D IS THE BEST ANSWER.

Answers A, B and C are all untrue. The Sarbanes–Oxley Act required the Securities and Exchange Commission [SEC] to create regulations governing the professional responsibility of lawyers who represent corporations which issue publicly-traded securities. The regulations found in 17 CFR Part 205¢k¢k address a lawyer's duty to act in matters before the SEC. The duties described in answers A, B, and C are those imposed by Rule 1.13, not by the SEC regulations. Most of the regulations impose broader duties on the lawyer involved in an SEC matter than Rule 1.13 requires of the lawyer for the entity. Unlike Rule 1.13(b), which applies to all lawyers representing an entity, the SEC Regulations apply only to people "appearing and practicing" before it and includes people who give securities advice. **Answer A is incorrect**. The lawyer's duties under Rule 1.13 must relate to the representation of the entity. Under the SEC Regulations, after a lawyer appears and practices before the SEC, she must follow the Sarbanes–Oxley Act procedures regardless of whether what she knows relates to her representation of her client. **Answer B is incorrect**. While Rule 1.13 requires reporting of a violation that is likely to cause substantial injury to the entity, the broader SEC Regulations require the lawyer to report any "material violation" of federal or state (securities) law regardless of potential harm to the entity. Rule 1.13(b) requires the lawyer to "know" someone is engaged in wrongdoing before being required to report that person, but the SEC Regulation is triggered when the lawyer merely "becomes aware" of evidence of a material violation of law, even though it will be difficult for the lawyer to evaluate the risk to the entity. **Answer C is incorrect**. None of the reporting requirements applies to a lawyer who has been retained by the entity to investigate wrongdoing that is reported by someone else.

PROBLEM #42. ANSWER D IS THE BEST ANSWER.

Answer D is an incomplete explanation of the nature of the consent necessary to proceed with the conflicting representations. To resolve a conflicts of interest when the interests of one client are directed adverse to another client, Rule 1.7(b) has four requirements. Lawyer Lemon must (1) independently decide whether she can competently and diligently represent all the affected clients, (2) decide whether some other law precludes her from accepting the representation, and (3) not represent one client against another client "in the same litigation," and (4) each of her affected clients must give her "informed consent, confirmed in writing."

For a consent to be "informed," Lawyer Lemon must explain to each of her affected clients the "material risks" and "reasonably available alternatives" of going forward with or without you as her counsel. Rule 1.0(e). It is insufficient for each of her clients simply to be aware of her other representation. In order for a consent to be informed, it is also possible that Lawyer Lemon would have to have to disclose to one client confidential information from the other client. If her other client refuses to permit that disclosure, no consent can occur and the representation cannot go forward. Lawyer Lemon's clients' consent must be confirmed in writing, which has a broad meaning. The requirement of a written consent should impress the client about the seriousness of the situation.

A is incorrect, because it is an accurate description of an additional factor necessary for a concurrent, directly adverse representation to continue. Lawyer Lemon must "reasonably believe" that she can provide competent, diligent representation to those clients whose circumstances present her conflict. Rule 1.7(b)(1). **B is incorrect**. Like A, it too is a statement of a relevant factor for determining whether Lawyer Lemon can proceed. If the contemplated representation is prohibited by law, her client's consent is irrelevant. Rule 1.7(b)(2). **C is incorrect**. Under Rule 1.7(b)(3), in any case before a tribunal, Lawyer Lemon cannot represent two or more clients who are asserting claims against each other. This provision obviously prevents her from representing both plaintiff and defendant in a civil case. It also prevents her from representing multiple defendants when one files a cross-claim against the other.

PROBLEM #43. ANSWER C IS THE BEST ANSWER.

Answer C describes a privileged communication. If a prospective client consults a lawyer, their preliminary communications are privileged even if the lawyer is not ultimately retained. When a lawyer is appointed to represent an indigent defendant, the communications between them are privileged even though the defendant pays no fee. A client enjoys the same evidentiary privilege even if she has not paid her lawyer's fees. **Answer A is incorrect**; it is not a privileged communication. In order for the lawyer-client privilege to be invoked, the client must communicate with the lawyer. The client's communication may be oral, written, electronic, or any other method of transmitting information. Excluded from the privilege are physical characteristics of the client, such as her hair, fingerprints, complexion, demeanor, and her dress, which are observable by anyone who talked with the client. **Answer B is incorrect**; it also is not privileged. Whether a communication is confidential depends on the client's intent in disclosing the information to her lawyer. For the lawyer-client privilege to apply, the client must intend for the information to be treated as confidential. If a client writes or speaks to her lawyer, while seeking legal advice, and gives her permission for the lawyer to disclose that information to a third party, the client's communication is not made in confidence. If the client makes statements to unknown persons in her lawyer's reception area, the privilege does not apply even if the persons work for the lawyer. The privilege does not apply if a client makes statements to her lawyer in the presence of others who hear the statements. **Answer D is incorrect;** because C is correct but A is not correct.

PROBLEM #44. ANSWER D IS THE BEST ANSWER.

A and B are each incorrect but true. All contingent fee arrangements must be in writing and signed by the client, in order to avoid later claims that the client never saw a written agreement. Answer **C is incorrect**. The contents of a contingent fee agreement must include whether the percentage to be charged depends on how far the case proceeds. In addition, an agreement must state the percentage of the recovery the lawyer will earn, whether expenses are to be deducted before or after the fee is calculated, and which expenses the client must pay if he gets no recovery. When the representation is concluded, a lawyer must also furnish a detailed statement in writing to her client. Rule 1.5(c).

PROBLEM #45. ANSWER B IS THE BEST ANSWER.

The Rules distinguish between a lawyer's roles as an advisor and as an evaluator. If a lawyer's client asks her to conduct a title search for the benefit of the prospective buyer of a piece of property, the lawyer is an evaluator if her opinion is given to the buyer or is made public. Rule 2.3. The lawyer is an advisor, per Rule 2.1, if her opinion is offered exclusively for the use of the lawyer's client. If Client Cotton asks Lawyer Lawson to write an opinion letter for the benefit of a third party, Lawyer Lawson's duty of loyalty is to Client Cotton but she also may have assumed obligations to third parties who will rely on her evaluation. If she gives a negligent opinion that results in damage to the third party recipient of her title opinion, the recipient can sue her even though he was not her client when she wrote the title opinion letter. **A is incorrect**, because as mentioned. The lawyer-as-advisor does not offer an opinion for anyone other than the client. **C is incorrect**, because an opinion letter is not part of a negotiation even though it could lead to a negotiated resolution of the commercial transaction. **D is incorrect**. A third-party neutral does not represent either party to a dispute, but is seeking to promote the resolution of that dispute through the use of alternative dispute resolution (ADR) proceedings. If a lawyer acts as a third-party neutral, she must disclose to unrepresented parties that she is not representing them to remove potential confusion about her role. Rule 2.4(b).

PROBLEM #46. ANSWER A IS THE BEST ANSWER.

Instead of applying to the lawyer's role as an evaluator, answer A describes a duty of the lawyer when she is acting as an advisor to a client. As an advisor, she has a duty to tell her litigation clients about any forms of dispute resolution that might serve as reasonable alternatives to litigation. Rule 2.1, Comment 5. Because answers B, C, and D are prescribed ethical duties of a lawyer acting as an evaluator, those answers are incorrect. **B is incorrect**. A lawyer acting as an evaluator must have a reasonable belief that doing an evaluation is consistent with other aspects of the lawyer-client relationship with her client. Rule 2.3(a). **C is incorrect**. A lawyer must obtain her client's informed consent to be evaluator if she knows "or reasonably should know" doing an evaluation likely will affect her client's interests in a material and adverse manner. Rule 2.3(b). The lawyer's disclosure to her client must include information about the effect of evaluating a matter for disclosure to a non-client. **D is incorrect**. Disclosure of the evaluation to a third party necessarily removes client confidentiality for any information in the evaluation. Other information, however, that relates to the evaluation but which is not included in the evaluation remains confidential under Rule 1.6. Rule 2.3(c). To disclose the latter type of confidential information to the third party requires that the lawyer obtain her client's informed consent.

PROBLEM #47. ANSWER D IS THE BEST ANSWER.

When acting as a negotiator on behalf of a client, a lawyer's ethical duties relate to the statements in answers A, B, and C. Unlike the statement in answer D, a lawyer in the role of a negotiator is permitted to exaggerate about facts and values during a negotiation. ABA Formal Opinion 06–439. **A is incorrect**. A lawyer has no ethical duty either to do any research for the other side of the litigation or transaction or to volunteer factual information that possibly could weaken her client's position. Rule 4.1(a) **B is incorrect**. The Rules prohibit a lawyer from making false statements of material fact. **C is incorrect**. In a negotiation, if a lawyer states that her client will not settle a case for less than a certain amount when the lawyer knows that is not true, her client's intentions "as to an acceptable settlement of a claim" are not considered to be a material fact. Therefore, the negotiator may make such a statement. Rule 4.1, Comment 2.

PROBLEM #48. ANSWER D IS THE BEST ANSWER.

In order for Lawyer Longfellow to represent Client Allen at trial and cross-examine an adverse material witness like Client Bruce who is also her client, there must be written consent from *both* clients even if Client Bruce's case is unrelated. The cross-examination ordinarily would constitute a conflict under Rule 1.7(a)(1). Vigorous cross-examination violates the duty of loyalty to Client Bruce, the witness, and failure to cross-examine forcefully violates the duty to represent Client Allen zealously. ABA Formal Opinion 92–367. D is correct because the conflict arose only after the representation of Client Allen began; Lawyer Longfellow would have to withdraw from representing both of her clients. **A and B are incorrect**, because under Rule 1.7(b)(4) each of Lawyer Longfellow's affected clients would have to give informed consent to waive the conflict of interest; the Rule requires that the consent be in writing. **C is incorrect** as well, because written (not oral) consent must be obtained from both Client Allen and Client Bruce.

PROBLEM #49. ANSWER D IS THE BEST ANSWER.

When a lawyer's workload begins to interfere with her competent and diligent representation of her existing clients, the lawyer must decline new cases and/or seek assistance to properly represent her clients. Thus, a lawyer is subject to discipline by accepting new cases when she already knows that her workload precludes competent representation. **A is incorrect**. One way for a new lawyer to become competent is to work with an experienced lawyer who already is competent, especially in order for her to develop trial practice and negotiation skills. Rule 1.1, Comment 2. **B is incorrect**. A lawyer does not have to be experienced in a particular area of the law in order to be considered competent in that legal matter. How does a new lawyer become experienced without having particular types of cases for the first time? It is important to remember that a new lawyer has graduated from law school, where she learned about the value of precedent, the rules of procedure and evidence, and how to analyze legal problems. Rule 1.1, Comment 2. **C is incorrect**. A lawyer does not have to be competent enough to represent a client when she accepts the client's case. She may agree to take the employment from a client and thereafter become sufficiently competent through research and preparation in a new area of law practice. Rule 1.1, Comment 2.

PROBLEM #50. ANSWER D IS THE BEST ANSWER.

ABA Formal Opinion 06–441 addresses the ethical obligations of lawyers who represent indigent defendants and have excessive caseloads. Lawyers must control their workload to avoid impairment of the obligations they owe to your existing clients. If her workload begins to affect those duties, the lawyer must find assistance or reduce her workload. **A is incorrect**. The ABA Opinion allows the lawyer to ask "the court to refrain from assigning the lawyer any new cases until such time as the lawyer's caseload has been reduced to a level that she is able to provide competent legal representation." **B is incorrect**. If the public defender has an excessive caseload, she must inform her supervisor about the problem and seek relief, such as help with discharging the public defender office's duties to its existing clients. **C is incorrect**. If the public defender's supervisor fails to provide relief for her, she should move up the chain of command within the public defender organization. If that effort proves to be ineffective, the ABA Opinion prescribes that Lawyer Lofton seek relief from the court with jurisdiction over her cases. The difference between answers C and D is in the "may" versus "must" of her obligation to withdraw from her current cases. The ABA Opinion states that she may seek to withdraw; she does not have to withdraw. If no one affords relief for Lawyer Lofton, she must continue to represent her clients to the best of her ability.

PROBLEM #51. ANSWER B IS THE BEST ANSWER.

When a lawyer represents a client, she must act with reasonable diligence, which includes a zealous lawful and ethical commitment to accomplish her client's objectives "despite opposition, obstruction, or personal inconvenience" to her. **A is incorrect**. She may be disciplined for her offensive courtroom tactics. A lawyer's duty "does not require the use of offensive tactics or preclude the treating of all persons involved in the legal process with courtesy and respect." Rule 1.3, Comment 1. **C is incorrect**. Reasonable diligence requires that a lawyer assess the work that needs to be done on her client's behalf and to exercise reasonable promptness in completing that work. A lawyer may agree "to a reasonable request for a postponement that will not prejudice" her client. Rule 1.3, Comment 3. Lawyer Light's requests for continuances are not reasonable. **D is incorrect**. A lawyer is subject to legal discipline for neglecting her clients only when there is a pattern of action or inaction.

PROBLEM #52. ANSWER B IS THE BEST ANSWER.

Lawyer Lopez is subject to discipline for deciding that she must withdraw from representing the non-paying client under Rule 1.16(a). Mandatory withdrawal is appropriate in three circumstances for Lawyer Lopez: 1) her continued employment would result in violating the ethical rules or other law, 2) her physical or mental condition has a materially adverse effect on your client, and 3) the client fires her. None of those circumstances exists in this situation of an unpaid fee. **A is incorrect**. If a client intentionally fails to pay the lawyer's fee, the lawyer may withdraw from representing the client, but only after the lawyer takes reasonable steps to protect the client's interests. Rule 1.16(b)(4) and (d). In a case pending before a court, the lawyer must obtain the court's permission to withdraw. Until the court consents, the lawyer cannot neglect the client's case. Rule 1.16(c). **C is incorrect**. While a client may waive many of the ethics rules that exist for his protection, the Rules do not authorize a lawyer to request that a client waive the right that he has to have lawyer act with reasonable promptness or diligence. **D is incorrect**. Rule 1.16, Comment 9 notes that "a lawyer must take all reasonable steps to mitigate the consequences to the client [even after being discharged by the client]. The Comment goes on to state that an exception, which permits a lawyer to keep the client's documents until the fee is paid, to the extent permitted by law.

PROBLEM #53. ANSWER A IS THE BEST ANSWER.

The Rules are consistent with Supreme Court case law which states that any type of communications by a lawyer must be true and not misleading. For example, a lawyer cannot make affirmative statements in her ads that misrepresent the law or facts or omissions of fact that result in the statement as a whole being materially misleading. Rule 7.1. Lawyer Larabee cannot state that she worked as a lawyer with a law firm when in fact she worked there only as a runner who delivers messages to and from office workers and lawyers there. **B is incorrect** because that statement in her ad is misleading. Lawyer Larabee is subject to discipline for stating that she graduated from Harvale Law School in 1995 because it suggests that is the place she attended law school for three years; the ad omits the fact that she attended only a summer program there. **C is incorrect**. When she claims that her fees are 25% lower than other lawyers in Madison County, she is subject to discipline for that statement if she has no basis for making that comparison. **D is incorrect**. It is true that she has never lost a workers' compensation case in court, but because such cases are not resolved by a court the statement is misleading.

PROBLEM #54. ANSWER A IS THE BEST ANSWER.

Because the ethical duty requires disclosure under these facts and the constitutional duty does not require disclosure, **B, C, and D are incorrect**. This hypothetical is the basis of ABA Formal Opinion 09–454, which explored the scope of a prosecutor's pretrial disclosure obligation. That opinion stated that information known to Prosecutor Pincus would be favorable to Dogman but not necessarily material under *Brady v. Maryland*, 373 U.S. 83 (1963) and its progeny, which require Prosecutor Pincus to disclose favorable evidence so that Dogman can decide on its usefulness. Rule 3.8(d) requires a prosecutor to "make timely disclosure to the defense of all evidence or information known to the prosecutor that tends to negate the guilt of the accused or mitigates the offense.… " It is more demanding than the constitutionally-based *Brady* rule, because "it requires the disclosure of evidence or information favorable to the defense without regard to the anticipated impact of the evidence or information on a trial's outcome. The Rule thereby requires prosecutors to steer clear of the constitutional line, erring on the side of caution." The information from the two eyewitnesses and the informant who disputed Dogman's involvement is known to Prosecutor Pincus and tends to negate Dogman's guilt regardless of the strength of the other evidence and even if Prosecutor Pincus is not persuaded about their testimony. The disclosure must occur as soon as reasonably practicable so that Dogman can make effective use of it in deciding whether to pled guilty and how to conduct its investigation.

PROBLEM #55. ANSWER B IS THE BEST ANSWER.

The judge must report the reimbursement on his periodic public financial disclosure statement, although reporting would not cure the impropriety of the reimbursements. A judge may accept reasonable compensation for extrajudicial activities permitted by the CJC or other law, unless accepting it would create an appearance of impropriety. CJC Rule 3.12. She also cannot accept anything of value, if acceptance is prohibited by law or would create the appearance of impropriety. CJC Rule 3.13(A). (She may, however, accept things of value such as ordinary social hospitality, gifts from friends or relatives, publications sent to her for her official use, or commercial opportunities as long as all persons have the same opportunities.) Reimbursements of expenses by the owners of Public Service Corrections would create the appearance of impropriety because it will be viewed as a payback or as an future incentive for the award of the renewable three-year contract. Thus, although a judge can accept reimbursement of necessary and reasonable expenses for travel, food, lodging, or other incidental expenses from sources other than her employing entity, that reimbursement is prohibited if it violates CJC Rule 3.13(A) or other law. CJC Rule 3.14(A). Reimbursement of expenses here also is prohibited because it is limited to the actual costs reasonably incurred by the judge. CJC Rule 3.14(B). The ten percent "appreciation bonus" compounds the unethical nature of accepting the reimbursement from Public Service Corrections. Nevertheless, judges must report reimbursement of expenses in public reports and make a judgment about whether reimbursement is acceptable as required by Rule 3.15. CJC Rule 3.14(C). As part of this process, the judge "must undertake a reasonable inquiry to obtain the information necessary to make an informed judgment about whether acceptance would be consistent" with the CJC. Because B is correct, the foregoing descriptions show how the other choices involving combinations of reimbursement and reporting are incorrect thereby making answers **A, C and D incorrect**.

PROBLEM #56. ANSWER A IS THE BEST ANSWER.

Law clerk Lubell is not a lawyer but she does work for a law firm that employs her and has sent her to interview a prospective witness likely to testify at trial for opposing counsel. (A *lawyer* has an ethical obligation is to withdraw if she is "likely to be called as a necessary witness," but she is not a "necessary" witness if her testimony is not cumulative of other information and it is unobtainable elsewhere as from the prospective witness for opposing counsel in this problem. Rule 3.7.) When law clerk Lubell interviews the prospective witness, she should first identify herself as a representative of the law firm that represents a party in the lawsuit in which he is likely to be called as a witness at trial. If law clerk Lubell knows that the prospective witness has a lawyer, she must obtain that lawyer's consent in order to talk to her. If she knows that the witness does not have her own lawyer, she cannot state or imply that she is disinterested when speaking to him. Rule 4.3. If he misunderstands law clerk Lubell's role as an employee of Lawyer Latham, she must make reasonable efforts to correct his misunderstanding. Otherwise, she does not have to disclose that she works for Lawyer Latham who represents a client in the lawsuit. She should not provide legal advice to an unrepresented person if she knows or reasonably should know that the interests of her employer and his client and the unrepresented person have a "reasonable possibility of being in conflict." Rule 4.3. **B is incorrect**. Law clerk Lubell's status as a nonlawyer does not automatically dispose of an ethical issue. Lawyer Latham is subject to discipline for failing to monitor adequately his employee's conduct. He has a duty to instruct his nonlawyer employees like law clerk Lubell about the ethical aspects of her employment. The Rule applies to any law partner, lawyers with managerial authority, and lawyers who supervise nonlawyer employees or independent contractors such as law clerks. Rule 5.3(a). **C is incorrect**. Lawyers are not subject to discipline for delegating litigation tasks to others. They are permitted to send employees and independent contractors to complete tasks that lawyer could do but have chosen to delegate instead. **D is incorrect**. Rule 3.7 applies to lawyers and witnesses for any party, not just the witnesses for a specific lawyer.

PROBLEM #57. ANSWER B IS THE BEST ANSWER.

A lawyer may refer to herself as "Of Counsel" for a law firm on stationery and other communications, as long as there is an ongoing general relationship between her and the firm. ABA Formal Opinion 90–357.

> A lawyer who is of counsel to a firm often has more limited access to confidential client information than firm partners and associates and usually a smaller financial stake in the firm. Nonetheless, the incentive to misuse confidential information, the difficulty of determining when it has been misused, the ostensible professional relationship, as well as the administrative ease of a definite rule, justify extending imputation to lawyers having an of-counsel status.

Restatement § 123 cmt. c(ii). When any lawyer is disqualified from representing a client, generally none of the lawyers with whom the disqualified lawyer is affiliated can represent that client. Rule 1.10. "In consequence there is attribution to the lawyer who is of counsel of all of the disqualifications of each firm, and, correspondingly, attribution from the of counsel lawyer to each firm, of each of those disqualifications.... [T]he effect of two or more firms sharing an of counsel lawyer is to make them all effectively a single firm, for purposes of attribution of disqualifications." ABA Formal Opinion 90–357. If Lawyer Lubinsky is Of Counsel to both the New York and the Los Angeles law firms, the conflicts of interest of each firm are imputed to the other firm. **A is incorrect**. The conflicts of one firm are imputed to the other firm as a result of the common Of Counsel relationship. **C is incorrect**. A lawyer is permitted to serve as Of Counsel for more than one law firm. **D is incorrect**. Ethical rules are applicable to all lawyers in a law firm, not merely to the lawyers who are directly responsible for creating the situation that has prompted the application of imputed disqualification standards.

PROBLEM #58. ANSWER C IS THE BEST ANSWER.

C is not an acceptable resolution of the ethical problem. When the other client advised the Large Law Firm that he or she was opposed to the project, a conflict developed under Rule 1.7(a)(1). The representation of the developer at that point was directly adverse to another client. Large Law Firm acted properly by telling both clients immediately of the conflict and declining to accept the representation of the other client in opposing the zoning variance application. The disclosure does not fully resolve the problem, because the other client remains a client of Large Law Firm although in an unrelated matter and the other client still opposes the development project. Through no fault of either client or of the firm, a conflict exists that involves the duty of loyalty to both clients. Loyalty to the developer would require that Large Law Firm continue its work. Loyalty to the other client would require that the firm not represent the developer. The "hot potato" rule in general disallows a law firm from discharging a client for the purpose of eliminating a conflict where it desires to accept the representation of another client such as the developer. One exception to the "hot potato" rule is referred to as the "thrust upon exception." Comment 5 to Rule 1.7 states in part: "Unforeseeable developments, such as changes in corporate and other organization affiliations or the addition or realignment of parties in litigation, might create conflicts in the midst of a representation, as when a company sued by the lawyer on behalf of one client is brought by another client represented by the lawyer in an unrelated matter." That exception does not apply here, because it was foreseeable that persons could emerge to oppose the development project.

All other options are acceptable ethical solutions for Large Law Firm and therefore are incorrect. **A is incorrect**. Withdrawal by Large Law Firm from further representation of the developer in connection with any aspect of the development project would impose a hardship on the developer. Large Law Firm could remain as counsel to both clients in other matters. This solution would remove the conflict, and Large Law Firm would be loyal to each client in declining to advance or oppose the other's views. Unfortunately for the developer, the work that he will have paid for will have to be replicated by a new lawyer or law firm. **B is incorrect**. This alternative is less prejudicial to the developer but the developer would have to hire a new lawyer to appear at zoning and other hearings on behalf of the developer. The law firm could remain as counsel by the developer in all other matters relating to the development project. **D is incorrect**. The other client would be asserting a position adverse to the developer in the proceeding before the zoning tribunal. It could even reach the point where the other client would have to be cross-examined by a member of Large Law Firm.

PROBLEM #59. ANSWER C IS THE BEST ANSWER.

Rule 1.13(a) provides that the client is the corporation, not the CEO. Therefore, Lawyer Lyle's obligation is to the corporation. She represents the organization, not its directors, officers, employees, members, shareholders, or other constituents. To represent the corporation, Lawyer Lyle must communicate with the corporation to permit informed decisions about the representation under Rule 1.4(b), and to take steps to prevent foreseeable harm to the corporation, per Rule 1.13(b). As the corporation's lawyer, if Lawyer Lyle knows that someone associated with the corporation is acting in a manner related to the representation that violates the law and can be reasonably imputed to the corporation and is likely to result in substantial injury to the corporation, she must do what is reasonably necessary in the best interest of the corporation. Any measures she takes must be designed to minimize disruption to the corporation. Such measures may include asking reconsideration of the matter; advising that a separate legal opinion on the matter be sought for presentation to appropriate authority in the corporation, and referring the matter to higher authority in the corporation. Lawyer Lyle ***first*** should attempt to dissuade Corman from the threatened misconduct. She should discuss with him the corporation's duty to comply with court orders and applicable law, any relevant corporate policies such as those involving ethical obligations and document retention, the lawyer's recommendation that a second opinion be obtained regarding the implications of the threatened conduct, and the lawyer's intent to refer the matter to higher authority in the corporation if he does not change his mind. **A is incorrect**. Lawyer Lyle may continue to represent the corporation despite Corman's threat to destroy documents. Her representation may prevent a violation of law by her client. She may continue representing the corporation and is not required to withdraw merely because the officer suggests improper conduct. Rule 1.16. **B is incorrect**. If Corman refuses to withdraw his threat, Lawyer Lyle should refer the matter to higher authority in the corporation. Assuming that if Corman carries out his threat to destroy that documents that are subject to a discovery order would be "a violation of law which reasonably could be imputed to the [corporation], and that is likely to result in substantial injury to the organization," Lawyer Lyle must do what is necessary to protect the best interest of the corporation, taking into account Rule 1.13(b). The specifics depend on the governance structure of the corporation, the degree of independence of the board, and the Corman's relationship with the board. If he refuses, she should consult the corporation's board of directors. She should also advise the board that her ethical obligations would likely require withdrawal from representing the corporation, and appropriate disclosure to the tribunal, if the CEO carries out the threat. **D is incorrect**. She should refuse to return copies of the documents in her possession until the matter is resolved so as not to assist in the unlawful destruction or concealment of evidence. If Lawyer Lyle reasonably believes after counseling the board that Corman will not retract his threat, she should preserve any pertinent documents until the matter of discovery compliance is resolved. Otherwise, the lawyer risks violating Rule 3.4(a), which provides that a lawyer shall not "unlawfully obstruct another party's access to evidence; unlawfully ... destroy or conceal a document ... or assist another person to do any such act." Returning the documents may also assist the client in conduct she knows to be illegal or fraudulent, per Rule 1.2(c). (Threatening to destroy the documents is not an illegal or fraudulent act or unlawful destruction, per 1.2(c) or 3.4(a).)

PROBLEM #60. ANSWER C IS THE BEST ANSWER.

Even if Lawyer Dickens must be disqualified for the reasons discussed below, imputing Lawyer Dickens's disqualification to the other members of the Dickens, Edwards & Frank firm can be avoided if Lawyer Dickens is properly screened and written notice is given promptly to the district attorney's office in accordance with Rule 1.11(b). **D is incorrect** because C is correct. **A and B are incorrect**. Rule 1.11(a) prohibits Lawyer Dickens from representing criminal defendants in matters in which she "participated personally and substantially" while a government prosecutor. Thus, if Lawyer Dickens did no work on a particular matter or acquired no material confidential information from Lawyer Dickens's "former client" (the state) while at the district attorney's office, neither Lawyer Dickens nor the Dickens, Edwards & Frank law partnership would be limited in the subsequent handling of the matter. If, however, Lawyer Dickens worked on a matter or acquired information protected by Rule 1.6 that is sufficiently capable of adverse use, the Rules would prohibit Lawyer Dickens from handling the matter absent informed consent, confirmed in writing. The reference in Rule 1.11(c) to information that "the government .. has a legal privilege not to disclose" may encompass information that could not otherwise constitute confidential client information under Rule 1.6, but which the government is not required to disclose. Absent government consent in the case of government-privileged information, Lawyer Dickens may not work on a matter in private practice in which Lawyer D had previously acquired "confidential government information."

PROFESSIONAL RESPONSIBILITY

Answer Key for Exam #3—Answers and Explanations

PROBLEM #1. ANSWER D IS THE BEST ANSWER.

A, B and C are all correct. Lawyer Dean's clients' interests are in conflict. The nature of the CERCLA investigation and the potential liability of each client for the entirety of the cleanup of the hazardous substances at the disposal site clearly indicates conflicts among their respective interests. Even if the CERCLA case law suggests that the different functions performed by the various PRPs dictates a percentage range of their respective liabilities, there may be significant conflicts between the PRPs as to whether each client is liable and whether each is liable on the high or low side of the damage range for the cleanup. **Answers A and B are correct.** Rule 1.7 prohibits a lawyer from concurrently representing clients whose interests are "directly adverse to another client," or "there is a significant risk that the representation of one or more clients will be materially limited by the lawyer's responsibilities to" other clients. **Answer C is also correct.** Despite the presence of a conflict of interest, she may represent multiple clients if she "reasonably believes" that she "will be able to provide competent and diligent representation to each affected client" and each of the represented clients consents in writing after being informed of the conflict by the lawyer.

PROBLEM #2. ANSWER A IS THE BEST ANSWER.

Keeping in mind that the question here asks about which of the listed answers is not correct, A is the best answer. Rule 1.7 does not require that another lawyer become involved in order for waiver of the conflict to be proper. **B is incorrect.** To represent these PRPs at the same time, Lawyer Dean or another lawyer should provide each of them with adequate information so that each can make an informed decision about whether to consent to the concurrent representation or to seek another attorney. Included within this

193

information should be the nature and scope of the conflicting interests as well as the fact that Lawyer Dean may have to withdraw from representing one or more, if not all, of the PRPs at some later time. This advice should include full disclosure of the circumstances and advice about any actual or reasonably foreseeable adverse effects of those circumstances upon the representation. **C and D are also incorrect.** The scope of the consent which Lawyer Dean should obtain from each client is two-fold, which include Answers C and D: consent to the representation of their conflicting interests, and consent to the disclosure of each client's confidential information to the other clients. Even if the clients consent to her representation of their conflicting interests, it is important for her to seek from them an additional consent that she can share the confidential information of each with the rest of the clients. Such consent will probably enable her to be better prepared for any litigation because it will not be necessary for every client to be present at the time that she consults with any one of them.

PROBLEM #3. ANSWER D IS THE BEST ANSWER.

All three of the preceding options are accurate statements. Unless specific conditions are met, a third person (including another client) cannot compensate an attorney for representing a client. Because of the appearance that someone than the client or the attorney would be involved in making or influencing important decisions relating to the representation, Rule 1.8(f) prohibits an attorney from accepting compensation from a third person for representing a client unless *three specific conditions* are met.

Each of the other answers is too narrow. **Answer A** states, the lawyer first must disclose to the client that a third party is compensating the lawyer for representing the client, who must thereafter consent to such payment. Rule 1.8(f)(1). At a minimum, the disclosure by Lawyer Dean should inform the client that payment of the fee by another will not affect (1) the lawyer's independent judgment; (2) the relationship between the lawyer and the client; or (3) the duty of confidentiality owed by the lawyer to the client. The client must then consent to the compensation of Lawyer Dean by someone other than the client. **Answer B** describes the second condition is that the payment will not interfere with the attorney's independent professional judgment or with the attorney-client relationship. Rule 1.8(f)(2). Only Lawyer Dean as the attorney in this case can make the determination to prevent such interference. **Answer C** describes the third part of the ethical requirement: despite such payment by a third party, the lawyer must preserve information relating to the representation. Rule 1.8(f)(3). This requirement merely reinforces the tradition that Lawyer Dean must preserve the confidentiality of information relating to the representation of any client. D is the correct answer because all three conditions must be met in order for Lawyer Dean to accept her fee from MIS.

PROBLEM #4. ANSWER D IS THE BEST ANSWER.

Under Rule 1.11, a former government attorney cannot represent a private client in connection with a matter in which the lawyer either participated personally and substantially as a government lawyer or has acquired confidential governmental information as a government attorney, unless the appropriate governmental agency consents after consultation. In addition, a lawyer with information that she knows is confidential government information about a person which she acquired as a public employee cannot represent a private client in a matter in which the information could be used to the material disadvantage of the government. The facts state that Lawyer Starks on several occasions heard the prosecutor who is responsible for the Ewald investigation talking with investigators and other assistant prosecutors about evidence in the case and litigation strategy. That type of information probably qualifies as "confidential government information" under Rule 1.11(c), because Lawyer Starks's knowledge about Grace's case was gained by her "under government authority" and is not otherwise available to the public. The language of Rule 1.11(c) suggests that Lawyer Starks cannot represent Ewald because she has information that she knows is confidential government information about Page's investigation and litigation strategy which could be used to the government's material disadvantage. **Answer A is incorrect.** The first issue to be addressed is whether Lawyer Starks participated personally and substantially as a government attorney in the prosecution of Grace Ewald. Although Grace was indicted while Lawyer Starks worked as a public prosecutor and shared office space with the assistant prosecutor who conducted the Ewald investigation, Lawyer Starks herself did not participate in the investigation of Ewald. She would not be disqualified under Rule 1.11(a). **Answers B and C are both incorrect.** Similarly, the ethics standard do not require Lawyer Starks's later disqualification merely because at the time of Grace's indictment she was a prosecutor for the governmental unit which indicted Grace or because she shared office space with the prosecutor who personally handled Grace's case.

PROBLEM #5. ANSWER A IS THE BEST ANSWER.

Answer A describes the proper standards for screening a disqualified prosecutor. **Answers B and C are incorrect** because each of them too narrowly the conditions for permitted screening. **D is**

incorrect because the Model Rules do permit screening under limited circumstances. Even if a former government attorney is disqualified, a firm with which that attorney is associated may represent the private client if the disqualified lawyer is screened from any participation in the case and receives no part of the fee from the representation. The language of Rule 1.11(b) states that a law firm with which Lawyer Starks is associated may represent Grace in her case only if Lawyer Starks is screened from any participation in the matter and is apportioned no part of the fee generated by the Grace representation. No written notice to the government is required. The important and difficult issue here is that proper method for screening Lawyer Starks from Grace's case. Any effort by the firm to screen Lawyer Starks from Grace's case should attempt to insure that none of the confidential government information she possesses would be used to the government's disadvantage. The most important aspect of the effort is that the firm took action before any sharing of information occurred and certainly before any motion is made by the prosecutor to disqualify the entire firm. In addition, the firm should deny Lawyer Starks access to the files in Grace's case, and admonish her and all other firm personnel not to discuss the case when Lawyer Starks is present. As to compensation, if Lawyer Starks is a salaried attorney, she may continue to receive her regular compensation. If she is a partner, she should not share in the profit from Grace's representation.

PROBLEM #6. ANSWER D IS THE BEST ANSWER.

According to Rule 8.2(a), a lawyer who makes a false statement about the qualifications or integrity of a judge, judicial candidate, or public legal officer is subject to discipline if she makes that statement knowingly or with reckless disregard for the truth. The Comments note the importance of improving the administration of justice by encouraging you to express "honest and candid opinions." Rule 8.2, Comment 1. There is no violation if the lawyer (1) tells the truth about the judge, even if she does so out of a sinister motive, or (2) speaks falsely but does not know of the falsity of the statement, unless the statement is reckless. **A is incorrect**, because it is irrelevant if he practices before Judge Ito. **B is incorrect**. The Rule includes judicial candidates. **C is incorrect**, because nothing in the Rule requires publication of the comments.

PROBLEM #7. ANSWER D IS THE BEST ANSWER.

Either Rule 1.9(a) and 1.9(b) alone provides the basis for D being correct. If Lawyer Perot used to represent a client like Clinton in a matter, Lawyer Perot cannot represent a new client like Dole in the same or substantially related matter if Dole's interests are "materially adverse" to Clinton's. Rule 1.9(a). The Rule recognizes loyalty and client confidences as the two interests of the client that must be protected. Under Rule 1.9(b), even if the former and current cases are not similar enough to be considered substantially related, an attorney cannot use confidential information to the disadvantage of a prior client like Clinton without her consent. **A is incorrect**; the imputed disqualification Rules do not permit Lawyer Perot, the disqualified lawyer, to hand off the case to his law partner. Lawyers like Perot who are disqualified under Rule 1.9 are not permitted under Rule 1.10 to screen themselves from representing a client like Dole so that his law partner can represent that client. **B is incorrect**. Assuming that Lawyer Perot is disqualified from representing Dole under Rule 1.9, that Rule nonetheless permits him to represent Dole if Clinton the former client gives informed consent. B is incorrect for two reasons. First, to be able to represent Dole, it is insufficient for Lawyer Perot merely to inform Clinton. As mentioned Lawyer Perot must obtain Clinton's informed consent. Second, it is unnecessary for Lawyer Perot to notify Dole about the situation before proceeding to represent Dole. **C is incorrect.** Although it is plausible for Lawyer Perot to refer Dole to another lawyer when Perot is disqualified from representing Dole, the use of a referral fee is unethical because Perot would be receiving a fee for something he was not ethically permitted to do, i.e., represent Dole. Even if Lawyer Perot were permitted to represent Dole but decided to refer the case to Nader the nature of fee sharing arrangement here is improper. Lawyers in different firms may divide fees only under specified conditions. First, the division must either be divided in proportion to the services performed by each lawyer or have each of them assume joint financial and ethical responsibility for the case. Second, Dole would have to agree in writing to the division, including the share for Nader and Perot. Rule 1.5, Comment 7. Finally, as with all fees, the total fee must be reasonable. Rule 1.5(e)(1)–(3).

PROBLEM #8. ANSWER B IS THE BEST ANSWER.

Lawyer Hillary cannot place the funds in her personal account. Rule 1.15 seeks to protect the property of others in the lawyer's possession and to maintain both the fact and appearance of the lawyer's honesty. Lawyers must keep separate identifiable trust fund accounts of clients' funds and they must not be commingled with the lawyer's money. Rule 1.15(a). A lawyer cannot deposit a settlement check in her personal account. The settlement check first must be deposited into the trust fund account for client funds. The lawyer also must promptly pay or deliver to the client any trust funds or property to which she is entitled. With a contingent fee, the lawyer must make a written accounting to the client, stating "the outcome of the matter, and if there is a recovery, showing the payment to the client and the method of its determination." Here, Lawyer Hillary has a choice of either forwarding the check to Farmer, or depositing the check in Farmer's trust account, informing Farmer of that deposit (**answer A**), and sending Farmer a check for Farmer's amount of the settlement (**answer C**).

PROBLEM #9. ANSWER B IS THE BEST ANSWER.

The lawyer-client privilege arose at common law and has been defined and refined through evidentiary rules and judicial precedent. Under the privilege, case law determines if the information sought is privileged, but a lawyer may reveal privileged materials or communications if compelled by legal process. The privilege protects communications made in confidence to a lawyer by a client for the purpose of seeking or obtaining legal advice. The lawyer-client privilege belongs to the client. The ethical duty of confidentiality prohibits a lawyer from talking about a client's case to anyone in the course of the representation, except as the client authorizes. The rationale for the ethical duty encourages a client to tell her lawyer all the information she knows about her case and also encourages a lawyer to learn additional information about her case from other sources. The ethical duty to protect information about a client's case applies to all information relating to the representation, whatever its source. A lawyer must maintain confidentiality whether she learns the information from the client, a third party, the media, or elsewhere. Primary distinctions between the evidentiary privilege and the ethical duty follow:

- Scope: For the privilege to apply, the client must communicate information to the lawyer, and intend that the communication to be in confidence. The ethical duty applies whether or not the client has told others the same information that she had told to her lawyer.

- Source: Only information obtained from the client or her agent is privileged. Any information relating to the representation of the client is protected by the ethical duty.

- Disclosure: No privileged information can be disclosed, even involuntarily, unless the client consents or the information is within the lawyer's discretion to disclose. For the ethical duty, a lawyer cannot voluntarily disclose; only by court order, consent, or by a discretionary exception can a lawyer disclose information relating to the representation.

The worksheets prepared by the accountant as Lawyer Jones's agent and given to Lawyer Jones contain information learned from talking with Smith and examining Smith's records. The worksheets also include other information relating to the representation of Smith, such as the accountant's expert advice about the best way to defend Smith's case. The information in **answers A, C and D** are all subject to the ethical duty of confidentiality only. The privilege is inapplicable to that information, which Lawyer Jones did not learn from his client Smith. Instead, he learned it learned from looking at public records and an old newspaper, and from talking to a taxi driver.

PROBLEM #10. ANSWER D IS THE BEST ANSWER.

Under Rule 5.3, a lawyer has a duty to instruct her nonlawyer employees about the ethical aspects of their employment, because a lawyer must exercise "reasonable care" to prevent them from violating confidentiality norms. The essence of a Rule 5.3 disciplinary violation is the failure to supervise the employee, even if the lawyer improperly discloses no confidential information. If the employee does improperly disclose, the lawyer has no ethical responsibility if the lawyer adequately supervised her. When a lawyer hires outside contractors for nonlawyer tasks, the lawyer must exercise care in selecting those people because they may have access to client information. If a breach of confidential information were to occur, the lawyer may have to inform the affected clients. ABA Formal Opinion 95–398.

A is incorrect. He does not have to do the work within his office but instead is permitted to hire an independent contractor to do the work subject to the Rule 5.3 standards discussed above. **B is incorrect**. As with answer A, a lawyer is not required to tell his client to make the copies for discovery. The lawyer may choose to do that, but it is unnecessary. As the discussion in the previous paragraph suggested, **C is incorrect**. Part of the reason for hiring a trustworthy copying firm is so that the lawyer does not have to physically be with them as they do their work.

PROBLEM #11. ANSWER D IS THE BEST ANSWER.

Under CJC Rule 2.11, she may preside in the cases described in answers A, B and C. In **answer A**, although Judge Jane knows the witness, that alone does not require that Judge Jane disqualify herself from presiding over th case. In **answer B**, recusal is required when the judge or a person within the third degree of relationship such as the judge's mother has more than a *de minimis* interest that could be substantially affected by the proceeding. CJC

2.11(A)(2)(c). The interest of the judge's mother is "not more than a *de minimis* interest," equaling to ownership of 100 shares out of three million shares issued. In **answer C**, recusal is required when the judge has an economic interest in a party to the proceeding. CJC 2.11(A)(3). However, the definition of an "economic interest" explicitly does not include "an interest in the issuer of government securities held by the judge." Because the judge owns $2,000 worth of general obligation bonds that were issued by the City of Air Authority, her interest does not qualify as an economic interest which requires her recusal. CJC 2.11, Comment 6. Thus, she may preside in answer C.

PROBLEM #12. ANSWER D IS THE BEST ANSWER.

Under Rule 1.16(b), a lawyer may withdraw if the client persists in a course of action that the lawyer reasonably believes is criminal or fraudulent. **A is incorrect**, because Rule 1.16(a)(1) states that a lawyer *must* (not may) withdraw from representation if her continued employment would result in violating the ethical rules or other law. **B is incorrect**. Under Rule 1.16(b)(3), a lawyer *may* (not must) withdraw if the client has used the lawyer's services to perpetuate a crime or fraud. **C is incorrect**. When representing a client would impose an unreasonable burden on a client, the lawyer may withdraw but the Rules do not require her to withdraw. (Regardless of whether a lawyer resigns or is fired, the lawyer must make reasonable efforts to protect the client's interests, such as turning over her papers and property. Rule 1.16(d).)

PROBLEM #13. ANSWER D IS THE BEST ANSWER.

As an exercise of their police powers, the states regulate the legal profession because it affects the public interest. The courts of each state have the inherent power to regulate members of the legal profession for their conduct, both in-court and elsewhere. The highest court of each state has adopted standards of professional ethics based on models created by the American Bar Association. The highest court in each state also regulates other aspects of the legal profession, such as admission standards and disciplinary enforcement. That court may delegate responsibility to the state bar association and to the Board of Bar Examiners for regulating bar admissions and disciplinary enforcement. **B and C are incorrect**, because neither the state bar association's power nor the Board of Bar Examiner's power is inherent. **A is incorrect**, because the state legislature lacks inherent power to regulate the practice of law which belongs to the judicial branch.

PROBLEM #14. ANSWER C IS THE BEST ANSWER.

While a lawyer is subject to discipline for wrongful conduct committed while she is acting in her capacity as a lawyer, she also may be disciplined for misconduct outside her capacity as a lawyer. Discipline in the latter category is limited to misconduct that functionally relates to your capacity to practice law, as with illegal conduct or conduct "involving dishonesty, fraud, deceit, or misrepresentation." Rule 8.4(c) prohibits lawyers from engaging in "dishonesty, fraud, deceit, or misrepresentation." Thus, even if the misdemeanor committed by Attorney Alex arose in a context completely unrelated to being admitted to practice, Alex is subject to discipline for such misconduct. In that regard, **A is incorrect** because the relationship of the misdemeanor to law practice is irrelevant. What is relevant is that the misconduct may involve engaging in dishonesty or deceit. **B is incorrect** because bar discipline may be imposed for criminal or non-criminal acts; classification of the misconduct as a felony is not relevant to the concern for honesty and trustworthiness. Because C is the correct answer, **D is incorrect**.

PROBLEM #15. ANSWER B IS THE BEST ANSWER.

Under Rule 1.10(b), if Attorney Joe leaves his law firm after having represented Stove, Inc., Bates and Bates may represent Oven, Inc. whose interests are materially adverse to Stove, Inc., as long as Oven, Inc.'s case is not the same or a substantially related matter as the one for which the firm had represented Stove, Inc. and no one remaining with Bates and Bates has confidential information from Stove, Inc. Rule 1.10(b). If everyone who had confidential information about Stove, Inc. has left Bates and Bates, it can represent Oven, Inc.

A is incorrect, because it is too broadly worded. As the aforementioned point about answer B indicated, despite the current matter for Oven, Inc. being materially adverse to its former client, Stove, Inc., as long as no one left at Bates and Bates has confidential information about Stove, Inc., neither Wishbone nor any other lawyer at Bates and Bates is subject to discipline for later representing Oven, Inc. **C is incorrect** for similar reasons. Even if the current case for Oven, Inc. is substantially related to matters handled by Joe while he was at Bates and Bates, no lawyer remaining at Bates and Bates is subject to discipline is none of them has confidential information about their former client Stove, Inc. **D is incorrect**. Screening lawyers who have confidential information is not recognized in the general imputed disqualification Rules like Rule 1.10; although screening is recognized by some court decisions, the Rules reserve its use for specific situation such as those described in Rules 1.11 and 1.12.

PROBLEM #16. ANSWER A IS THE BEST ANSWER.

Per Rule 1.11(a), after a lawyer leaves government employment, he can never represent a client in connection with a matter in which he

participated personally and substantially as a government employee, unless the appropriate government agency consents in
writing. Rule 1.11(a)(2). If LaVar knew only of the existence of the
Reds investigation and litigation while working at the Department
of Justice, it cannot be said under Rule 1.11 that he participated in
the Reds matter personally and substantially. A lawyer must have
"had such a heavy responsibility for the matter in question that it is
likely [he] became personally and substantially involved in the
investigative or deliberative processes regarding that matter." ABA
Formal Opinion 342 (1975). **Answer B is incorrect**. It cannot be
said that LaVar had any confidential government information about
the Reds matter, due to his lack of knowledge about that case.
Because LaVar did not participate at all in the Reds matter and has
no confidential information, it is unnecessary for the Department of
Justice to consent to his representation of Reds at Fine and Dart. **C
is incorrect**. As already discussed LaVar is not subject to discipline
in representing Reds at Fine and Dart, because of his lack of
personal and substantial participation in the Reds case while at the
Department of Justice. *If* LaVar had been disqualified from representing Reds at Fine and Dart under Rule 1.11, every other lawyer
at Fine and Dart is not disqualified. They may represent Reds if
LaVar is "screened" from any participation in the matter and LaVar
received no part of the fee from that matter. Rule 1.11(a). No
governmental consent to screening is required. **D is incorrect**,
because Rule 1.11 does not specify a time period for determining
whether a lawyer is subject to discipline for a conflict of interest.
Federal statutes do use time periods following government service
in an attempt to avoid a conflict of interest. In contrast to the Model
Rules, 18 U.S.C. § 207 restricts senior personnel of the federal
executive branch and federal agencies even after they have left
government service. That statute does not preempt state versions of
the MRPC, but it is broader than the Rules because it applies to
former government officials even if they are not lawyers. The
sanctions for violating § 207 are criminal rather than disciplinary.
The federal statute is inapplicable here because it applies only when
the former government official acted "personally and substantially
as a government official." Although it has a provision restricting
communications by a former government lawyer with his former
agency, that ban applies only to senior personnel. Because LaVar
had no such responsibility in the Reds matter and was at the
Department of Justice for only two years, the statute does not apply
to him.

PROBLEM #17. ANSWER B IS THE BEST ANSWER.

In a matter in which she is working "personally and substantially"
(such as *Sterling v. American Cigarette Corp.*), a judge or other

adjudicative official like Judge Dale cannot negotiate for employment with anyone involved as a party (here, American Cigarette Co.) or the lawyer (here, the Queeg and Constant firm) for a party. Rule 1.12(b). The standard applies to both trial judges and appellate judges. By contrast, as long as she *first* notifies the judge for whom she works, while working for the government, a judicial law clerk may negotiate for private work with a party who is involved in a matter in which the clerk participated personally and substantially. Rule 1.12(b). Thus, under the facts, Judge Dale is subject to discipline but Draper is not. For that reason, **A is incorrect**, because only Judge Dale is subject to discipline. **C is incorrect**. Having violated Rule 1.12(b), Judge Dale is subject to discipline regardless of whether Judge Dale goes to firm or is screened from the *Sterling* case. Draper is not subject to discipline because the facts indicate that Draper has complied with Rule 1.12(b) by notifying Judge Dale prior to negotiating with the Queeg firm. As a former judicial law clerk, Draper is disqualified from later representing either Sterling or American Cigarette because Draper worked with Judge Dale on the case of those parties personally and substantially on the merits. Rule 1.12(a). Any disqualification of Draper under Rule 1.12 is *not* imputed to any lawyer in the Queeg firm if Draper is screened from the disqualifying matter, and is apportioned no fee from that case. Second, the Queeg firm must promptly notify in writing the appropriate tribunal which can decide the sufficiency of the screening. Rule 1.12(c). For the aforementioned reasons, **D is incorrect** because Judge Dale is subject to discipline for having violated Rule 1.12(b).

PROBLEM #18. ANSWER B IS THE BEST ANSWER.

A lawyer has a duty to voluntarily disclose to the tribunal any legal authority in the controlling jurisdiction that he knows is directly adverse to his client's position and which his adversary has not disclosed. Rule 3.3(a)(2). A case directly on point from an adjacent state does not have to be disclosed. Because Townes must be aware of the adverse legal authority before he can be disciplined, the Rule does not punish the inept researcher. A competent researcher must ask whether any judicial decision that "opposing counsel has overlooked [is] one which the court should clearly consider in deciding the case". ABA Formal Opinion 280 (1949). A good advocate will distinguish any case precedent, argue that it should be overruled, or challenge the soundness of the precedent's reasoning. The duty to disclose adverse legal authority extends to the conclusion of the proceedings. Rule 3.3(c). **A is incorrect**, because the facts state that the cases directly against Townes's client's position are from the jurisdiction where the motion was filed and will be heard. **C is incorrect**. The Rules impose a duty on counsel to disclose adverse legal authority when the adversary counsel has failed to cite that authority. It is important for the judge to base any decision on all pertinent legal authority, because her decision may serve as precedent for other parties in later cases. **D is incorrect**, primarily because of the statement's breadth. While it is true that Townes is an officer of the court, the search for truth might suggest that he be required to disclose adverse legal authority from a broader geographic area than the jurisdiction where the lawsuit was filed and the motion is pending.

PROBLEM #19. ANSWER B IS THE BEST ANSWER.

One of the ethical duties for a prosecutor is the obligation to make a "timely disclosure" to the defendant of exculpatory evidence, i.e., evidence that "tends to negate the guilt of the accused or mitigate the punishment." Rule 3.8(d). Such evidence includes evidence related to guilt or innocence, as well as impeachment evidence. This ethical duty is similar to the prosecutor's constitutional duty to disclose exculpatory evidence established in *Brady v. Maryland*, 373 U.S. 83 (1963), which requires disclosure of evidence that is favorable to the accused and material to either guilt or punishment. Benson recently believed that the fire in this case was caused by an explosion in the furnace rather than the prosecution's current theory that arson caused the fire that Drew is charged with setting. Ford has an ethical duty to disclose this information about Benson to Drew's counsel. **A is incorrect**. The ethical duty for the prosecutor is to disclose the information to the defendant. In addition to discharging this duty, Ford may choose to recommend to his superior what he believes to be the appropriate disposition about the case but that is not his ethical duty. **C is incorrect**. Rule 3.8(d) refers to a "timely disclosure" of exculpatory information, suggesting that Ford's ethical duty is self-executing without the necessity of waiting for Drew's counsel to request such information. **D is incorrect**. Ford's duty to disclose is not dependent upon how he intends to present his case for the prosecution.

PROBLEM #20. ANSWER D IS THE BEST ANSWER.

Rule 4.2 prohibits a lawyer from communicating with a person known by the lawyer to be represented by counsel, unless counsel consents. The rationale for the Rule is to prevent you from unduly influencing the other person. Therefore, if the hotel manager still worked for Hotel International, Rule 4.2 might apply. However, Rule 4.2 is inapplicable to the situation here involving a former employee of a party. A related issue here involves the application of Rule 4.3. If a person has no lawyer, on behalf of a lawyer's client a lawyer cannot state or imply that she is disinterested. If the former hotel manager misunderstands the Lawyer Leland's role as a lawyer for the estate of the deceased, Lawyer Leland must make reasonable efforts to correct the former manager's misunderstanding. Otherwise, Lawyer Leland does not have to disclose that he represents his client. If the former manager were to ask Lawyer Leland for legal advice, Lawyer Leland should not provide such advice to the former manager if he knows or reasonably should know that the interests of his client and the unrepresented person have a "reasonable possibility of being in conflict." Rule 4.3. Finally, the former manager's memorandum sent to the home office of the owner of Hotel International (Hotels Are Us, Inc.) complaining about the maintenance and sprinkler issues was not a privileged document. Nor was the other information given by the former manager to Lawyer Leland privileged. The document was not sent to a lawyer for the Hotels Are Us; it was sent to the former manager's supervisor.

A is incorrect. As discussed, the information given by the former manager to Lawyer Leland was not privileged. Even if it was privileged, the former manager could decide whether to waive the application of the privilege. **B is incorrect**. The former manager's lack of counsel does not determine whether the motion to disqualify will be granted. As mentioned, Lawyer Leland has an ethical obligation to the former manager under Rule 4.3 in dealing with an unrepresented person. **C is incorrect**. If the hotel manager had still worked for Hotel International at the time of the interview, Rule 4.2 would apply, and Lawyer Leland would be subject to disqualification if he talked to the former manager without having obtained the consent of the counsel for Hotels Are Us.

PROBLEM #21. ANSWER A IS THE BEST ANSWER.

When Samantha told Lawyer Hester in confidence about abusing her children, that information was both privileged under the lawyer-client privilege and confidential under Rule 1.6. Lawyer Hester would be subject discipline if he reported Samantha's past child abuse to the police. **B is incorrect**. There are discretionary provisions for disclosure of confidential information, but none of them is categorized specifically as being in the interests of justice. **C is incorrect**. Although there is a state policy favoring child protection, lawyers have no duty under that statute or policy to disclose abuse. If lawyers were included in the statutory language, Lawyer Hester would be able to disclose what he knew about Samantha's misconduct. Rule 1.6(b)(6) permits a lawyer to disclose confidential information in order "to comply with other law or a court order." If a state law, like the child abuse reporting requirement here, requires that a lawyer disclose confidential client information, Rule 1.6(b)(6) overrides the general confidentiality requirement. **D is incorrect** for two reasons. First, the confidentiality requirement applies to information about past crimes. On the other hand, Rule 1.6(b)(1) permits Lawyer Hester to disclose "information relating to the representation of a client to the extent the lawyer reasonably believes necessary" to "prevent reasonably certain death or substantial bodily harm." The language enables a lawyer to disclose client information to prevent *future* death or bodily harm, but not Samantha's past misconduct. Second, answer D is incorrect because the Rule 1.6(b)(1) is discretionary rather than mandatory.

PROBLEM #22. ANSWER D IS THE BEST ANSWER.

Even if it could be said that a lawyer-client relationship existed here, the privilege does not apply to Simpson's admission to her. The lawyer-client privilege protects communications made in confidence to a lawyer by a client for the purpose of seeking or obtaining legal advice. In this case, there was a communication by Simpson made in confidence to Lawyer Giesel. If a prospective client consults a lawyer, their preliminary communications are privileged even if the lawyer is not ultimately retained. Rule 1.18. In this case, however, when Simpson admitted the robbery to Lawyer Giesel, she had already told him that she would not represent him because she does not handle criminal cases. Thus, his statements to her about having committed the crime cannot be said to have been primarily for obtaining Lawyer Giesel's legal advice or services. Therefore, no lawyer-client privilege attached to the statements Simpson made to Lawyer Giesel.

A is incorrect. One of the ways in which a lawyer-client relationship with a client is created occurs when a client intentionally wants a lawyer to provide legal services to him and the lawyer and the client agree. In this case, Lawyer Giesel never agreed to provide services to Simpson, but merely recommended to him ten lawyers who represent criminal defendants. **B is incorrect**, because there never was a lawyer-client relationship that existed. **C is incorrect**, because D is correct. The lawyer-client privilege is inapplicable to the statements by Simpson to Lawyer Giesel about committing the robbery.

PROBLEM #23. ANSWER B IS THE BEST ANSWER.

B is false. Because a judge is prohibited from serving as the family member's lawyer in any forum, CJC Rule 3.10, Judge Audra cannot serve as the lawyer for her brother's estate. **A is incorrect**, because it is true. A judge cannot accept an appointment to a fiduciary position such as an executrix, except for the estate, trust, or person of a member of the judge's family, as long as such service will not interfere with the proper performance of her judicial duties. CJC 3.8(A). She also cannot serve as the executrix if she as a fiduciary will likely be engaged in proceedings that would ordinarily come before her, or if the "estate, trust, or ward becomes involved in adversary proceedings in the court on which the judge serves, or one under its appellate jurisdiction." CJC Rule 3.8(B). Thus, Judge Audra may serve as executrix for her brother's estate. **Answer C is incorrect**, because it is true. Like anyone, Judge Audra may receive a bequest from a family member like her brother. **D is incorrect**, because it is true. Even though a judge cannot practice law, CJC Rule 3.10 permits her to "give legal advice to and draft or review documents for a member of [her] family." Therefore, the Code of Judicial Conduct permits Judge Audra to prepare her older brother's will.

PROBLEM #24. ANSWER C IS THE BEST ANSWER.

When a lawyer represents a client in either a litigation or a nonlitigation setting, she cannot knowingly "make a false statement of material law or fact to a third person." Rule 4.1(a). When a lawyer like Lawyer Lucy communicates with the defense lawyer in this case, her statements cannot be misleading or half-truths. **A is incorrect**. During a negotiation, a lawyer may exaggerate about facts and values. ABA Formal Opinion 06–439. However, the statement in the facts is not mere posturing between lawyers in a case. It is a false statement. **B is incorrect**. In a vehicular accident case, the speed of each vehicle is material to the case. For example, if a party is driving a vehicle over the speed limit, the party is negligent *per se* rather than merely negligent. **D is incorrect**, because Lawyer Lucy's statement is a false statement of material fact. It is true, however, that under generally accepted conventions in negotiation, certain types of statements ordinarily are not taken as statements of material fact. For example, estimates of price or value placed on the subject of a transaction and a party's intentions as to an acceptable settlement of a claim are ordinarily in this category.

PROBLEM #25. ANSWER D IS THE BEST ANSWER.

Both **A and B are incorrect**, but accurate. A is true. In an *ex parte* proceeding, a lawyer must disclose *all* material facts, adverse or otherwise, and all applicable law to the tribunal so that the court can make an informed decision. Rule 3.3(d). Lawyer Dove's increased duty of disclosure is necessary to offset the absence of an adversarial position presented by the other side. Rule 3.3, Comment 14. B is also true. Rule 3.3, Comment 3 states: "[t]here are circumstances where failure to make a disclosure is the equivalent of an affirmative misrepresentation." Nondisclosure may breach the duty of candor where the silent lawyer has unique knowledge of critical facts not known to the court and the court will be deceived about the actual facts on a key aspect of the matter if the lawyer keeps quiet. **C is incorrect**. A lawyer's duty not to make false statements of fact applies to both oral presentations to the court as well as to representations she makes in documents filed with the court. As discussed regarding statement II, the duty of candor to the court may be violated by a knowing error of omission as well as by an affirmative, knowing false statement of fact.

PROBLEM #26. ANSWER A IS THE BEST ANSWER.

The issue here is what constitutes the scope of "false" evidence for purposes of Rule 3.3. A lawyer cannot submit pleadings or other materials that she knows to be false. A document may contain "false" evidence if the document is not what it purports to be, even if the facts contained in the document are technically accurate. Here, the ethics violation is based on Lawyer Lemon's submission of interrogatory answers that she knew did not reflect the client's position, because she both unilaterally changed his initial responses and did not submit the changed answers to him for his approval prior to returning them to the adversary party. All of the alternative answers are incorrect. As the court observed in *In re Shannon*, 876 P.2d 548 (Ariz. 1994), the truth or correctness of the revised answers was not the issue. **B is incorrect**, because the facts suggest that the interrogatory answers she filed were correct. **C is incorrect**, because the factual accuracy of the answers does not relieve Lawyer Lemon of disciplinary sanctions. **D is incorrect**, because Lawyer Lemon knew that the interrogatory answers she submitted were not those from Client Donaghy.

PROBLEM #27. ANSWER D IS THE BEST ANSWER.

A and C are both incorrect, though true. Answer A is true. Lawyer Adkins knowingly made a false statement of fact to the court when she asked the court for maintenance for herself, based on being married to George. Answer C is also true. Rule 3.3(a)(3) states: "If a lawyer, ... has offered material evidence and the lawyer comes to know of its falsity, the lawyer shall take reasonable remedial measures, including, if necessary, disclosure to the tribunal." Although she had violated Rule 3.3(a)(1) by making a false statement of fact, she did not violate Rule 3.3(a)(3). When she realized that her claim for maintenance was based on a false premise, she took a reasonable remedial measure by her decision to dismiss her claim against George for maintenance and health insurance. **B is incorrect** and untrue. Lawyer Adkins took reasonable remedial measures to correct the false evidence she had already offered.

PROBLEM #28. ANSWER C IS THE BEST ANSWER.

Rule 1.8(h)(2) states: "A lawyer shall not ... settle a claim or potential claim for [malpractice] liability with an unrepresented client or former client unless that person is advised in writing of the desirability of seeking and is given a reasonable opportunity to seek the advice of independent legal counsel in connection therewith." Any discussion should stop short of an offer to settle a dispute, unless lawyer advises the client to seek independent counsel. Lawyer Jordan's offer was a general statement of her intent to compensate Client Davis for the amount he would have recovered if Lawyer Jordan had filed a lawsuit. Lawyer Jordan's statements related to the general idea of a settlement, rather than a specific dollar amount. **Answer A is incorrect**, because the advice to seek independent legal counsel does not apply unless Lawyer Jordan is discussing a specific settlement with Client Davis. **B is incorrect**. Rule 1.8(h)(2)'s reference to an unrepresented client means that the Rule applies when a lawyer is discussing dispute resolution with a current or former client without having advised that unrepresented person to seek independent counsel. Another lawyer does not have to be present; the Rule merely requires that the lawyer advise the unrepresented client that it may be a good idea to have another lawyer to consult for advice about the dispute. **D is incorrect**, because B is not true.

PROBLEM #29. ANSWER A IS THE BEST ANSWER.

With his old law firm, Lawyer Toner knew all the information about all the clients of the old law firm. If Lawyer Toner changes law firms knowing confidential information about every one of his old law firm's clients, including the commuter airline, he cannot represent one of the injured passengers in a substantially related matter based on the same accident for two reasons. First, he cannot represented an injured passenger if his old firm had previously represented the commuter airline whose interests are materially adverse to Lawyer Toner's new client. Second, he cannot represent a passenger because he has confidential information about the commuter airline. Rule 1.9(b). **B is incorrect**; any consent by the commuter airline to permit Lawyer Toner to represent the new passenger in the latest lawsuit against the airline must be in writing. Lawyer Toner as the otherwise disqualified lawyer may represent the passenger against the airline if the airline gives informed consent in writing. Rule 1.9(b). An informed consent requires the law old firm to explain to the airline the relevant risks, as well as their significance. Rule 1.0(k). **C is incorrect**. Under the Model Rules, screening Lawyer Toner from the case is not permitted. (Some case law and some state disciplinary codes permit the use of screening if this type of conflict of interest exists, to remove the imputation of disqualification by walling off the disqualified lawyer and permitting his colleagues to proceed with the representation.) **D is incorrect.** Even if Lawyer Toner were to leave the new large law firm right away, his knowledge of the commuter airline's confidential information would be imputed to the rest of the lawyers in the new law firm. In this type of conflict of interest, screening Lawyer Toner from the other lawyers would not prevent the others from also being disqualified from representing the new passenger.

PROBLEM #30. ANSWER C IS THE BEST ANSWER.

If Lawyer Dennehy leaves her law firm after having represented Drugs B Good, her old firm may represent the Estate of Jones whose interests are materially adverse to Drugs B Good, as long as the Estate of Jones's case is not the same or a substantially related matter as the one for which the firm had represented Drugs B Good *and* no one remaining with Lawyer Dennehy's old firm has confidential information from Drugs B Good. Rule 1.10(b). If everyone who had confidential information about Drugs B Good has left the old firm, it can represent the Estate of Jones. Lawyer Dennehy was the only lawyer at her old law firm who had represented Drugs B Good, and she is no longer practicing there. Thus, answer C is true. The old law firm's client, the Estate of Jones, has an interest materially adverse to Drugs B Good, the old client. The lawsuit by the Estate of Jones is not the same or substantially similar to any lawsuit upon which the old firm had represented Drugs B Good, because this law suit is the first of its kind involving the specific pharmaceutical. **Answers A and B are incorrect**. As discussed above, Rose and Lind can represent the plaintiff, the Estate of Jones. Because answer C is true, the unqualified nature of answer A prohibiting *any* lawsuit by the plaintiff is not true. **D is incorrect**, because neither A nor B is correct.

PROBLEM #31. ANSWER A IS THE BEST ANSWER.

Under Rule 1.2(a), a defendant's wish to forego further appeals and accept the death penalty, like other decisions relating to the objectives of litigation, is essentially his decision which his lawyer must respect. As the agent for her client, Client Convict, Lawyer Lani must follow his "decisions concerning the objectives of representation." After Client Convict sets the goals for Lawyer Lani's representation, she is responsible for deciding the necessary means to accomplish those objectives. Rule 1.2(a). **B is incorrect**. She will not be subject to discipline if she has a reasonable and objective basis to doubt Client Convict's competency to make a decision foregoing further appeals. If that is true, Lawyer Lani must, in a timely fashion, inform the trial court and request the court to make a judicial determination of Client Convict's competency. Rule 1.14(b). She will have to demonstrate an objective and reasonable basis for believing that Client Convict cannot act in his own interest. For similar reasons, **C is incorrect**. As a threshold matter, seeking to have a court question his competency requires that Lawyer Lani have a good faith belief that he is not competent to participate in decisions relating to seeking further relief. **D is incorrect**. She may enlist his family's assistance to persuade him not to give up his appeals, but Rule 1.6 prohibits her from disclosing his confidential communications to his family.

PROBLEM #32. ANSWER D IS THE BEST ANSWER.

D is the correct answer. The law firm will not be subject to discipline if it keeps Able's name in the firm name. The Model Rules standards for advertising apply not only to traditional advertising methods such as television and radio, but they also apply to professional designations in media like websites. A lawyer or law firm may use the name of a deceased or retired member of the law firm in the firm name in a line of succession. Rule 7.5, Comment 1. **A is incorrect**, because changing the firm name to Unites States Lawyers is misleading. Under the Rules, a law firm cannot use a firm name, letterhead or other professional designation that is false or misleading. For example, a firm may use a trade name, e.g., "Fourth Street Clinic," as long as it is not false or misleading, *and* does not suggest a connection with either a governmental agency or a legal services organization. Rule 7.5(a). Calling the firm United States Lawyers may suggest that the firm is connected with the federal government. **B is incorrect**, because that statement is misleading. When a law firm has offices in more than one state, it may use the same firm name in all its offices. If the lawyers are admitted to practice in fewer than all of the states where the law firm has its offices, each lawyer's jurisdictional limits must appear on the law firm letterhead and law firm publicity. Rule 7.5(b). The statement that all of its lawyers practice are admitted to practice everywhere in the United States is misleading for two reasons. First, the firm has only six offices and the offices are east of the Mississippi River. Second, the law firm's lawyers are not all admitted to practice in all six of the states where the law firm's offices are located. **C is incorrect**. If Baker holds a public office such as United States Senator, the law firm cannot continue to use his name in the firm name because he does not have an active, regular practice with the firm. Rule 7.5(c). Otherwise, it is misleading for the firm to use his name in its communications.

PROBLEM #33. ANSWER A IS THE BEST ANSWER.

A lawyer cannot give anything of value in exchange for a recommendation of her services. Rule 7.2(b)(1). Lawyer Dudley cannot pay anyone to promote her services or to distribute her business cards, and she cannot pay her support staff an amount connected to the amount of business he sends to her. Lawyer Dudley must supervise any nonlawyer employed by her so that he does not violate the Rules. Rule 7.2, Comment 5. **Answer B is incorrect**; it will not subject her to discipline. Lawyer Dudley is permitted to pay the "usual charges" of a lawyer referral service conducted by a legal services plan, a not-for-profit, or a qualified lawyer referral service. Rule 7.2(b)(2). Unless the referral plan is a not-for-profit or a qualified plan, she cannot become involved in paying an entity for referring cases to her. **Answer C is incorrect**; it also will not subject Lawyer Dudley to discipline. She may enter into reciprocal referral agreements with another lawyer or nonlawyer professional, if that agreement is not exclusive and her client is told about the existence and nature of the agreement. Rule 7.2(b)(4). Otherwise, she cannot pay anyone for sending professional work her way. Rule 7.2, Comment 6. The purpose of these Rules is that she must be independent of other persons. Because both answers B and C are incorrect, answer **D is incorrect**.

PROBLEM #34. ANSWER C IS THE BEST ANSWER.

The scope of a lawyer's duty to report misconduct does not include a duty to report any and all misconduct. The Rule focuses on conduct that raises a "substantial question" about the other lawyer's "honesty, trustworthiness or fitness as a lawyer." Rule 8.3(a). A lawyer's duty includes the exercise of judgment about the seriousness of the violation. Lawyer Milligan's duty includes reporting any lawyer like Lawyer Richardson who is suspected of alcoholism, drug addiction, or other mental impairment. ABA Formal Opinion 03–431. If Lawyer Milligan recognizes the symptoms of mental impairment that significantly harm Lawyer Richardson's ability to represent clients, Lawyer Milligan has the discretion to consult with Lawyer Richardson, members of her law firm, mental health professionals, or members of an established lawyer assistance program. There are two contexts when the Rule 8.3(a) duty to report is extinguished. It is superseded by the duty of confidentiality under Rule 1.6, as when Lawyer Milligan's client tells her that another lawyer has engaged in serious misconduct, or when as here Lawyer Milligan represents Lawyer Richardson who has herself committed serious misconduct. In each instance, Lawyer Milligan learned the information during the lawyer-client relationship. Rule 8.3, Comment 5. It would violate the lawyer-client relationship for Lawyer Milligan to report her client to the appropriate professional authority. For the reasons just discussed, both **A and B are incorrect**. By representing Lawyer Richardson, Lawyer Milligan's duty or discretion to report Lawyer Richardson is extinguished. **D is incorrect**. Any duty to report Lawyer Richardson is not dependent upon criminal charges being lodged against her.

PROBLEM #35. ANSWER B IS THE BEST ANSWER.

Generally, a lawyer or her firm cannot share legal fees with a nonlawyer, in order to control nonlawyer involvement in the delivery of legal services. Rule 5.4(a). That Rule recognizes several exceptions to the general Rule, one of which permits Lawyer Richards's firm to pay money to his estate for a reasonable period of time after his death. Rule 5.4(a)(1). Because answer A is the opposite of the correct answer B, **A is incorrect**. **C is incorrect**. Although the law firm may pay money to Lawyer Richards's estate or to another person such as his widow, the Rules do not require payment of those fees directly to a nonlawyer like Lawyer Richards's widow. **D is incorrect**. Another of the exceptions to the general Rule against sharing legal fees with a nonlawyer permits Lawyer Willard to buy the law practice of Lawyer Richards and pay the purchase price to the Lawyer Richards's nonlawyer executor of the estate. Rule 5.4(a)(2).

PROBLEM #36. ANSWER B IS THE BEST ANSWER.

Subject to several exceptions, the general ethical standard bans a judge from two types of communications: (1) initiation, permission or consideration of *ex parte* communications; or (2) consideration of other communications made to the judge outside the presence of the parties or their lawyers, concerning a pending or impending case. CJC Rule 2.9(A). One of the exceptions to the general rule states that "[a] judge may obtain the written advice of a disinterested expert on the law applicable to a proceeding before the judge, if the judge gives advance notice to the parties of the person to be consulted and the subject matter of the advice to be solicited, and affords the parties a reasonable opportunity to object and respond to the notice and to the advice received." CJC Rule 2.9(A)(2). In this case, Judge Ice could afford the parties the opportunity to respond by filing additional briefs in the case. **A and C are incorrect**. CJC Rule 2.9(A)(3) permits Judge Ice to consult with other judges, but says nothing about having to inform the parties before or after that consultation. **D is incorrect**. CJC Rule 2.9(A)'s exceptions list several methods for a judge to receive additional advice about rulings. In addition to the aforementioned methods, it is true that the customary method for a judge to learn more about legal issues is to request the parties to submit additional legal briefs. However, the Code of Judicial Conduct also permits a judge to consult with "court staff and court officials whose functions are to aid the judge in carrying out the judge's adjudicative responsibilities.... "

PROBLEM #37. ANSWER B IS THE BEST ANSWER.

Rule 1.18(a) states that "[a] person who discusses with a lawyer the possibility of forming a client-lawyer relationship with respect to a matter is a prospective client." However, a lawyer has a duty of confidentiality to the prospective client like Client Callie, no matter how brief was their initial conference. Rule 1.18(b). The confidential information obtained from her cannot be disclosed unless she agrees in writing that the content of the conversations are not to be treated as confidential. If Lawyer Linus declines the representation, the Rules treat Client Callie as a former client regarding the confidential information she disclosed to him, and he cannot use that information to her disadvantage. Rule 1.9; Rule 1.18. Rule 1.18 differs from the other Rules for imputed disqualification. Whereas Rule 1.10 attributes a lawyer's conflict of interest to all the lawyers with whom he practices, Rule 1.18(d)(1) is not as broad. Unless Lawyer Linus has information that "could be significantly harmful" to Client Callie, anyone with whom Lawyer Linus practices can represent someone else in the matter. Rule 1.18(c). Even if his colleagues are subject to disqualification, however, they may obtain informed consent waivers from both the national hotel chain and Client Callie in order to represent the national hotel chain. Rule 1.18(d)(1). If the national hotel chain and Client Callie *both* do not waive the conflict of interest, Rule 1.18(d)(2) nevertheless permits Lawyer Linus to be screened from his colleagues in order for them to represent the national hotel chain. Screening is possible only if his colleagues take "reasonable measures to avoid exposure to more disqualifying information than was reasonably necessary to determine whether to represent the [former] prospective client." Rule 1.18(d)(2). Several steps are necessary for an effective screen. First, it must be set up in a timely manner, ideally before anyone else raises the issue. Second, Lawyer Linus's colleagues must promptly inform Client Callie in writing. Third, they must notify the national hotel chain, describing the subject about which Lawyer Linus consulted Client Callie as well as the screening methods to be used. Rule 1.18, Comment 8. Finally, Lawyer Linus cannot receive any part of the fee paid by the national hotel chain. **A is incorrect**. As Rule 1.18(a) makes clear, Client Callie was a prospective client of the law firm because she discussed with Lawyer Linus "the possibility of forming a client-lawyer relationship with respect to a matter.... " **C is incorrect**. As with any confidential disclosures, Client Callie may consent to disclosure of what she told Lawyer

Linus. The previous discussion indicates that the law firm may thereafter represent the national hotel chain if Lawyer Linus and the confidential information he possesses are effectively screened. **D is incorrect**. Without an effective screen, it is true that Client Callie's information is imputed to all others in the law firm. However, the previous discussion indicates that an effective screen cures that imputed disqualification.

PROBLEM #38. ANSWER D IS THE BEST ANSWER.

Under Rule 1.10(a), when a lawyer moves from private practice in one office to a law firm or corporate law office that represents a client with interests adverse to his former client, the lawyer's new firm can use an ethics screen and avoid imputed disqualification without obtaining or asking for the consent of his former client. The new law firm must provide written notice of the screen to Lawyer Niles's former client. The notice must (1) describe the screening procedures, (2) promise that both the new firm and Lawyer Niles will comply with the Rules, (3) state that judicial review of the screen is available, and (4) include an agreement that responds to Lawyer Niles's former client's concerns. Upon written request of his former client, Lawyer Niles and a partner at his new law firm periodically must certify compliance with the screening procedure. **A is incorrect**, both because D is correct and because there are likely to be other cases in which the new law firm may continue to represent its old client when the interests of Lawyer Niles's former client are not relevant. **B is incorrect**. Again, the issues regarding the disqualification of Lawyer Niles and his new law firm extend only to the situation in which the new firm is representing its longstanding client and the adverse interests of Lawyer Niles's former client are involved. **C is incorrect**. As the earlier discussion indicated, Rule 1.10(a)'s provision for screening requires notice to Lawyer Niles's old client but not its consent in order for the new law firm to screen Lawyer Niles from information about the representation of the new firm's old client.

PROBLEM #39. ANSWER B IS THE BEST ANSWER.

Except for agreements for retirement benefits, the Rules prohibit agreements that restrict a lawyer's right to practice after she leaves her law firm. Lawyer Nancy cannot offer or make a contract restricting her right to practice law after the termination of the relationship created by a partnership, operating, shareholder, or employment agreement. Rule 5.6(a). (The exception to Rule 5.6(a) permits a restriction on her right to practice that is part of an agreement on retirement benefits. ABA Formal Opinion 06–444. If she is retiring, she would not be available to represent clients anyway. A court will examine the benefits and restrictions as a whole to decide whether a law firm has properly used the retirement label to implement a covenant not to compete with the remaining lawyers.) **A is incorrect**, because it is a variant of the opposite of answer B, which is correct. **C is incorrect**. Restrictive covenants can subject you to discipline even if they are reasonable in length and geographic area. ABA Formal Opinion 300 (1961). Courts likewise will not enforce such restrictive covenants. **D is incorrect**. No one, including a lawyer, can restrict her right to practice law as part of the settlement of a client's case. Rule 5.6(b). This Rule qualifies the language of Rule 1.2(d), which requires a lawyer to go along with her client's decisions about settlements. The rationale for the Rule relates to both the lawyer's freedom and her client's freedom.

PROBLEM #40. ANSWER D IS THE BEST ANSWER.

Answers A and B are both true. **Answer A is incorrect** but true. What the client reveals to his lawyer may be covered by the lawyer-client privilege, but that information may not qualify as information "prepared in anticipation of litigation." On the other hand, many facts developed during trial preparation do not come from the client and therefore are not privileged. **Answer B is incorrect** but true. The lawyer-client privilege protects communications between clients and their lawyers, thus encouraging an open dialogue. The work product doctrine is broader and precludes lawyers from capitalizing on an adversary's work efforts. While the work product doctrine is codified as to tangible items, such as letters, in Federal Rule of Civil Procedure 26(b)(3)¢k¢k, work product also is aimed at protecting a lawyer's legal theories and strategies developed in preparation for litigation. **Answer C is incorrect**. Like the lawyer-client privilege generally, work product is protected even after the termination of the litigation for which it was prepared. *F.T.C. v. Grolier, Inc.*, 462 U.S. 19 (1983)¢k¢k. Work product extends to subsequent litigation. The rationale is that FRCP 26¢k¢k, which governs discovery, does not explicitly confine the work product privilege to the litigation in which it is sought.

PROBLEM #41. ANSWER C IS THE BEST ANSWER.

Under CJC Rule 3.13(A)-(B), a judge may accept things of value such as ordinary social hospitality, or gifts from friends or relatives as long as acceptance would not "appear to a reasonable person to undermine the judge's independence, integrity, or impartiality." **A is incorrect.** The frequency of the lawyer's appearance in the judge's court would not prevent him from giving a wedding present to his friend. **B is incorrect**, because as long as the gift does not undermine Judge Chen's independence, integrity or impartiality, CJC Rule 3.13(B) permits Judge Chen to accept the wedding gift without publicly reporting its receipt. **D is incorrect**. The CJC does not use a dollar value to measure the propriety of the gift.

PROBLEM #42. ANSWER C IS THE BEST ANSWER.

A lawyer cannot engage in an *ex parte* communication with a judge, unless a law or court order specifically permits it, e.g., *ex parte* communications with a judge for scheduling purposes. Rule 3.5(b). **A is incorrect**, because a local rule allows for an *ex parte* conversation for scheduling purposes. **B is incorrect**. While a lawyer may be disciplined for intentionally delaying legal proceedings (see Rules 3.2 and 8.4(d)), there is no evidence that Lawyer Penelope intended to delay these proceedings; she simply forgot that she had a scheduling conflict with the pretrial conference date that the judge had set during the pretrial. **D is incorrect**; some judges and some local rules do require lawyers to carry their calendars for ease of scheduling and to avoid the situation described in this problem. However, the Model Rules do not include this requirement.

PROBLEM #43. ANSWER B IS THE BEST ANSWER.

Answer B is not an accurate statement of the duties imposed under Rule 1.13 and the SEC regulations. The statements in B are the opposite of accurate statements about the extent of a lawyer's knowledge before she has a duty to report wrongdoing. Rule 1.13(b) requires the lawyer to "know" someone is engaged in wrongdoing before being required to report that person, but the SEC Regulation is triggered when the lawyer merely "becomes aware" of evidence of a material violation of law, even though it will be difficult for the lawyer to evaluate the risk to the entity. **A's statements are incorrect but true**. The lawyer's duties under Rule 1.13 must relate to the representation of the entity. Under the SEC Regulations, after a lawyer appears and practices before the SEC, she must follow the Sarbanes–Oxley Act procedures regardless of whether what she knows relates to her representation of her client. **C's statements are incorrect but true**. While Rule 1.13 requires reporting of a violation that is likely to cause substantial injury to the entity, the broader SEC Regulations require the lawyer to report any "material violation" of federal or state (securities) law regardless of potential harm to the entity. **Answer D is incorrect but true**. The lawyer's reporting duties under the SEC Regulations are more specific than the Rule 1.13 standards. The lawyer must report a problem to the entity's chief legal officer who then must investigate the problem. Next, unless the reporting lawyer is told that there is no problem or that steps are being taken to prevent its recurrence, that lawyer must report the problem to the entity's audit committee or a different regulatory compliance committee set up by the entity. If the reporting lawyer receives inappropriate responses, she must explain that to the chief legal officer. If she is fired for reporting the problem, she may notify the entity's Board or the compliance committee about her termination and its reason. Thereafter, she may disclose the entity's conduct to the SEC to prevent or rectify conduct "likely to cause substantial injury to the financial interest of property of the issuer or investors." If the lawyer who learns the information works under the supervision of another lawyer, she may report the problem to her supervisor, who then must proceed through the aforementioned steps.

PROBLEM #44. ANSWER C IS THE BEST ANSWER.

After a lawyer leaves government employment, she can never represent a client in connection with a matter in which she participated personally and substantially as a government employee, unless the appropriate government agency consents in writing. Rule 1.11(a)(2). Here, Lawyer Powell lacked substantial responsibility over the lawsuit a matter if she did not directly supervise the Environmental Protection Division's litigation. For her to have had substantial responsibility, she must have "had such a heavy responsibility for the matter in question that it is likely [she] became personally and substantially involved in the investigative or deliberative processes regarding that matter." ABA Formal Opinion 342 (1975). **A is incorrect**. Because she was not involved in the oil company case substantially and personally, she is not subject to discipline even though the case is the same matter that was pending while she worked for the Attorney General. A "matter" is "any judicial or other proceeding, application, request for a ruling or other determination, contract, claim, controversy, investigation, charge, accusation, arrest or other particular matter involving a specific party or parties." Rule 1.11(e)(1). For Rule 1.11, a "matter" is broader than a case filed before a tribunal but narrower than a set of facts. **B is incorrect**. Lawyer Powell was not involved personally and substantially with the case against the oil company while she worked as General Counsel in the Environmental Protection Division at the Attorney General's office. Consent would be relevant only if she otherwise would be facing an ethical violation for switching sides in the same matter. **D is incorrect**, because the premise is untrue: Lawyer Powell was not participating personally and substantially in the oil company case. *If* the assumptions for answer D were true, then it would have been the correct answer. If Lawyer Powell were subject to discipline and disqualified from representing the oil company under Rule 1.11, every other lawyer in her new firm is not disqualified. They may represent the oil company if she is "screened" from any participation in the matter and she receives no part of the fee from that matter. Rule 1.11(a). No governmental consent to screening is required. The law firm would have to "promptly" notify the Environmental Protection Division in writing about the conflict and the screening so that it can be certain that the screening is effective. Rule 1.11(a)(2). If the imputation rules were strict, private clients' counsel choices would be limited when they want to employ a former government lawyer with significant experience and knowledge about how government works.

PROBLEM #45. ANSWER B IS THE BEST ANSWER.

If a client wants to recognize and reward a lawyer for her outstanding legal work, any gift transaction from him to her must meet general standards of fairness. If Client Carter does make a substantial gift to Lawyer Ford and the gift requires the preparation of a legal instrument such as a will, Lawyer Ford cannot draft it. Another reason that precludes Lawyer Ford's drafting a will for Client Carter would be if the funds for the vehicle constituted a large percentage of Client Carter's assets; Rule 1.8(c) prevents her from drafting a will for Client Carter when the will gives her a disproportionate percentage of his assets. **A is incorrect**. Although agency and fiduciary duty law treat client gifts to a lawyer as presumptively fraudulent, Rule 1.8, Comment 6, as described in the earlier discussion such gifts are allowed under limited circumstances. **C is incorrect.** Ethically, the idea for a "substantial gift" needs to come from the client and not from his lawyer, who cannot solicit a substantial gift, even in his will. Rule 1.8(c). **D is incorrect**, because of the explanation about why B is the correct answer—a client cannot make a substantial gift to his lawyer if the lawyer drafts an instrument in connection with the gift. Because of Rule 1.8(k)'s imputed disqualification provision, a lawyer in a different law firm should draft the instrument. That lawyer's obligation to the client includes an explanation to the client that he is not obligated to give any gift to his lawyer.

PROBLEM #46. ANSWER C IS THE BEST ANSWER.

Although a lawyer is subject to discipline for having a sexual relationship with a client, he may not be subject to discipline if a consensual sexual relationship already existed prior to the beginning of the lawyer-client relationship. Rule 1.8(j). Comment 18 states: "Sexual relationships that predate the client-lawyer relationship are not prohibited. Issues relating to the exploitation of the fiduciary relationship and client dependency are diminished when the sexual relationship existed prior to the commencement of the client-lawyer relationship. However, before proceeding with the representation in these circumstances, the lawyer should consider whether the lawyer's ability to represent the client will be materially limited by the relationship. See Rule 1.7(a)(2)." Because of his extended relationship with Client Cardio, Lawyer Lee's independent professional judgment may have become impaired. Thus, in the words of Rule 1.7, Lawyer Lee should seriously consider whether to withdraw from representing Client Cardio, because his ability to represent her is materially limited by their romantic relationship. **A is incorrect**, because as mentioned, a lawyer is not necessarily subject to discipline for having sexual relations with a client that predate their lawyer-client relationship. **B is incorrect**. Sexual relations with a client create an ethical problem for a lawyer because of his potential undue influence and the client's emotional vulnerability, both of which affect his independent personal judgment and rebut the client's meaningful consent. **D is incorrect**. While his sexual relationship with Client Cardio predated his lawyer-client relationship with her and therefore relieves him of an ethical problem under Rule 1.8(j), he may still have a conflict of interest problem under Rule 1.7 if continues to represent her while their romantic relationship continues.

PROBLEM #47. ANSWER B IS THE BEST ANSWER.

When a lawyer represents a client, she must act with reasonable diligence. Diligence includes a zealous lawful and ethical commitment to accomplish her client's objectives "despite opposition, obstruction, or personal inconvenience" to the lawyer. Reasonable diligence requires that a lawyer assesses the work that needs to be done on her clients' behalf and to exercise reasonable promptness in completing that work. A statute of limitation, a rule of procedure, or your client's schedule may affect a timetable for completing her work. Delays happen in law practice. Lawyers who represent indigent defendants often have excessive caseloads which adversely affect their duties of diligence and competence. A lawyer must control her workload to avoid impairment of the obligations she owes to her existing clients. ABA Formal Opinion 06–441. Likewise, if her workload begins to affect those duties, she somehow must find assistance or reduce her workload. **A is incorrect**. Lawyer Landy's supervisor has an obligation under Rule 5.1 to exercise his supervisory authority to ensure that Lawyer Landy acts diligently in all of her appointed cases. At a minimum, her supervisor has a duty to monitor her caseload, assessing the type and complexity of those cases, her experience and ability, the resources she has for support, and any other duties assigned to her in the Public Defender's law office. ABA Formal Opinion 06–441. **C is incorrect**, because Lawyer Landy cannot ask her clients to waive the duty of diligence that she owes to them. **D is incorrect**, because a court has the supervisory authority to appoint any lawyer to represent an indigent party or any other person in need of representation. If Lawyer Landy's supervisor fails to provide relief for her, she should move up the chain of command within her organization and then seek relief from the court with jurisdiction over the case. If no one can offer relief, she must continue to represent her clients to the best of her ability.

PROBLEM #48. ANSWER A IS THE BEST ANSWER.

When a sole practitioner dies or becomes disabled, the possibility exists that her clients may be harmed. Accordingly, the duty of diligence may require that a solo practitioner should have a plan to protect her clients' interests and to assure that their cases are not neglected. ABA Formal Opinion 92–369. The plan should designate a lawyer who would notify the clients, review the files only to identify the clients, and decide which cases needed immediate attention. Rule 1.3, Comment 5. That Comment also refers to Rule 28 of the American Bar Association Model Rules for Lawyer Disciplinary Enforcement, which provides "for court appointment of a lawyer to inventory files and take other protective action in absence of a plan providing for another lawyer to protect the interests of the clients of a deceased or disabled lawyer." **B, C, and D are incorrect**. The Comment to Rule 1.3 does not prescribe any of the alternative courses of action. While Lawyer Lana may consider each of those courses, none of them is required or even suggested by the Rules.

PROBLEM #49. ANSWER A IS THE BEST ANSWER.

Sending an email to a represented person, and simultaneously sending a copy of the communication to his lawyer, is impermissible under Rule 4.2, unless the represented person's lawyer already has consented to the communication. By itself, simultaneously sending an email to a represented person and her lawyer does not satisfy the prior consent requirement. An email is a "communication" covered by Rule 4.2, which requires that a lawyer have the "prior consent" of a represented person's lawyer before communicating directly with that person. Prior consent is consent obtained in advance of the communication. Rule 4.2 embodies principles of fairness. "[T]he anti-contact rules provide protection of the represented person against overreaching by adverse counsel, and reduce the likelihood that clients will disclose privileged or other information that might harm their interests." ABA Formal Opinion 95–396. Sending a simultaneous copy of the communication to the opposing lawyer does not eliminate the risk that the represented person will be subject to overreaching. There is no assurance that an email sent simultaneously to a lawyer and his client will be received by them at the same time. The lawyer might not receive his copy of the communication until after the client has received it and made a direct uncounseled response. More important, permitting a lawyer to communicate directly with a represented person by email, even if a copy is also sent to counsel, would undermine the role of the represented person's lawyer as spokesperson, intermediary and buffer. Under Rule 4.2, a represented person is entitled to be insulated from any direct communications from opposing counsel. All other communications relating to the subject matter of the representation, whether in person, by letter or via email, must proceed through the represented person's lawyer absent prior consent. **B is incorrect**. There is no rule requiring that settlement offers be in writing. Often, such offers are made orally, in person or by phone. **C is incorrect**. The anti-contact rule applies regardless of the type of communication being sent to the party who is known to have a lawyer. **D is incorrect**. As noted, the fact that the simultaneous copy of the email is sent at the same time does not assure that the recipients will receive them at the same time, thereby creating a risk that the adversary will respond without first consulting his lawyer.

PROBLEM #50. ANSWER B IS THE BEST ANSWER.

Under Rule 1.18(b), a lawyer must neither disclose nor make adverse use of confidential information learned from a prospective client. In addressing whether a lawyer who participates in a bidding process with a prospective client should later be personally disqualified from representing a client with materially adverse interests in a substantially related matter, Rule 1.18 provides that "[a] lawyer ... shall not represent a client with interests materially adverse to those of a prospective client in the same or a substantially related matter if the lawyer received information from the prospective client that could be significantly harmful to that person in the matter.... " Lawyer Fisher from the Law Firm Carey & Dyson participated in the bidding process and is not personally prohibited from representing Company Bates because she did not receive any confidential information from Company Abner during the bidding process. Therefore, she may represent Company Bates in the lawsuit brought against it by Company Abner. **A is incorrect**, because it is nonsensical. **C is incorrect**, because it is assumed that the basic facts do not include confidential information. **D is incorrect**, because it is nonsensical.

PROBLEM #51. ANSWER C IS THE BEST ANSWER.

An assistant city law director is prohibited from representing criminal defendants in proceedings in which the state is prosecuting. Specifically, an assistant city law director is prohibited from representing criminal defendants in proceedings in which the state is a plaintiff because the representation is directly adverse to the state which is a conflict of interest under Rule 1.7(a)(1) that cannot be waived under Rule 1.7(b), because, even with client consent, Rule 1.7(c)(1) does not permit a representation prohibited by law. A lawyer is prohibited from representing a criminal defendant in a proceeding prosecuted by another lawyer in the same law firm because such conduct is prejudicial to the administration of justice in violation of Rule 8.4(d). Otherwise, no one would have any confidence in the justice system. If the assistant law director is disqualified, are the lawyers in her law firm likewise disqualified? To determine whether a conflict of interest of an assistant city director of law is imputed to law firm partners or associates, a lawyer must look at several rules. The general rule of imputation, Rule 1.10(a) imputes a prohibited conflict of interest under Rule 1.7 (or Rule 1.9) to lawyers associated in a law firm unless the conflict of interest is based on a personal interest of the prohibited lawyer and does not present a significant risk of materially limiting the representation of the client by the remaining lawyers in the firm. However, the general rule of imputation, Rule 1.10(a), does not apply to lawyers associated in a law firm with former or current government lawyers. Rule 1.10(f) states that "[t]he disqualification of lawyers associated in a firm with former or current government lawyers is governed by Rule 1.11." Rule 1.11(c) applies to current government lawyers, but Rule 1.11(c) does not impute the disqualification of a current government lawyer to the lawyers associated in a law firm with the current government attorney. While it is true that by law many states disqualify a lawyer practicing with a prosecutor from representing clients in an adversarial position to that prosecutor in the jurisdiction of that lawyer, the conflict of interest is not directly imputed by Rule 1.11(c) to law firm partners or associates who wish to privately represent criminal defendants outside the jurisdiction of the city law director.

PROBLEM #52. ANSWER C IS THE BEST ANSWER.

Rule 1.16(d) provides, in part: "The lawyer must provide, upon request, the client's file to the client." Comment 9 to Rule 1.16 states:

> Upon termination of representation, a lawyer shall provide, upon request, the client's file to the client notwithstanding any other law, including attorney lien laws. It is impossible to set forth one all-encompassing definition of what constitutes the client file. However, the client file generally would include the following: all papers and property the client provides to the

lawyer, litigation materials such as pleadings, motions, discovery, and legal memoranda; all correspondence; depositions; expert opinions, business records; exhibits or potential evidence; and witness statements. The client file generally would not include the following: the lawyer's work product such as recorded mental impressions; research notes; legal theories; internal memoranda; and unfiled pleadings.

Thus, a former client's right to material that constitutes the client file is almost always unrestricted, despite a concern over a client's reaction to or subsequent use of expert's evaluations or reports, discovery, correspondence, crime scene photos and other papers. However, information or material received by Lawyer Likins that is restricted by statute, court rule or court order is not a part of the "client file" that the former client has a right to receive. Rule 1.2(d) contains an exception to unrestricted access that applies to former clients making requests for information in his client file. "A lawyer shall not counsel a client to engage, or assist a client, in conduct that the lawyer knows is criminal or fraudulent, but a lawyer may discuss the legal consequences of any professional conduct with the client and may counsel or assist a client to make a good faith effort to determine the validity, scope, meaning or application of the law." If Lawyer Likins knows that material in a client file will be used in conduct that is criminal or fraudulent, she may decline to assist the client by withholding the material, but she must inform him about her belief and the reasons for withholding information in his file that he would otherwise have unrestricted right to receive. For former clients, then, parts of the client file may be withheld to prevent fraudulent or criminal conduct. **A is incorrect**. As the foregoing discussion suggests, generally a lawyer is not subject to discipline by turning over her client's file to him upon request. **B is incorrect**. When a former client requests material from his client file, the lawyer ethically lacks discretion to make the disclosure decision based on what she believes to be offensive to anyone, including the victim. Only if the law were to reflect that same concern would she be acting within the ethics rules. **D is incorrect**. Her client's right to his file's contents is broader that what Lawyer Likins received from him during the representation.

PROBLEM #53. ANSWER D IS THE BEST ANSWER.

Lawyer Lyons's other business interests in the real estate transaction gives rise to a conflict under Rule 1.7(a)(2), because there is a significant risk that these other roles would interfere with her representation of Client Cedric. Lawyer Lyons's interest in fees or income from these other roles, if not also her liability concerns from those other roles, create a significant risk that her ability to "exercise independent professional judgment and render candid advice" would be compromised. Rule 2.1. Lawyer Lyons can undertake multiple roles only if she can and does comply with each of Rule 1.7's requirements. It also is important to identify the significant overlap between Rules 1.7(b) and 1.8(a). For example, both rules would apply whether Lawyer plays the nonlawyer role (or roles) as the owner or co-owner of a non-law business or as an employee or independent contractor for such a business. In addition, both rules require Lawyer Lyons to obtain Client Cedric's informed consent in writing. Rules 1.7(b)(4), 1.8(a)(3). The informed consent requirements under Rule 1.8(a)(3) are more stringent. First, it is not enough that Lawyer Lyons confirm Client Cedric's waiver by a writing sent by Lawyer Lyons, as would be the case under Rule 1.7. She must also receive Client Cedric's informed consent "in a writing signed by the client." Second, Lawyer Lyons's writing must clearly set forth each aspect of Lawyer Lyons's business relations with Client Cedric and the role that she Lawyer will play in each, as well as the role that she will have as his lawyer. For example, the writing would include the fees that she would earn in each capacity and the circumstances under which each fee would be payable, e.g., at the real estate closing. Third, in addition to recommending that Client Cedric consult independent counsel, Lawyer Lyons must expressly inform him in writing that consultation is desirable and she must ensure that he has a reasonable opportunity to obtain such advice from another lawyer.

The terms of the business aspects of the transactions between Lawyer Lyons and Client Cedric must be "fair and reasonable" per Rule 1.8(a)(1). We assume that this requirement will be met if Client would be unable to obtain the same services from another under more favorable terms. Lawyer Lyons also must "reasonably believe[ ] that [she] will be able to provide competent and diligent representation to" Client Cedric under Rule 1.7(b)(1). In other words, her subjective belief must be objectively reasonable under the circumstances. **A is incorrect**, because the Model Rules do address concerns about a lawyer's multiple roles including non-lawyer roles which may affect the lawyer's ability to deliver legal representation to her client. **B is incorrect**, because lawyers are permitted to assume non-lawyer roles under Model Rules, but only if the lawyer has engaged in the foregoing discussion with her client. **C is incorrect**, because it is too narrow. The client's informed consent must be in writing, but in addition she must encourage him to consult independent counsel for advice.

PROBLEM #54. ANSWER D IS THE BEST ANSWER.

When a lawyer becomes a government employee, such as Lawyer Abner's employment with the district attorney's office, Rule 1.11(d) controls the analysis regarding imputation of the conflict and screening, if Lawyer Abner is personally disqualified because consent to a conflict is not given. Comment 2 to Rule 1.11 explains: "Because of the special problems raised by imputation within a government agency, paragraph (d) does not impute the conflicts of a lawyer currently serving as an officer or employee of the government to other associated government officers or employees, although ordinarily it will be prudent to screen such lawyers." Thus, Lawyer Abner's disqualification is not imputed to the other lawyers in the district attorney's office.

C is incorrect, because D is correct. **A is incorrect**. When Lawyer Abner leaves Abner, Becker & Collins, Lawyer Abner will have a "former client" relationship with the firm's clients under Rule 1.9. 1.9(a) prohibits a lawyer from acting adversely to a former client if the current and former matters are the same or substantially related. Matters are "substantially related" within the meaning of Rule 1.9 "if they involve the same transaction or legal dispute or if there otherwise is a substantial risk that confidential factual information as would normally have been obtained in the prior representation would materially advance the client's position in the subsequent matter." Rule 1.9, Comment 3. Absent written, informed consent, a lawyer who has been directly involved in a client's specific legal proceeding or transaction cannot later represent other clients with materially adverse interests in that same proceeding or transaction. By contrast, a lawyer who has handled several matters of a type for a client is not thereafter precluded from representing another client in a factually distinct matter of the same type, even if the subsequent client's interests are adverse to the interests of the former client. If Lawyer Abner brought a robbery prosecution against a former client and the robbery appeared to be part of a pattern of robberies, and if Lawyer Abner previously defended the former client in one of those robberies, the new prosecution would be substantially related to Lawyer Abner's prior defense of the former client and would constitute a former client conflict under Rule 1.9(a).

B is incorrect. Former client conflicts can arise from sharing confidential information. For example, suppose that while Lawyer Abner was at her old firm Lawyer Becker asked her for advice about a case that Lawyer Becker was handling. After Lawyer Abner left the firm, she could not represent a new client in the same or substantially related matter that Lawyer Becker had consulted her about if the former client's interests and Lawyer Abner's new client are adverse and if Lawyer Abner had acquired confidential information material to the new case. Rule 1.9(b). For example, if the robbery defendant previously had been defended by Lawyer Becker in a DUI case, there would be a conflict if Lawyer Abner acquired confidential information while representing Lawyer Becker's client that could materially advance the prosecution of the robbery case. Rule 1.9(b). Otherwise, neither Lawyer Abner nor any other lawyer in the district attorney's office would be disqualified from handling the matter. Even if such a conflict existed, on obtaining informed consent, confirmed in writing, both Lawyer Abner and the other lawyers in the office could proceed.

PROBLEM #55. ANSWER C IS THE BEST ANSWER.

As the phrase "confidential information" is used in the Model Rules, judges do not acquire such information from the parties litigating before them when they preside over cases in open court. Instead, lawyers practicing cases before Judge Good have gained confidential information from their clients during the lawyer-client relationship with those clients. Thus, C is a nonsensical answer. **A is incorrect**. Lawyer Good's subsequent representation of litigants is limited by Rule 1.12(a), which states in part: "a lawyer shall not represent anyone in connection with a matter in which the lawyer participated personally and substantially as a judge ... , unless all parties to the proceeding give informed consent, confirmed in writing." The "personal and substantial participation" requirement means that Lawyer Good must have become "personally involved to an important, material degree" before Lawyer Good will be disqualified. See ABA Formal Op. 342 (1975). In the ordinary course of judging, however, Lawyer Good must have done something more than review the status of a matter in court before her involvement will be deemed to have been personal and substantial. If Lawyer Good did not participate personally and substantially in a matter as a judge, neither Lawyer Good nor the other lawyers in the firm of Good, Hanks & Isaacs would be limited in their handling of the matter. **B is incorrect**. Rule 1.12(a) provides that if Lawyer Good participated personally and substantially as a judge, Lawyer Good may not work on a matter without the informed consent of all parties, confirmed in writing. **D is incorrect**. Lawyer Good's disqualification is imputed to the other members of the firm under Rule 1.12(c), unless Lawyer Good is screened from the matter. Rule 1.12(c) provides:

> If a lawyer is disqualified by paragraph (a), no lawyer in a firm with which that lawyer is associated may knowingly undertake or continue representation in the matter unless: (1) the disqualified lawyer is timely screened from any participation in the matter and is apportioned no part of the fee therefrom; and (2) written notice is promptly given to the parties and any appropriate tribunal to enable them to ascertain compliance with the provisions of this rule.

Thus, if Lawyer Good is properly screened and written notice is provided in accordance with Rule 1.12(c), the other lawyers in Good, Hanks & Isaacs may proceed with the representation.

PROBLEM #56. ANSWER B IS THE BEST ANSWER.

The conflict of interest check between the three firms is required because of imputed disqualification under Rule 1.10, which provides (with very limited exception) that the conflict of one member of a firm becomes the conflict of all members of a firm. Thus, if an individual is a member of more than one firm, the conflict of any member of any of the involved firms becomes the conflict of all the members of the involved firms. **A is incorrect**. Upon formation of the new partnership, Rule 1.7 requires that an ongoing conflict of interest check be done between the clients not only of each firm, but also between the clients of all three law firms. **C is incorrect**. Because there are different firms involved, the dictates of client confidentiality under Rule 1.6 require that each firm obtain a client's or potential client's informed consent, as defined under Rule 1.0(e), to circulate enough information outside the firm to the other firms involved in order to do the required conflicts check. **D is incorrect**. Rule 1.9, dealing with former clients, mandates consideration of potential conflicts with them as well.

PROBLEM #57. ANSWER C IS THE BEST ANSWER.

The proposed arrangement is a business transaction between the Client and the lawyers, and thus is governed by the provisions of Rule 1.8(a). In exchange for the lawyers' agreement to begin the representation, the Client is agreeing to both pay a fee and to hold the lawyers harmless for any misfeasance vis-à-vis third parties. Therefore, the attorneys must form an opinion as to whether this agreement is fair and reasonable to the client. If they do, then they must fully disclose the terms in a comprehensible writing to the client, advise the client of the desirability of seeking independent legal counsel on the transaction, and obtain the client's informed consent in a writing which describes the essential terms of the transaction and the lawyer's role. **A is incorrect.** By its terms, Rule 1.8(h) applies only to agreements with respect to the liability of the lawyer to the client, which is not intended. Rule 1.8(h) is not a bar to the proposed agreement. **B is incorrect**. As the foregoing suggests, if the requirements of Rule 1.8(a) are satisfied, a law firm can contract to hold their lawyers harmless. **D is incorrect**. Any decision by a client to limit the lawyers' liability belongs to the client and must comply with the requirements of Rule 1.8(h). If such an agreement complies with Rule 1.8(h), it may be used regardless of whether other agreements also limit the lawyers' liability.

PROBLEM #58. ANSWER A IS THE BEST ANSWER.

Lawyer Lang is bound to follow Client Calhoun's directions with respect to the handling of the lawsuit. Her responsibilities in this situation are governed by Rule 1.2 (a) which states, in pertinent part: "Subject to paragraphs (c) and (d), a lawyer shall abide by a client's decisions concerning the objectives of the representation and, as required by Rule 1.4, shall consult with the client as to the means by which they are to be pursued." The provisions of Rule 1.2 (a) are subject to Rule 1.4(a)(2) which obligates a lawyer to "reasonably consult with the client about the means by which the client's objectives are to be accomplished." Also germane to Lawyer Lang's concerns is Rule 1.2(c) under which such a consultation would necessarily involve an explanation to the client of the extent to which Lawyer Lang's representation of her interests in this matter might be limited by the terms of the insurance contract and an informed consent under Rule 1.8 (f). Client Calhoun has discussed with Lawyer Lang and understands the potential adverse consequences of such a "limited defense" position and has directed Lawyer Lang to continue to proceed as directed. Under the circumstances, Lawyer Lang is bound to honor the Client Calhoun's decision. For the foregoing reasons, **B and C are incorrect. D is incorrect**, because Client Calhoun is Lawyer Lang's client, not the insurance company.

PROBLEM #59. ANSWER D IS THE BEST ANSWER.

Both plans implicate Rule 7.2(c), which prohibits a lawyer from giving "anything of value to a person for recommending the lawyer's services," subject to four exceptions that are inapplicable here. Rule 7.2, Comment 6 reiterates that a lawyer may not pay another for "channeling professional work." The prohibition applies even though the Comment also states: "A lawyer may compensate employees, agents and vendors who are engaged to provide marketing or client-development services such as publicists, public relations personnel, business development staff and website designers." Whether a percentage of fees collected or a flat amount, the reward is something of value to the firm employee and is prohibited. A referral reward plan for nonlawyer firm staff giving a paid day off would be something of value and, therefore, should not be used. What about rewards for clients who refer other clients? A fee reduction to current clients also would be something of value impermissible under Rule 7.2(c). In summary, both referral plans are inconsistent with the express terms of Rule 7.2(c) and are not benefited by the exceptions stated in the Rule. This conclusion is correct, even though under Rule 7.2 a lawyer may spend substantial sums on marketing and advertising and in employing personnel who are specialized in those fields.

PROBLEM #60. ANSWER D IS THE BEST ANSWER.

Lawyer Linker did not engage in an *ex parte* communication with the court. It was Client Cox who had an *ex parte* communication with the judge without Lawyer Linker's knowledge. Thus, there were no violations of Rules 3.5(b) or 8.4(a). Lawyer Linker fulfilled her obligation to her client by seeking a hearing to address her client's possible uninformed waiver of the lawyer-client privilege. It was then up to the judge to decide how to handle the matter. Apparently, the judge decided to abort the unintended waiver of the privilege and to reject Client Cox's attempted *ex parte* communication by returning all of the materials. Lawyer Linker's obligation is to contact Client Cox immediately, explain the potential adverse consequences of his conduct, and advise him not to make any more *ex parte* contacts with the judge. Lawyer Linker's obligation to maintain her client's confidences under Rule 1.6 would prevent her from disclosing Client Cox's letter or its enclosures to opposing counsel. Therefore, **A, B and C are incorrect.**

†